P9-AOT-653

Fair *and* Foul

Fair *and* Foul

Beyond the Myths and Paradoxes of Sport

D. Stanley Eitzen

ROWMAN & LITTLEFIELD PUBLISHERS, INC.
Lanham • Boulder • New York • Oxford

0829732

ROWMAN & LITTLEFIELD PUBLISHERS, INC.

Published in the United States of America
by Rowman & Littlefield Publishers, Inc.
4720 Boston Way, Lanham, Maryland 20706

12 Hid's Copse Road
Cumnor Hill, Oxford OX2 9JJ, England

Copyright © 1999 by Rowman & Littlefield Publishers, Inc.

All rights reserved. No part of this publication may be reproduced, stored in a
retrieval system, or transmitted in any form or by any means, electronic, mechanical,
photocopying, recording, or otherwise, without the prior permission of the
publisher.

British Library Cataloguing in Publication Information Available

Library of Congress Cataloging-in-Publication Data

Eitzen, D. Stanley.
    Fair and foul : beyond the myths and paradoxes of sport / D. Stanley Eitzen.
       p.   cm.
    Includes bibliographical references and index.
    ISBN 0-8476-9170-5 (cloth : alk. paper). — ISBN 0-8476-9171-3 (pbk. : alk.
paper)
    1. Sports—Sociological aspects. 2. Sports—Psychological aspects. I. Title.
GV706.5.E567   1999
796—dc21   98-49895
                                               CIP

Printed in the United States of America

♾ ™The paper used in this publication meets the minimum requirements of
American National Standard for Information Sciences—Permanence of Paper for
Printed Library Materials, ANSI/NISO Z39.48–1992.

Contents

0829073ϡ

Acknowledgments

My sociological approach to sport and other social arenas results in large measure from the contributions of a number of friends, colleagues, and collaborators over a career. They have questioned me, cajoled me, challenged me, helped me, taught me, enlightened me, and inspired me. They are (in alphabetical order) Maxine Baca Zinn, Jay Coakley, Jo Anne Drahota, William Flint, James Frey, Kenneth C. W. Kammeyer, Craig Leedham, Marston McCluggage, Michael Messner, Stephen Pratt, Dean Purdy, Julie Raulli, Timothy Rouse, George Sage, John Schneider, Eldon Snyder, Elmer Spreitzer, Kathryn Talley, Doug Timmer, Prabha Unnithan, and Norman Yetman.

Especially important to this project were reviewers Mike Litwin, sportswriter for the *Rocky Mountain News,* and sport scholars/sociologists Michael Messner and George Sage. They were extremely helpful in keeping me on the desired path and providing suggestions for improvement. My editor, Dean Birkenkamp, is simply the most author-oriented editor in my experience. Dean is the only editor, of the many I have worked with, who actually read the manuscript line by line, offering keen observations and suggestions. Dean's dedication to this project led him to read and critique three chapters of it while he was on his honeymoon! You may not want to marry this guy, but you sure would want him as your editor.

Chapter 1

The Duality of Sport

The very weekend I wrote the first draft of this introduction, my team, the Denver Broncos, winless in four previous Super Bowls and a two-touchdown underdog to the defending champion Green Bay Packers, won this biggest of all football games. Victory is sweet! Life is good! The media attention, the pageantry, and the knowledge that this is the most watched American television event (sport and nonsport) of the year magnify the game. The Super Bowl is viewed by 800 million fans in 188 countries worldwide. The game was brimming with great drama, heroics, excellent team play, and an uncertain outcome. And this game was vitally important. It was important to the Denver fans who had suffered from previous humiliations in this game of games. It was important that our hero, quarterback John Elway, a mortal lock to be a Hall of Famer, would finally win the championship that had eluded him throughout his stellar fifteen-year career. For these and many other reasons, the Super Bowl embodies all sport—and shows why sport is so infectious to me and so many others.

But there is another side to the Super Bowl, a side that diminishes sport for me. A sports event, a physical competition between opponents, is decided by differences in abilities, strategy, and chance. The effort to win under these conditions is the essence of sport, whether a playground basketball game, a school physical education class, a church league slow-pitch softball game, the Michigan–Ohio State annual football game, or the Super Bowl. But as the level of sport becomes more sophisticated, sport shifts from play to work and from pleasurable participation to pageantry meant to please fans, owners, alumni, and other powerful people. Today, sport has become a spectacle; sport is big business.

In this transformation sport has become corrupted. Each year the city hosting the Super Bowl benefits from the $200 million in business generated by this mega-event. Over $5 billion is bet on this single sports event. Teams are owned either by wealthy individuals or, increasingly, by large corporations. Television networks pay enormous sums for the broadcasting rights to the Super Bowl

1

and then sell advertising (at $1.8 million per 30 seconds for the 1998 Super Bowl). The NFL has a $200 million marketing contract with Nike. The sale of NFL memorabilia during Super Bowl week brings in more money than the players will make for playing the game. John Elway, although he had never won the big one until late in his career, makes nearly $5 million a year in salary, a figure eclipsed by additional income from endorsements, personal appearances, and autograph signings.

But other Broncos make $125,000 a year and have few opportunities after very short careers. The owner of the Broncos, Pat Bowlen, especially wanted to win this Super Bowl because a win would increase the odds of the Denver metropolitan population's voting favorably to increase taxes for building a new Bronco Stadium. (Bowlen would put up 25 percent of the money but would receive almost 100 percent of the proceeds.) The cost of attending the Super Bowl includes $275 for the ticket, travel expenses, hotel accommodations, and food at rates in the host city that escalate dramatically during Super Bowl week. Even if average fans could afford such a package, corporations nevertheless hold the bulk of the tickets, which they use to reward their top employees and key business clients.

Some of the players cheat by taking anabolic steroids and other banned substances that give them a chemically induced physical advantage. During the course of the game there are cheap hits aimed at injuring an opponent. Similarly, there are numerous instances of trash talking and other intimidating behaviors. Some athletic heroes are thugs and rapists off the field. Racism is evident at the Super Bowl, in the race of the players at various positions, the race of the coaches, assistant coaches, trainers, owners, publicists, and media personnel. Likewise, the Super Bowl represents the sexist side of sport as it glorifies athletes, coaches, teams, owners, broadcasters, and newspaper writers, all of whom are male. Women provide supporting roles. Their bodies are used to heterosexualize the festival as cheerleaders, dancers, half-time performers, and promotional sex objects.

The 1998 Super Bowl was particularly important to Denver fans because we had lost the three previous tries. We Americans emphasize the outcome of games rather than the process. We glorify winners and vilify losers. Fran Tarkenton, a phenomenal quarterback whose team lost three Super Bowl attempts, carries the stigma of the Super Bowl loser. As John Madden, former NFL coach and current television game analyst, has said, "The biggest gap in sports is between the winner of the Super Bowl and the loser in the Super Bowl."

The Super Bowl symbolizes the fundamental sports paradox for me: It is both unifying and divisive, inclusive and exclusionary, expansive and exploitative. These agony and ecstasy elements of sport form the subject of this book.

I begin with a paradox: Sport, a seemingly trivial pursuit, is important. Sport is a fantasy—a diversion from the realities of work, relationships, and survival.

Sport entertains. Why then do we take it so seriously? First and foremost, sport mirrors the human experience:

> Sport elaborates in its rituals what it means to be human: the play, the risk, the trials, the collective impulse to games, the thrill of physicality, the necessity of strategy; defeat, victory, defeat again, pain, transcendence and, most of all, the certainty that nothing is certain—that everything can change and be changed.[1]

Second, sport mirrors society in other profound ways as well. It shares with the larger society the basic elements and expressions of bureaucratization, commercialization, racism, sexism, homophobia, greed, exploitation of the powerless by the powerful, alienation, and ethnocentrism. American sport embodies American values—striving for excellence, winning, individual and team competition, and materialism. Parents want their children to participate in sport because participation teaches them the basic values of American society and builds character.[2]

Third, sport is compelling because it combines spectacle (there appears to be a universal human social tendency to combine sport and pageantry) with drama (the outcome is not perfectly predictable), excellence (the physically most able compete), and clarity (we know exactly who won, by how much, and in what manner). We also know who lost and why.

Finally, there is the human desire to identify with something greater than oneself. For athletes, this is being part of a team, working and sacrificing together to achieve a common goal. For fans, identifying with a team or a sports hero bonds them with others who share their allegiance; they belong and they have an identity.[3]

Sport is a pervasive aspect of American society. Participation rates are high. Most children are involved in organized sport at some time in their lives. Sport is the subject of much conversation, reading material, leisure activity, and discretionary spending. Over one-tenth of the *World Almanac* is devoted annually to sport, more than is allotted to politics, business, and science. *USA Today,* the most widely read newspaper in the United States, devotes one-fourth of its space to sport. Even the *Wall Street Journal* has a weekly sports page. Several cable television networks provide twenty-four-hour sports coverage. Annually, the most watched television event in the United States is the Super Bowl. The amount of sports betting is staggering, with unknown billions waged legally and illegally.

We sports fans read the daily sports page with a keen interest in the latest scores, win-loss records, favorite athletes, and possible new college recruits or trades that improve our beloved professional teams. We know a great deal about sport. We know point spreads, current statistics, play-off probabilities, biographical information about athletes and coaches, and more. As children, many of us learned sports information, memorizing incredible amounts of trivia.

Moreover, most of us play sports, whether as individuals or on organized teams, throughout much of our lives.

But do we truly understand sport? Can we separate the hype from the reality and the myth from the facts? Do we question the way sport is organized? Unfortunately, many fans and participants alike have a superficial, uncritical attitude that takes much for granted.[4] Sportswriter Rick Reilly wrote in *Sports Illustrated* that "sport deserves a more critical examination. We need to ask more probing questions about sport."[5]

As a sociologist, I am prone to examine all social arrangements critically. A sociologist asks questions such as, How does sport really work? Who has power and who does not? Who benefits under the existing social arrangements and who does not? These questions scrutinize existing myths, stereotypes, media representations, and official dogma. The answers to them enable us to demystify sport and truly understand it, which is the goal of this book. My inquiry is guided by critical questions. I examine sport and the beliefs surrounding it, holding them to the light of current research findings and critical thinking to demythologize them. I focus on showing how sport really works and in the process identify a duality in it, which exists in all human institutions. That is, sport has positive *and* negative outcomes for individuals and society. My approach will probably raise questions, doubts, resistance, and even anger among some readers, demonstrating the power of myth. In the process, though, readers will see sport from a new angle, one that brings new interpretations and insights to what they experience in sport.

Paradoxes of Sport

The subtitle of this book refers to the paradoxes of sport. The *Random House Dictionary of the English Language* supplies the following definition of paradox: (1) "any person, thing, or situation exhibiting an apparently contradictory nature" and (2) "any opinion or statement contrary to commonly accepted opinion."[6]

This book is titled *Fair* and *Foul* [7] because sport is beset by a number of contradictions (definition 1), and the common understanding of sport is often guided by myth. My goal is to demythologize sport by calling into question the prevailing beliefs about this phenomenon (definition 2). These two dimensions of the term "paradox" constitute the organizing principle—the essence—of this book.

Sport is inherently contradictory. On the one hand, sport provides excitement, joy, and self-fulfillment for the participants. As former athlete Kenny Moore put it:

> To celebrate sport is . . . to celebrate sheer abandon, to savor moments when athletes surrender themselves to effort and are genuinely transformed. This is when

sport takes loneliness, fear, hate and ego and transmutes them into achievement, records, art, and powerful example.[8]

But there is also a dark side, as Moore concedes:

[Sport also presents us with] cocaine deaths, steroid cover-ups, collegiate hypocrisies, gambling scandals, criminal agents, and Olympic boycotts. Such failings show that sport's civilizing, freeing effect on us is incomplete. Not everyone is following the rules. Not everyone is trying.[9]

Put another way, sport provides examples of courage, superhuman effort, extraordinary teamwork, selflessness, and sacrifice. Yet the images conveyed through sport—contempt for authority, greed, exploitation, selfishness, and violence—are not always uplifting.[10]

Sport is clearly appealing. We are fascinated by the competition and the striving for excellence. Sport is compelling because it transcends our everyday, routine experiences with excitement, heroics, and unpredictability. But there is also much about sport that is appalling. But, paradoxically, fans often find the appalling appealing—the violence, the incredible amounts of money, and the outrageous behaviors by some athletes, coaches, and owners.

Each chapter in this book takes up a particular paradox of sport. First, sport is both unifying and divisive. Sport can unite warring factions and bring different social classes and racial groups together. But it can also reinforce the barricades that separate groups.

Second, the names, mascots, logos, and rituals associated with sports teams evoke strong emotions of solidarity among followers. But these sports symbols have a potentially dark side as well. Many Native Americans are offended by the use of Native American names (like the Washington Redskins), war paint, tomahawks, war chants, and mascots dressed in native costume. They feel that these practices stereotype, demean, and trivialize the traditions and rituals of Native Americans. Similarly, the names given to women's teams raise parallel questions concerning stereotyping (the name Rambelles hardly refers to athletic skills) and trivialization (Wildkittens as a diminutive of Wildcats). Then there is the use of the rebel flag—the symbol of the Confederacy, racial segregation, and African-American enslavement—as the rallying symbol for sports teams at some Southern schools. Proponents see the Confederate flag as an inspirational symbol of Southern heritage and Old South pride and tradition. Opponents of this practice see this symbol as sending an inflammatory message about a tradition of racial oppression and exclusion.

Third, sport is a rule-bound activity organized and supervised by authorities and organizations to promote fair play. It includes a socialization process whereby participants learn to play by the rules, commit themselves to hard work and teamwork, and practice good sportsmanship. These positive attributes of sport have given rise to the common assumption that sport builds character. Yet they are counteracted by unethical coaches and players, the widespread use of performance-enhancing drugs, the pampering of athletes, hatred among opponents, and the debasement of fair play.

Fourth, sport promotes good physical health. Obviously, the physical exercise that sports participation requires is beneficial because it promotes endurance, coordination, weight control, muscle strength, strong bones, joint flexibility, and increased aerobic (lung and heart) capacity. At the same time, however, participants get hurt during sporting activities. Sport can also damage the health of athletes through overtraining, rapid weight loss to meet weight requirements, excessive weight gain, and the use of drugs that promote muscle mass, strength, and endurance. Demanding coaches may expect too much from their athletes. Parents may drive their child athletes too hard, too fast. Elite young athletes are especially vulnerable to excessive training and even sexual abuse from adult authorities.

Fifth, social control is necessary for stability in society and all social groups. Social control, which is a central feature in sport, has two contradictory consequences. Its positive functions lead to consensus and cooperation as everyone pulls together to achieve a common goal, as well as stability on the team, in the organization, or in the society. The maintenance of the status quo, however, is not always good for everyone. Sport, for example, supports tradition but in so doing helps to reinforce traditional gender roles and compulsory heterosexuality. It helped to maintain racial segregation until after World War II and continues to allow considerable discrimination against racial minorities in some sports even to this day.

Sixth, we live in a democracy, but our schools present a contradiction when it comes to democracy. Formally, schools cherish and nourish the values and traditions of society and teach them to each succeeding generation. Schools, though, are undemocratic, and team sports are the most undemocratic part of the schools. Coaches are often tyrants who demean and degrade student-athletes. Athletes' lives are regimented by authorities, and they are often denied fundamental freedoms. If people learn democracy by practicing it, then the schools and their sports teams, in particular, have the opposite effect.

Seventh, sport is an integral part of higher education in the United States. Big-time college sport supplies full-ride scholarships to athletes and generates many millions of dollars for their institutions, their communities, and corporate America. Big-time college sport unites its supporters, provides free publicity for the schools, and gives good athletes from economically disadvantaged backgrounds the chance for a college education. And it is a training ground for future professional athletes. Does it, however, fit with the educational mission of these universities?

A strong case can be made that sport is actually detrimental to academics. For example, most of these schools actually lose money, since scholarship moneys and other economic resources are channeled away from academics and toward athletics; the athletes admitted tend to perform below the student body average on test scores and graduation rates; athletes are often athletes first and students second; occasional scandals hurt the image of the schools involved; the programs and resources are disproportionately for the male athletes in the revenue-producing sports; gender equity is denied; and athletes are exploited under the guise of amateurism. The overarching contradiction is that big-time school sport is organized as a commercial entertainment activity within an educational environment. This arrangement may have certain positive consequences, but it compromises educational goals.

Eighth, sport is a mechanism of social mobility. Athletes can parlay their skills and achievements into college scholarships, careers as professional athletes, coaching positions, and other sports-related occupations. Huge amounts of money are made by special athletes, many of whom come from lower socioeconomic backgrounds. However, the odds of any athlete's achieving these rewards are very slim.

The fact is that achieving a professional sports career is extremely difficult, no matter how hard the individual works. Sport is a path out of poverty for only a very few. Racial minorities are especially vulnerable to the appeal of riches and fame through sport, but this is a false hope leading to failure for most. Women have even less chance of upward mobility through sport than men because fewer college scholarships are available to them, as well as fewer professional sport opportunities. Even those who do become professional athletes lack lifelong security.

Ninth, large cities either have professional sports franchises or actively seek them. In either case, the cities subsidize or offer to subsidize the teams and their wealthy owners, typically by providing arenas or stadiums, refurbishing these venues as needed, charging little or no rent, providing access roads, and giving generous percentages on concessions and parking, and the like. The rationale for such largesse is that professional teams benefit their host cities economically.

This raises some interesting questions: Who benefits economically from professional teams and who does not? Do the members of all social classes share in the benefits? Should wealthy owners and affluent athletes be subsidized by taxpayers, many of whom are not interested in sport? Do men and women in the community gain more or less equally from the arrangements? Does a city actually benefit economically from having professional teams? Is the profit margin so low for professional teams that they can only survive if subsidized by taxpayers? Is there a better alternative to professional teams' being owned by affluent individuals or large corporations who threaten to move the team to a city that offers more generous subsidies?

These nine paradoxes are considered in this book. Although each chapter focuses on a central paradox, it also explores related contradictions and myths. Issues of class, race, and gender are also considered in each chapter.

Do these contradictions and questions pique your interest about how sport really works? Or does their critical thrust make you defensive about sports? Both are likely reactions, indicating once again the contradictory nature of sport. My point is that anyone who truly wants to understand sport in American society must accept its inherent dualities.

Too often we focus on the bright side of the dualities present in sport, letting myths guide our perceptions and analyses. I intend to present the reality of sport, including the good and the bad. Indeed, I emphasize the negative aspects of sport in order to demythologize and demystify it. Yet I do not want to forget the magical nature of sport that is so captivating and compelling. Overcoming this basic contradiction—being critical of sport while retaining a love for it—will enable us to examine the negatives surrounding sport with the goal of seeking alternatives to improve this vital, interesting, and exciting aspect of social life.

Finally, sports organization can be changed, but this requires a plan, a strategy, and an organized effort (the topic of chapter 11). Sociologist Jay Coakley has put it this way:

> The growing importance of sports in contemporary society will lead more people to take a closer and more critical look at how sports have been defined, organized, and played. As this occurs, some of these people will call for changes in dominant forms of sports, or reject those forms and call for the development of alternative sports. But we should not expect this process to lead to widespread, revolutionary changes in sports. The process of social transformation is always tedious and difficult; it requires long-term efforts and carefully planned strategies. Transformation does not occur overnight, and it does not occur without an organized effort.[11]

Understanding sport must precede any effort to change it for the better. That is the goal of this book.

Notes

1. "Why Sports?" *The Nation,* August 10–17, 1998, p. 3.
2. Howard L. Nixon II and James H. Frey, *A Sociology of Sport* (Belmont, Calif.: Wadsworth, 1996), pp. 40–45. See also Howard L. Nixon II, *Sport and the American Dream* (Champaign, Ill.: Human Kinetics/Leisure Press, 1984).
3. David Shaw, "The Roots of Rooting," *Psychology Today* 11 (February 1978): 48–51.
4. David L. Andrews, "Rethinking Sports in America," *Center News* 14 (Spring 1996): 3. *Center News* is published by the Center for Research on Women, the University of Memphis.
5. Jay J. Coakley, "Beyond the Obvious: A Critical Look at Sport in the U.S.," *The World & I* 2 (October 1988): 589.
6. Jess Stein, ed., *Random House Dictionary of the English Language,* unabridged ed. (New York: Random House, 1966), p. 1046.

7. For an examination of another social institution using paradoxes as an organizing theme, see Judith Lorber, *The Paradoxes of Gender* (New Haven: Yale University Press, 1994).

8. Kenny Moore, "Uplifted, Gently, by Sport," *Sports Illustrated,* November 15, 1989, p. 234. See also George H. Sage, "Sports Participation as a Builder of Character?" *The World & I* 2 (October 1988): 641.

9. Ibid.

10. John Meyer, "Great Escapes . . . and Other Fantasies," *Rocky Mountain News,* January 9, 1982, p. 2B.

11. Jay J. Coakley, *Sport in Society: Issues and Controversies,* 6th ed. (New York: McGraw-Hill, 1998), p. 517.

Chapter 2

Sport Unites, Sport Divides

We took a city that was known for last place and united it. Blacks and whites, Marylanders, Virginians and Washingtonians, Democrats and Republicans, they all were pulling together for the same thing.

— George Allen, coach of the Washington Redskins

To play this game you must have fire in you, and there is nothing that stokes fire like hate.

— Vince Lombardi, coach of the Green Bay Packers

The 1985 European soccer championship in Brussels caused a riot between the fans representing the two teams in the finals — Liverpool, England, and Turin, Italy.[1] About forty-five minutes before the scheduled start of this important match a clash broke out between English fans and Italian fans. The fans were separated from each other only by a wire fence. They were dressed in their team colors, carrying flags and banners of their respective countries and singing nationalistic songs and chants. The escalating nationalistic fervor erupted in threats and obscenities being directed at opposing fans, and soon bottles started to fly across the barrier. The Liverpudlians began pushing against the fence, which collapsed.

By the time the riot ended, thirty-eight people had been killed, with over four hundred injured. Fearful of triggering another riot if they called off the match, officials of the Union of European Football Associations decided to play the match, despite the carnage that preceded it. The Italian team, by the way, won 1–0 with a penalty kick in the fifty-eighth minute of play.

Adapted from D. Stanley Eitzen, "Sport Unites, Sport Divides: Sport in a Multicultural World" (speech presented at North Central College, Naperville, Ill., October 17, 1995); and D. Stanley Eitzen and George H. Sage, *Sociology of North American Sport,* 6th ed. (Madison, Wis.: Brown and Benchmark, 1997), chap. 9.

Two opposing forces are at work throughout the world today: increasing intoler-ance, ideological purity, exclusion, and conflict, on the one hand, as well as many signs of tolerance, cooperation, compromise, acceptance of differences, and in-clusion on the other. Just as the world is moving toward becoming a global com-munity, it is torn by parochial hatreds dividing nations and regions into warring ethnic enclaves.[2] Sport too embodies these contradictory elements as it increas-ingly pulls people apart on the one hand and pulls them together on the other.

The Role of Sport in Unity and Division among Nations

Sport Unites

International events bring together people from different countries and differ-ent racial, ethnic, and religious backgrounds, promoting understanding and friendships across these social divides. The U.S. government uses athletes to promote international goodwill. The State Department, for example, sponsors tours of athletes to foreign countries for these purposes. Sport has also been used to open diplomatic doors. In the 1970s, when Communist China and the United States did not have diplomatic relations, the leadership of the two na-tions agreed that their athletes could compete in each country. After this "ping pong" diplomacy broke the ice, the two countries eventually established nor-mal relations. In 1998 U.S. wrestlers were invited to participate in a seventeen-nation tournament in Iran, the first American athletic team to visit Iran since the 1979 Islamic revolution. Wrestling is Iran's national sport, and Iran's new pres-ident, Mohammed Khatami, encouraged this breakthrough to crack "the wall of distrust between the two nations." Thomas Omestad described an important symbolic act that may help to bridge the antagonism between Iran and the United States that has existed for nearly two decades:

> It was only a small, spontaneous gesture. But it worked emotional magic. After winning a silver medal . . . American Larry "Zeke" Jones waved a hand-sized Iran-ian flag, and the 12,000 fans packed into a Tehran arena went wild with delight. "America! America!" They chanted in response—a sudden, unscripted reversal of the ritual "Death to America!" chorus that Iranians usually chant at public events.[3]

Thus sport was a wedge helping to break down the hostility between these two countries. Perhaps it is a prelude to normalizing relations between the United States and a former enemy. In June 1998 Iran upset the United States in a first-round World Cup soccer match in Lyon, France.[4] The Iranians celebrated their unexpected victory wildly but not (and this is crucial) with taunts directed at the United States. President Bill Clinton congratulated the Iranians, and the Iranian president was a gracious winner. (Clinton's gesture was facilitated by the fact that soccer is not yet an important sport to Americans.)

Sport can be used to unite groups within one country, as Adolph Hitler used the 1936 Olympic Games in Berlin to unite the German people through the accomplishments of Germany's athletes on the world stage. According to Richard D. Mandell in his book *The Nazi Olympics*, the Olympic festival was a shrewdly propagandistic and brilliantly conceived charade that reinforced and mobilized the patriotism of the German masses.[5] The successes of the German athletes at those Olympics (they won eighty-nine medals, twenty-three more than U.S. athletes and more than four times as many as any other country) was "proof" of German superiority.

Cuba provides a contemporary example of the great potential sport has as a mechanism for promoting domestic unity.[6] Fidel Castro, Cuba's leader, has decreed that sport is a right of the people. No admission is ever charged to a sporting event. The most promising athletes are given the best coaching and training. The Communist leadership in Cuba uses sport to unite its people through pride in its athletic achievements. Cuba devotes 3 percent of its national budget to a sports ministry that encourages and trains elite athletes. In the Pan American Games, Cuban athletes, from a country with half the population of California, win many times more medals than U.S. athletes on a per capita basis. The Cuban athletes are sports heroes and heroines, evoking intense nationalistic pride in the Cuban people and, indirectly, support for the ruling elite.

Racially, South Africa is a nation deeply divided. Sport has helped to break down this division, at least in part, in two ways. First, when the whites in South Africa held an election to decide whether to dismantle apartheid, 69 percent voted to give up their privilege, marking a rare peaceful transition of power. One reason for the favorable vote was South African President F. W. de Klerk's warning that failure to pass the measure would return the country to isolation in business and sport.[7] South Africa had last participated in the Olympics in 1960 and had been barred since then from international competition. Its apartheid racial policies had made it a pariah country in everything from politics to sport for three decades. With apartheid dismantled, South Africans could once again show their athletic prowess. This was a compelling argument for many whites. Subsequently, South Africa has been allowed to compete in the Olympics and in other worldwide competitions, especially rugby, which is very important to its people.

After the formal fall of apartheid and the election of Nelson Mandela, the sports world accepted South Africa. The World Cup in rugby was held in South Africa in 1995. President Mandela used the rugby World Cup as an opportunity to bring the races somewhat closer together within his country. The national rugby team, the Springboks, and rugby itself had symbolized white South Africa, so Mandela encouraged black Africans to think of this team as their team. In speaking to a black audience, Mandela, wearing a Springbok cap, said, "This Springbok cap does honor to our boys. I ask you to stand by them tomorrow because they are our kind." Mandela inspired *Sports Illustrated* to comment:

Our kind. Not [black]. Not white. South African. The rugby team became a symbol for the country as a whole. . . . given the right time and place, sport is capable of starting such a process in a society. It is only a start, of course. The hard work lies ahead, after the crowds have dispersed and the headlines have ceased. South Africa's racial and economic woes are not behind it. Far from it. But thanks to the common ground supplied by a rugby pitch, those problems appear less imposing than they did only a month ago.[8]

The Springboks, by the way, went on to win the World Cup, defeating the world's two rugby powers—Australia and New Zealand—in the process. For the first time in South Africa's troubled history, whites and blacks found themselves unified by a sport. Of course, this kind of unity is superficial and temporary, but it is nevertheless an instrument that can promote the achievement of unity in an otherwise divided country.

Sport Divides

But sport also has the capacity to divide peoples. Phillip Goodhart and Christopher Chataway argue that there are four kinds of sport: sport as exercise, sport as gambling, sport as spectacle, and representative sport. Representative sport is

limited conflict with clearly defined rules, in which representatives of towns, regions, or nations are pitted against each other. It is primarily an affair for the spectators: they are drawn to it not so much as the mere spectacle, by the ritual, or by an appreciation of the skills involved, but because they identify themselves with their representatives. . . .

Most people will watch [the Olympic Games] for one reason only: there will be a competitor who, they feel, is representing them. That figure in the striped singlet will be their man—running, jumping, or boxing for their country. For a matter of minutes at least, their own estimation of themselves will be bound up with his performance. He will be the embodiment of their nation's strength or weakness. Victory for him will be victory for them; defeat for him, defeat for them.[9]

This keen identification with national athletes clearly frames the contest as a symbolic battleground between "us" and "them." This attitude, of course, is exclusionary rather than inclusionary.

Sport can encourage division rather than unity. Tensions generated in sports matches, such as those that erupted between El Salvador and Honduras and between Gabon and the Congo after soccer matches, have contributed to the outbreak of war. A full-scale war between El Salvador and Honduras followed the clash between fans at the elimination round of the 1970 World Cup and concluded with bombing raids, troop movements and, eventually, 2,000 dead. Obviously, the matches themselves did not start these conflicts, since the matches occurred in an already tense context over land disputes and other controversies.

A sports event between two quarreling countries can (and occasionally does) provide the catalyst for actual war between them.

Losing an international match can cause deep internal division, whereas unity typically accompanies victory. When Colombia lost a recent World Cup, riots occurred in the country because the people were distressed over their team's play. Incredibly, a player who had inadvertently scored a goal for the opposition was murdered, presumably for his failure in sport.

An interesting development to watch is the emergence of a European economic community with a common currency, open borders, and transgovernmental units to oversee commerce among the member nations. Will sporting events among these nations drive a wedge between them, making cooperative transnational efforts difficult or impossible? Will sport inflame contentious nationalistic impulses, causing fragmentation rather than unity? Or can sport help these nations transcend their nationalistic tendencies by somehow enhancing the goals of transnational unity among these countries?

Unity and Division through Sport in the United States

Does sport unify or divide Americans? Distinguished sports commentator Frank Deford makes a strong case for the negative: "It is time to recognize the truth, that sports in the United States has, in fact, never been so divisive. Uniquely today, sports has come to pit race against race, men against women, city against city, class against class and coach against player."[10]

Let's examine how sport unites and divides the United States, looking at the three major hierarchies in society: class, race, and gender. Does sport lead to greater harmony within these systems of social stratification? Or does sport increase division? As we shall see, it has the potential to work both ways. I emphasize the divisive nature of sport because its divisiveness goes counter to the prevailing myth.

Class

The lines dividing the social classes in the United States are quite fuzzy, except for those that delineate the very rich and the very poor. Money separates. The affluent tend to live in enclaves that are barricaded, at least symbolically, from those with whom they do not want to associate. They tend to send their children to private schools rather than public schools, which restricts their interaction with people who possess fewer economic resources. Even in the public schools, class segregation occurs when tests privileging the mainstream culture are used to determine what courses students take. Class segregation for the affluent also occurs at play. The wealthy play golf and tennis, and swim in exclusive country clubs and ski and sail at expensive resorts. Does sport break down these economic and social barriers between social unequals or does it re-inforce them?

When Ronald Reagan accepted the Theodore Roosevelt Award, the highest honor bestowed on an individual by the National Collegiate Athletic Associa-tion, in 1990, he said:

> When men and women compete on the athletic field, socioeconomic status disap-pears. African American or white, Christian or Jew, rich or poor . . . all that mat-ters is that you're out there on the field giving your all. It's the same way in the stands, where corporate presidents sit next to janitors . . . and they high-five each other when their team scores. . . . which makes me wonder if it [status] should mat-ter at all.[11]

This observation, of course, is incredibly naive. It reinforces the myth that sport is egalitarian. According to the prevailing myth, sport provides opportunity for those with ability regardless of class origins and because it promotes interaction across the social classes. Let me, as sociologists are wont to do, demythologize.

Reagan asserts that sport provides opportunity for those with athletic ability regardless of class origin. Does it? The answer is a little yes but mostly no. First, sociologists know that upward mobility is limited to a few athletes (see chap-ter 9). Athletes of humble social origins can become incredibly wealthy. Michael Jordan, who makes over $33.1 million a year as a player and another $47 million a year from endorsements, is an obvious example. Many young males, especially African-American males, believe that they will become pro-fessional athletes if they work hard enough. How reasonable is this expecta-tion? In two words, not very! The odds of a male high school athlete becoming a professional athlete is about 1 in 10,000; for an African-American male the odds rise to 1 in 3,500.[12] Women, except for golf, tennis, basketball, and ice skating, do not figure into these statistics, since they are excluded from profes-sional sport in the United States.

Second, sociologists know that opportunity for upward mobility is limited to a few sports. Children from families with limited economic resources tend to participate in sports that require little equipment and are publicly funded, such as community youth programs and school sports. Thus they tend to excel in foot-ball, basketball, baseball, track, and boxing. Children of the affluent, on the other hand, have access to golf courses, tennis courts, and swimming pools, as well as coaching in those sports, through private country clubs, neighborhood associa-tions, and parental subsidies. Moreover, some sports such as gymnastics and ice skating require considerable money for coaching, access, equipment, and travel (young elite ice skaters, for example, spend as much as $60,000 annually). Iron-ically, most professional opportunities for women athletes are in sports in which the affluent have a tremendous advantage from childhood.

Ronald Reagan's remarks also suggested that sport encourages interaction across class lines? Does it? Again, the answer is that sport works both ways.

Yes, people of all sorts talk to each other about sports. Past or upcoming sports events are topics that transcend class lines. People in public places often shed the barriers of social class as they discuss past or future big games with strangers, acquaintances, and fellow workers.

Yes, players on teams may develop friendships with those from different social backgrounds, thus transcending social class. Yes, players from humble origins may be upwardly mobile, increasing their interaction with people across class boundaries. Certainly obtaining a college education, which athletic participation facilitates, increases interaction across classes.

But sport scholarships are for the very few. And attending college on an athletic scholarship does not necessarily lead to graduation. Athletes in the revenue-producing sports are less likely to graduate than their nonathlete peers (discussed further in chapter 8).

Historically, sport has been pursued mainly by the affluent, who alone had the time and the money for such non-income-producing activities. The notion of the sports "amateur" was a nineteenth-century invention[13] that the affluent used as a mechanism of class separation. The major competitions in Europe, including the Olympics, were limited to those who could afford the necessary travel, equipment, and coaching, and had the leisure to pursue athletic excellence. More than having the ability to participate, class origins precluded international competition for many. John Kelley, a world-class rower, was barred from the 1928 Olympics because as a bricklayer he had a physical advantage over those who either did not work at all or did not do manual labor. Ironically, the well-to-do in this case used their athletic prowess in international competitions as "proof" of their superiority over the lesser classes.

Unfortunately, the social classes are not proportionately represented at professional sports events. The cost of attending sports contests is too high for the poor. In 1997 the average cost of a ticket (not counting club seats or luxury boxes) for the National Football League (NFL) ranged from $30.16 for the New York Jets to $52.92 for the Washington Redskins. This meant that the cost for a family of four at an average game was $221 for tickets, parking, and refreshments.[14] The cost for a family of four to attend a National Basketball Association (NBA) game was $214.28 in 1997 (the average ticket price was $36).[15] The average for a National Hockey League (NHL) game in 1997 was $228.39. Attending a baseball game is cheaper, $114.82 for a family of four in 1997.[16] Obviously these amounts are prohibitive for many families. The cost for a family of four to attend an NBA, NFL, or NHL game amounts to about 30 percent of the average household's weekly earnings; attending a baseball game takes about 16 percent of that average household's weekly earnings.[17] Among those who do attend, contrary to Reagan's blurred vision, CEOs and janitors do not sit side by side. Seating is segregated by cost, in a very stratified arrangement. The very rich enjoy luxury suites that cost as much as $240,000 for a season or $100,000 for a tournament—the U.S. Open tennis tournament. At basketball games the affluent may sit in $1,500 courtside seats while the less well-to-do are dispersed by the cost of seating, with the cheapest seats farthest from the action. Even golf now has its version of sky boxes, called "Golf Watch," for tournaments.

> For [a single-ticket cost of] $1,500, patrons get to sit in a half-dozen pavilions—with food, drink, and TV monitors—that far outdo 18th-hole corporate tents. Usually elevated, pavilions overlook greens and tees. Roped-off lanes let patrons walk from one hole to the next in private.[18]

The poor, of course, are not in the seats or at the golf tournament at all. If they do attend, they likely are there as vendors and janitors, or they may help park cars.

John Underwood, writing in the *New York Times,* lamented the high cost of attending sports events:

> The greatest damage done by this new elitism is that even the cheapest seats in almost every big-league facility are now priced out of reach of a large segment of the population. Those who are most critically in need of affordable entertainment, the underclass (and even the lower-middle class), have been effectively shut out. And this is especially hateful because spectator sport, by its very nature, has been the great escape for the men and women who have worked all day for small pay and traditionally provided the biggest number of a sport's core support. As it now stands, they are as good as disenfranchised—a vast number of the taxpaying public who will never set foot inside these stadiums and arenas.[19]

Race

Progress in race relations has been slow and seems to be slipping. Cities are becoming more racially segregated. Schools are becoming more racially concentrated. The gap between whites and African Americans and Latinos is widening in terms of income, wealth, education, and employment. With growing immigration and economic hard times for the working poor, racial discord increases. Racial discrimination in housing, lending policies, job opportunities, and the criminal justice system infuriates minorities. What they believe to be the pathologies of racial minorities, such as crime, welfare dependency, teenage pregnancy, and drugs, motivate fearful whites to build walls, real and symbolic, that separate them physically from racial minorities and to support harsh political policies toward these minorities. The question here is, Given these racial realities in U.S. society, does sport reduce or exacerbate racial tensions? Is the playing field open or does it reinforce racial inequality?

In regard to racial harmony, sport works both ways. A 1993 Louis Harris poll showed that three-fourths of high school athletes, white and African-American, said that they had made friends across racial lines through sport. Other research has found that attitudes toward race are enhanced (1) when players from both races contribute more or less equally to team success and (2) when the team is successful.[20] Thus on integrated teams in which each race needs the other to succeed and the team does succeed, members of both races have positive feelings toward each other.

In many sports minority athletes are heroes cheered by their fans of all races. That is, fans tend to appreciate the athletes on their own teams, regardless of race. Michael Jordan, an African American, like Mohammed Ali before him, is, arguably, the most popular individual in America or even the world. (My grandson has lived all of his nine years in Xalapa, Mexico; when I asked him what Michael Jordan's number was, he unhesitatingly gave the correct answer—23.) But fans who adore their minority athletes may vent racial hatred on the minority athletes of opposing teams.

A strong case can be made that sport divides the races as well. Historically, desegregating a sport has intensified racial hostilities. Because of America's persistent racial divide, sport sometimes provides the context for episodes of racial hostility (in schools, parks, playgrounds, prisons). Similarly, games that involve teams representing white schools and teams representing African-American schools often provide a setting for racial taunts and violence by players and fans. This occurs with some regularity in metropolitan areas when mostly white suburban high schools play against high schools from the inner city that have a mostly African-American or Latino student body. It also occurs in small-town America. In 1998 high school students from Martinsville, Indiana, a town with a population of 12,000 whites and no African Americans, taunted opposing players with racial slurs and obscenities when competing against racially integrated teams. Martinsville High School, as a result, was placed on probation by its athletic conference.[21]

Race tends to be a factor in the choices that athletes make. That is, on integrated teams, players often segregate themselves voluntarily for meals, travel arrangements, and leisure activities, and they tend to select roommates of the same race. As whites and African Americans compete for positions on a team, each group may feel that the other race is getting special treatment, leading to various manifestations of "racial paranoia."

Integrated teams may be segregated by position, which is called "stacking." In football whites are more likely to play on offense and to play at the thinking and leadership positions that more often determine the game's outcome. African Americans overwhelmingly play on defense and at positions that require physical characteristics such as size, strength, speed, and quickness. This means that the members of one race spend most of their practice time with players of the same race.

Most African-American college athletes play for schools that are predominantly white (with African Americans constituting only 5 percent or so of the student body). They differ from the rest of the student body in color and size. They may also differ in academic preparation. They often differ in economic resources. Consider, for instance, a six-foot ten-inch, poor African-American basketball player from the inner city of Detroit. Although he took high school courses that did not prepare him for college, he is recruited to play at Tulane University, where the student body is mainly from a southern, rural background, 98 percent white, affluent, and with average SAT scores of 1100. He is marginal on a number of dimensions in this setting. This marginality from the rest of the student body is likely to drive him further into not just the athletic ghetto but, most particularly, the African-American athletic ghetto (see chapter 8).[22] Moreover, the African-American athletes are often segregated in athletic ghettos on campus (dorms, meals, courses, majors) and interact with other athletes but rarely with other students.

Is the playing field level for racial minorities? Does race restrict or is it irrelevant? If sport offers social mobility for minorities, it should help bring the races together so that minorities are found throughout the social structure, not disproportionately at the bottom. The answer to these questions, however, are not clear-cut, since a case can be made for both sides.

The case for the affirmative begins with history. There are opportunities now for African Americans in sport that were not present until after World War II. Today, for example, about 80 percent of the players in professional basketball (the NBA) are African Americans, as are 67 percent of professional football players and 18 percent of those in major league baseball (Latinos make up 18 percent of baseball players).[23] In big-time college basketball and football, about 60 percent of the players are African Americans. Clearly, sport does constitute a path of significant upward mobility for some African Americans.

There are African-American superstars who make incredible amounts of money from sport (Michael Jordan, Albert Belle, and Tiger Woods, among many others). There are African-American coaches, administrators, and referees, whose visibility suggests that African Americans are not subject to discrimination in sport. Sport appears to be an open system in which ability tells, instead of race restricting.

However, limits are placed on African Americans and other racial minorities, who are rarely found in certain sports (golf, tennis, bowling, skiing, ice skating, polo, auto racing). There are still barriers in these sports to full minority participation. Before 1990, for example, the U.S. Golf Association (USGA) and the Professional Golf Association (PGA) regularly played their golf tournaments at country clubs that did not allow minorities as members. When the various governing bodies in golf adopted antidiscrimination guidelines for their host clubs, eleven country clubs with tournaments refused to integrate. Since then, four of them have come into compliance, but seven clubs continue to discriminate openly.[24] Moreover, many of those that did integrate did so by admitting a token African American or two to silence the protesters.

As noted earlier, racial minorities are underrepresented in central leadership and thinking positions in team sports and are overrepresented in physical, reac-

tive positions. Stacking is one of the best-documented forms of discrimination in both U.S. college (men's football and women's volleyball) and professional ranks (football, baseball) and in other societies as well (Canadian football, British soccer, and Australian rugby). In 1997 fifty-nine of the sixty starting cornerbacks in the NFL were African Americans. Of the thirty starting quarterbacks, six were African Americans. Each Green Bay starting defensive player was African American. There were no African-American place kickers, or placekick holders. Are these differences in racial composition by position accidental, or are they based on actual performance criteria? Or are the decisions made by athletes, coaches, scouts, and general managers based on racial stereotypes?

Racial minorities rarely hold positions of authority in sport—head coaches, athletic directors, general managers, and owners. At the end of 1997 there were six head coaches and four athletic directors in the National Collegiate Athlete Association (NCAA) 106 top football programs (Division IA) who were African-American.[25] Of the twenty-three head coaching openings at Division IA schools at the end of 1996, only one was filled by an African American. Similarly, at the end of 1997 not one of the twelve head coaching jobs that had been filled since the end of the season went to an African American. Thus, in 1997, only 5 percent of the 112 Division I-A football schools had an African-American head coach, yet 57 percent of the players in the schools were black.[26] The situation is better in college basketball, as 61 of the 305 Division I coaches at the end of 1997 were African Americans. In 1997, three of the thirty head coaches in the NFL were African Americans. By mid-1998 the last eighteen head coaching openings in the National Football League were filled by whites. Of the men who were interviewed for those jobs, only one was African American. As *Sports Illustrated* editorialized:

> Though 68% of NFL players are African American, NFL owners, an all-white club, have given short shrift to well qualified [African American] candidates. . . . What really has to change is the close-mindedness of owners and general managers, who have long been practicing a pernicious form of racism.[27]

In major league baseball in 1997 there was only one African-American general manager (and he resigned early in 1998). The president of the National League is African American, and there are four African Americans managing out of twenty-eight teams. Frank Robinson became the first African-American manager in 1975. From that time through the 1994 season, 140 managers have been hired. Of these managers, twenty-five never played in the majors. All twenty-five were white. Moreover, the average playing experience of African Americans who became managers was twice as long as that of whites, sixteen years compared with seven (Latinos averaged almost thirteen years of playing experience). Clearly, the standards differ for whites and minorities.[28] Writing about American society and the changes that have occurred since Jackie Robinson broke through baseball's color line in 1947, Roger Angell has said:

This same pattern of minority impotence may be in force all across unstable corporate America, where African American or Latino C.E.O.s and board members are also hard to find, but pointing this out should be of no comfort to baseball. Nor should it be taken as disparaging what was accomplished by Jackie Robinson's courage and class; if anything, it tells us something about the size and the lumpish Jabba-the-Hutt immobility of racial prejudice in this country. What we can say is that baseball has changed, but not nearly enough; in too many ways, it's [racial prejudice] still the national pastime.[29]

African Americans are also underrepresented among assistant coaches, who tend to be assigned the less prestigious roles. In football, African-American assistant coaches are typically assigned to coach receivers, running backs, and defensive backs, positions dominated by blacks. Rarely are they offensive or defensive coordinators, the most important coaching positions after head coach. In major league baseball, minorities coaching the baselines overwhelmingly coach first base, where the responsibilities are much less important than at third base. This is significant because the third base coach is the most important on-the-field coach. When managing jobs open up, third base coaches have the best experience for moving to the top job.

There is a phenomenon that sociologists of sport call "unequal opportunity for equal ability," which means that minorities have to be better than whites to succeed in the sports world. African Americans with superior talent are not subject to discrimination but substars are. The data from baseball and basketball, which include records of practically every aspect of individual and team performance, show that African Americans as a group almost always outperform whites on these measures. The reason for this difference is that African Americans are much more likely to be starters, whereas whites are overrepresented as substitutes. In baseball the evidence is clear that the undistinguished African-American player is less likely to be on the roster than the undistinguished white player. As a result, when the statistics are compiled for African Americans and compared with those of whites, the former have superior statistics to the latter. In Jonathan Brower's words, "mediocrity is a white luxury."[30]

There is also unequal salary for equal ability. Studies from the 1980s for professional football and basketball found that when players of equal ability are compared, African Americans receive less salary than equivalent white players.[31] A recent study of the National Basketball Association found that this discrepancy continues to exist. The gap is not present among the superstars or non-starters, but it does occur among starters below superstar status. When players of equal ability are compared, whites make 18 percent more in salary than African Americans.[32]

African-American women who aspire to leadership positions as coaches and administrators of sport are victims of double jeopardy — their race and their gender. Few if any African-American women are head coaches in colleges and uni-

0829732

versities or of teams training for the Olympics. Few if any African-American women are athletic directors or NCAA executives or executive directors of the fifty governing bodies for U.S. Olympic sports.

How are these clear facts concerning racial discrimination in sport to be explained?[33] To understand how discrimination works, we need to ask, How are things normally done? Who gets preferential treatment under these normal arrangements? Who is automatically excluded because of these arrangements? The answers to these questions are not always easy to find because the arrangements are "natural" and the discrimination often unintentional or disguised. In short, discrimination in society and in sport is structured and institutionalized and is not purely the result of individual prejudices.

Gender

Ours is a patriarchal society. Women are second to men in power, earnings, and job opportunities. With few exceptions women occupy secondary roles at home, in corporations, in colleges and universities, and in voluntary associations. Women are discriminated against by lenders, by employers, and by the Social Security system, to name a few. Does sport reinforce this imbalance, or does it work to break down gender inequities? As with class and race, a case can be made for both sides on this question.

In 1972 Congress passed Title IX, which states that no person in the United States can be excluded, on the basis of sex, from participation in, can be denied the benefits of, or can be subjected to discrimination in any educational program or activity receiving federal financial assistance. As a result of this landmark legislation, there has been a boom in women's participation in school athletics. High school programs for girls went from about 300,000 participants in 1971 to 2.2 million now (there are 4.2 million boys). The money for women's sports programs in college went from virtually nothing before Title IX to about 30 percent of the athletic budget now. Before Title IX, women received no athletic scholarships, compared to about 50,000 for men. Now women receive about 35 percent of the athletic scholarships given by colleges and universities.

Although progress has been slow, a few women's teams have been successful in winning support from their schools and the fans. In some programs, women's teams actually have better support than men's teams (e.g., in women's basketball, Louisiana Tech). In the 1997–1998 basketball season, a women's basketball game between the defending national champion, the University of Tennessee, and a former champion and perennial contender, the University of Connecticut, was played before a crowd in excess of 24,000.

Women's professional tennis has at least as much fan support as men's tennis, as measured by attendance and television viewing. Women's professional golf is gaining popularity, although it does not generate the interest that men's golf does. In so-called amateur ice skating women are more popular than men. When the women's Olympic ice skating champion turns professional, she receives much more money than her male counterpart.

Despite these positives, in many ways sport perpetuates male dominance in society. What could be more striking than the shift in leadership that has occurred in women's athletics in only a few years. Ironically, after Title IX brought greater public attention and wider participation in women's sports, control over the teams shifted dramatically to men. Before Title IX 90 percent of collegiate women's teams were coached by women; now 49 percent are. And male coaches of female teams receive, on average, 27 percent more in salaries than female coaches of female teams. In 1972 more than 90 percent of women's intercollegiate programs were administered by a woman, but in 1994 only 21 percent were.[34]

Major inequities remain, despite the progress since Title IX. For example, whereas women constitute slightly over half of the undergraduate population, they make up only about 35 percent of the varsity athletes. Despite this obvious disparity, the male-dominated athletic establishment defines the situation as gender equity, since they do not include football (see chapter 8).

Sport also perpetuates male dominance through the media. The media guides compiled by athletic departments of various universities provide some useful hints. These guides, for example, basketball guides, give more attention to the men's team than to the women's team (in terms of number of pages, length of descriptions for coaches and players), use better-quality paper, and include more photographs and different types of photographs (action pictures for men and stills for women). The descriptions of the players differ, with men much more likely than women to be characterized as aggressive. Women's sports activities are viewed as secondary and relatively unimportant. *Sports Illustrated* and *USA Today* have the best record of the major journalistic outlets in providing coverage for women's sports, although they devote much less than half of their coverage to it. But even *Sports Illustrated* errs by giving too much emphasis to the nonathletic side of women. For example, in 1993 the fifty-two covers included only six featuring women. Who these women were and what they represent is quite instructive. The annual bathing suit cover objectifies feminine beauty of a nonathletic kind. The cover featuring tennis player Monica Seles showed a knife in her back. The third and fourth women were the nonathlete widows of Cleveland Indians pitchers Steve Olin and Tim Crews. The fifth was tennis player Mary Pierce, whose father beat her. The sixth was skater Nancy Kerrigan, who was clubbed on the knee by an assailant. Thus in one year *Sports Illustrated* displayed on its cover one beautiful model in a swimming suit and five women who were victims.[35] The media also treat men and women differently in their broadcasts. The play-by-play announcers and those providing the analysis are almost exclusively men. A few women roam the stadium looking for human interest stories or interviewing coaches, athletes, wives of the participants, and the like.

The announcers also refer to women differently than men. A study of play-by-play television commentary of women's and men's basketball and tennis by Michael A. Messner, Margaret Carlisle Duncan, and Kerry Jensen found some interesting and important differences.[36] In basketball, men's games were referred to as universal (the NCAA championship game, the Final Four) whereas women's games were always referred to as the NCAA *women's* national championship game or the *women's* Final Four: "The men's games and tournament were presented as the norm, the universal, while the women's were continually marked as the other, derivative (and, by implication, inferior) to the men's."[37]

Messner and colleagues also found a gendered hierarchy of naming. Both in basketball and tennis, the commentators commonly referred to women as girls, as young ladies, and as women. Men, on the other hand, were never referred to as boys but rather as men or young men. This difference tends to linguistically infantilize women while granting adult status to men. Similarly, when athletes were named, the commentators used women's first names far more often than men's. Both of these practices—referring to women as girls and by their first names—in effect make men the dominants and women the subordinates. In doing so, they both reflect and reconstruct gender inequality.

Male dominance is also perpetuated through the names given to women's teams. Some of these names make women athletes either invisible (i.e., are subsumed under a male name given the men's teams, such as Tomcats) or they are trivialized (e.g., the Pink Panthers rather than the Panthers).[38] (This form of sexism is discussed in detail in chapter 3.)

Sport also perpetuates male dominance by celebrating beautiful and sexy women. Women are used as entertainers at sports events. It is a rare sports event that does not feature majorettes, cheerleaders, and dancers dressed in sexy outfits who prance, shake, and titillate. The press coverage of sports disproportionately emphasizes the beauty of female athletes rather than their athletic attributes and accomplishments.

Men in sport are viewed as the achievers, the doers; women support them and achieve status from the men's exploits, not their own. Women are passive, men are aggressive; women are dependent, men are independent.

Male dominance is maintained when communities build very expensive stadiums and arenas to keep their professional teams or to entice other teams to move there (see chapter 10). These stadiums, costing a quarter to half a billion dollars in tax revenue, are for men. They are for male owners, male athletes, male coaches, male trainers, male media, male-controlled corporations, and mostly male fans. The symbolic message is clear: Men count for much more than women.

Is the Unity Achieved through Sport Always Good?

Most discussions of sport implicitly assume that unity is good and division is bad. This is not always the case.[39] The Nazi Olympics of 1936, for example, unified the Germans in their contempt for Jews, Gypsies, people of color, homosexuals, and non-Germans. This unity was achieved by separating the German people into superior/inferior categories. Soccer wars divide nations precisely because of soccer's ability to unite the people within national boundaries. The infamous black power fist statement by Tommy Smith and John Carlos on the victory stand during the playing of the national anthem in the 1968 Olympics was viewed by most Americans as a divisive gesture pulling white and black athletes apart. Many blacks and antiracists, however, interpreted this symbolic act as a powerful, unifying political statement. Depending on the audience, this act was divisive or unifying, unpatriotic or progressive. Thus it is not simply a matter of sport either uniting or dividing but how and under what circumstances sport unites and/or divides and with what consequences.

Sport does have a unifying function. This can be accomplished with progressive consequences if it is organized to make full participants of the members of all social classes, races, and genders. Sport does this to some degree, but for the most part sport reinforces the inequalities in society. Consider, for example, the statement by Mariah Burton Nelson from her book, *The Stronger Women Get, the More Men Love Football.* "We need to take sports seriously — not the scores or the statistics, but the process. Not to focus on who wins, but on who's losing."[40] By my count, the losers in sport have been and continue to be the poor, racial minorities, and women. And, as long as these folks lose, sport will more likely divide than unify.

Notes

1. Richard Lacayo, "Blood in the Stands,"*Time,* June 10, 1985, pp. 38–41.
2. Benjamin R. Barber, "Jihad vs. McWorld," *Atlantic Monthly* 269 (March 1992): 53–63.
3. Thomas Omestad, "Wrestling with Tehran: U.S., Iran Go to the Mat in a Replay of Ping-Pong Diplomacy," *U.S. News & World Report,* March 2, 1998, p. 44.
4. For the political background of this event, see Ian Thomsen, "Political Football," *Sports Illustrated,* June 1, 1998, pp. 66–69.
5. Richard D. Mandell, *The Nazi Olympics* (New York: Macmillan, 1971).
6. Steve Wulf, "Running on Empty: Cuba Maintains a Rich Sports Tradition Despite Shortages of Everything but Pride," *Sports Illustrated,* July 29, 1991, pp. 60–70.
7. "Rugby over Race," *Sports Illustrated,* March 30, 1992, p. 10.
8. E. M. Swift, "Bok to the Future," *Sports Illustrated,* July 3, 1995, p. 33.
9. Phillip Goodhart and Christopher Chataway, *War without Weapons* (London: Allen, 1968), p. 3.

10. Frank Deford, "Seasons of Discontent," *Newsweek,* December 29, 1997–January 5, 1998, p. 74.

11. Ronald Reagan, quoted in "Athletics a Great Equalizer, Reagan Tells NCAA," *NCAA News* 10 (January 1990): 1.

12. George H. Sage, *Power and Ideology in American Sport: A Critical Perspective* (Champaign, Ill.: Human Kinetics Books, 1990), p. 40.

13. D. Stanley Eitzen, "The Sociology of Amateur Sport: An Overview," *International Review for the Sociology of Sport* 24, no. 2 (1989): 95–105.

14. Associated Press, "Cost of Attending an NFL Game Rises to $221 for a Family of Four," *Denver Post,* August 30, 1997, p. 8C.

15. Mike Lopresti, "NBA Could Soon Choke on Its Troubles," *USA Today,* December 4, 1997, p. 3C.

16. "Major League Ticket Price Rises about 7 Percent," *USA Today,* March 3, 1997, p. 3C.

17. Dan McGraw, "Big League Troubles," *U.S. News & World Report,* July 13, 1998, p. 43.

18. "Skyboxes on the Greens," *Business Week,* March 31, 1997, p. 8.

19. John Underwood, "From Baseball and Apple Pie, to Greed and Sky Boxes," *New York Times,* October 31, 1993, p. 22.

20. McKee J. McClendon and D. Stanley Eitzen, "Interracial Contact on Collegiate Basketball Teams: A Test of Sherif's Theory of Super-Ordinate Goals," *Social Science Quarterly* 55 (March 1975): 926–938.

21. Carolyn White, "Indiana Racial Incidents Prompt Probation," *USA Today,* February 10, 1998, p. 12C.

22. Patricia A. Adler and Peter Adler, *Backboards and Blackboards: College Athletes and Role Engulfment* (New York: Columbia University Press, 1991).

23. Kenneth L. Shropshire, "Jackie Robinson's Legacy," *Emerge,* April 1997, p. 60.

24. Jaime Diaz, "Off-Limits," *Sports Illustrated,* February 10, 1997, pp. G10–14.

25. Jim Naughton, "Black Athletic Directors Remain a Rarity in NCAA's Division I," *The Chronicle of Higher Education,* July 3, 1998, pp. 29A, 31A.

26. Steve Wieberg, "Black Coaches Still Snubbed in Football," *USA Today,* January 9, 1998, p. 1C.

27. "The NFL's Numbers Problem," *Sports Illustrated,* March 31, 1997, pp. 29–30.

28. Shropshire, "Jackie Robinson's Legacy," p. 62.

29. Roger Angell, "Box Score: Has Baseball Fulfilled Jackie Robinson's Promise?" *New Yorker,* April 14, 1997, p. 6.

30. Jonathan J. Brower, "The Quota System: The White Gatekeeper's Regulation of Professional Football's Black Community" (paper presented at the annual meeting of the American Sociological Association, New York, August 1973).

31. James V. Koch and C. Warren Vander Hill, "Is There Discrimination in the 'Black Man's Game'?" *Social Science Quarterly* 69 (March 1988): 83–94; Richard E. Lapchick, "Blacks in the NBA & NFL," *Center for the Study of Sport and Society Digest* 1 (Summer 1989): 4.

32. Barton Hughes Hamilton, reported in David Leonhardt, "Color Line on the Court?" *Business Week,* December 22, 1997, p. 6.

33. The following description of institutional racism is from D. Stanley Eitzen and

Maxine Baca Zinn, *In Conflict and Order: Understanding Society,* 8th ed. (Boston: Allyn and Bacon, 1998), p. 294.

34. R. Vivian Acosta and Linda J. Carpenter, "Women in Intercollegiate Sport: A Longitudinal Study—Seventeen Years Update, 1977–1994" (manuscript, Department of Physical Education, Brooklyn College, 1994).

35. Lynda Truman Ryan, "Swimsuit Models or Victim Stories, Who Will Cover for Me?" *New York Times,* February 2, 1994, p. 20.

36. Michael A. Messner, Margaret Carlisle Duncan, and Kerry Jensen, "Separating the Men from the Girls: The Gendered Language of Televised Sports," *Gender and Society* 7 (1992): 121–137.

37. Ibid., p. 125.

38. D. Stanley Eitzen and Maxine Baca Zinn, "The De-athleticization of Women: The Naming and Gender Marking of Collegiate Sport Teams," *Sociology of Sport Journal* 6 (December 1989): 362–370.

39. My thanks to Mike Messner, who made these points in his review of the initial draft of this project.

40. Mariah Burton Nelson, *The Stronger Women Get, the More Men Love Football: Sexism and the American Culture of Sports* (New York: Harcourt Brace, 1994), p. 8.

Chapter 3

Names, Logos, Mascots, and Flags: The Contradictory Uses of Sport Symbols

The two teams that played in the 1995 World Series were the Atlanta Braves and the Cleveland Indians. Inside the stadium, the fans of the Braves did the "tomahawk chop" and enthusiastically shouted "Indian" chants. Similarly, the fans of the Indians united behind their symbol, Chief Wahoo, waved foam tomahawks, and wore war paint and other pseudo–Native American symbols. Outside the stadium, Native American activists carried signs in protest of the inappropriate use of their symbols by Anglos. Symbols have the power to both unite followers and divide groups into "us" and "them." They also can be interpreted as symbolic of past and continued oppression.

A symbol is anything (words, gesture, or object) that carries a particular meaning for the members of a group. A raised finger (which one is important), a green light, a whistle, a handshake, and a raised fist are all symbols with meaning. Some symbols, such as a wink, are trivial, others, like the flag of the United States, are vitally important.

A group's symbols serve two fundamental purposes—they bind together the individual members of a group, and they separate one group from another. Each of the thousands of street gangs in the United States, for example, has a group identity that is displayed in its name, code words, gestures, distinctive clothing, and colors. The symbols of these gangs promote solidarity and set them apart from rivals. These symbols are so important that the members may risk their lives in their defense.[1]

Using symbols to achieve solidarity and community is a common group practice, as the French sociologist Émile Durkheim showed in his classic analysis of primitive religions.[2] Durkheim noted that preliterate people in a locality believed that they were related to some totem, which was usually an animal but could be some other natural object as well. All members of a common group were identified by their shared symbol, which they displayed as the emblem of their totem. This identification with an animal, a bird, or another object is common in U.S.

schools. Students, former students, faculty members, and others who identify with the school adopt nicknames for the school's teams, display the school colors, wave the school banner, wear special clothing and jewelry, and engage in ritual chants and songs. These behaviors usually center around athletic contests. Sociologist Janet Lever connects these activities with Durkheim's notion of totemism:

> Team worship, like animal worship, makes all participants intensely aware of their own group membership. By accepting that a particular team represents them symbolically, people enjoy ritual kinship based on a common bond. Their emblem, be it an insignia or a lapel pin or a scarf with team colors, distinguishes fellow fans from both strangers and enemies.[3]

A school's nickname is much more than a tag or a label. It conveys, symbolically as Durkheim suggests, the characteristics and attributes that define the institution. In an important way, the school's symbols represent the institution's self-concept. Schools may have names that signify the school's ethnic heritage (e.g., the Bethany College Swedes), state history (University of Oklahoma Sooners), religion (Oklahoma Baptist College Prophets), or founder (Whittier College Poets). Most schools, though, use symbols of aggression and ferocity for their athletic teams (birds such as hawks, animals such as bulldogs, human categories such as pirates, and even the otherworldly such as devils).[4]

Although school names and other symbols evoke strong emotions of solidarity among followers, there is also a potential dark side to their use. The names, mascots, logos, and flags chosen by some schools may be derogatory to some group. The symbols may dismiss, differentiate, demean, and trivialize marginalized groups such as African Americans, Native Americans, and women. Thus they serve to maintain the dominant status of powerful groups and subordinate those groups categorized as "others." That may not have been the intent of those who decided on the particular names and mascots for a particular school, but their use diminishes these "others," thus retaining the racial and gender inequities found in the larger society.[5] School symbols as used in sports, then, have power, not only for maintaining in-group solidarity, but also for separating the in-group from the out-group and perpetuating the hierarchy between them. Three conspicuous examples of this phenomenon are the use of the Confederate flag at the University of Mississippi, the use of Native American names (Redskins, Scalpers) and other symbols (war paint, tomahawks, Native American dances), and the sexist names given to women's athletic teams.

Symbols of the Confederacy

At Nathan Bedford Forrest High School in Jacksonville, Florida, young African-American athletes wear the Confederate army's colors on their uniforms. They call themselves the Rebels. And the school they play for is named after the slave-trading Confederate general who became the original grand wizard of the Ku Klux Klan.[6]

There is a neo-Confederate culture in much of the South.[7] There are organizations dedicated to promoting the heritage of the Confederate States of America. They fight to retain Confederate symbols, like the Rebel battle flag, that have had a prominent place in many Southern states, most notably Alabama, Georgia, South Carolina, and Mississippi. The neo-Confederate culture and its symbols have two distinct meanings—one that promotes the South's heritage and another that symbolizes slavery, racial separation, and hate.

The Rebel battle flag, which some individuals and groups feel should still fly over state buildings, is an object of controversy. Several states have abandoned it after considerable struggle, but South Carolina continues to have the Rebel flag as its official flag.

The University of Mississippi displays the Rebel battle flag and sings "Dixie" at football games.[8] The practice began in 1948 after the Dixiecrats, rebelling against a strong civil rights plank in the Democratic platform, walked out of the Democratic convention. In that year the University of Mississippi adopted the Rebel flag, designated "Dixie" the school's fight song, and introduced a mascot named "Uncle Reb," a caricature of an Old South plantation owner. These symbols proclaimed its support for racial segregation (its sports teams were officially designated the Rebels in 1936). In 1962 James Meredith, despite the strong opposition of Governor Ross Barnett and other white leaders in the state, became the first black student at the school. There were demonstrations at that time that supported the governor and demonstrations that opposed the racial integration of the school. Through it all, the Rebel flag and the singing of "Dixie" were symbols of defiance used by the supporters of segregation.

Over the ensuing years, the use of these symbols at the University of Mississippi caused considerable debate. On the one hand, they represented the state's heritage and as such were a source of pride, inspiration, and unity among citizens of the South. The opposing position was that these symbols represented a history of oppression against African Americans, noting that the Rebel flag was also a prominent symbol of the Ku Klux Klan. Since almost one-third of Mississippians are African Americans (among the states, Mississippi has the nation's largest African-American population), the flagship university of that state should not use symbols that recall the degradation and demeaning of their ancestors. Is it proper, they ask, to use the key symbol of the Confederacy and African-American enslavement as a rallying symbol for the University of Mississippi's sports teams—teams composed of whites and African Americans?

As a compromise, in 1983, twenty-one years after the University of Mississippi integrated, its chancellor ruled that the Rebel flag was no longer the official banner for the school. Chancellor Porter L. Fortune Jr. made it clear, however, that students would have the right to wave the flag at football games. And that they have done. Sports team names such as "Rebels," as well as mascots such as "Uncle Reb" and songs such as "Dixie," have continued as official school symbols.

In 1997 the debate still raged. Use of the Rebel flag was opposed by the student government and the football coach, Tommy Tuberville, who urged fans to use a less divisive banner (one bearing the letter *M* studded with stars). Coach Tuberville, by the way, felt that the use of the flag was making it difficult for him to recruit blue-chip African-American players. To his dismay, however, there were groups organized to promote the use of the Rebel flag. "Under the racially charged heading 'Stop the Lynching of Ole Miss and Southern Heritage,' a Jackson, Mississippi, citizens' group recently sent out a mailing, with a Confederate flag on the envelope, asking for money to support its cause."[9] At games, Rebel flags vastly outnumber the Battle M flags. "If anything, the dispute over the university's symbols seems to make many whites more, not less, inclined to cling to the past."[10]

Charles W. Eagles, a University of Mississippi history professor, sums up the ongoing debate:

> For some of us—those who believe in the University of Mississippi—the symbols prevent the university from being everything it can be. Others—those that are faithful to Ole Miss [the traditionalists]—think that if you took the symbols away, there wouldn't be anything there. The symbols are seen as a real burden for the University. But they're the backbone of Ole Miss.[11]

This debate demonstrates vividly the power of symbols, not only the power to unite or divide but also the hold these symbols have on people, as seen in their resistance to change and in the organized efforts to change those symbols interpreted as negative.

The Use of Native American Names and Ceremonial Acts

Ray Franks did an exhaustive study of the names of athletic teams at all U.S. community colleges, colleges, and universities. He found that names associated with Native Americans predominated in popular use.[12] The actual number is not known, but Native American names probably dominate the nation's high school teams as well. Major professional teams have also adopted Native American names—in baseball, the Atlanta Braves and the Cleveland Indians; in football, the Washington Redskins and the Kansas City Chiefs; in basketball, the Golden State Warriors; and in hockey, the Chicago Blackhawks.

Native American names used for sports teams can be generic (Bryant College Indians, Rio Grande College Redmen), tribal (Florida State Seminoles, University of Alaska at Fairbanks Nanooks, Central Michigan Chippewas, Eastern Michigan Hurons, Mississippi College Choctaws, Utah Utes), or they can focus on some attribute (Bradley Braves, Marquette Warriors, Lamar High School [Colorado] Savages) or some combination (University of Illinois Fighting Illini, North Dakota Fighting Sioux).[13]

Defenders of Native Americans names, logos, and mascots argue that their use is a tribute to the indigenous peoples. Native Americans, the argument goes, are portrayed as brave, resourceful, and strong. Native American names were chosen for sports teams precisely because they represent these positive traits.

Other defenders claim that the use of Native American names and mascots is no different from the use of names and mascots that represent other ethnic groups, such as the Irish or the Vikings or the Norse. Because members of these ethnic groups accept the use of their names, Native Americans should also be proud of this recognition of their heritage.

But Native Americans do object to their symbols being used by athletic teams. Since the early 1970s individuals and organizations such as the American Indian Movement have sought to eliminate the use of Native American names, mascots, and logos by sports teams.[14] They use several key arguments, foremost, racist stereotyping. Names such as Indians, Braves, and Chiefs are not inherently offensive, but some names, logos, and mascots project a violent caricature of Native Americans (scalpers, savages). Teams that use Native American names commonly employ the tomahawk chop, war paint, and mascots dressed as Native Americans. This depiction of Native Americans as bloodthirsty warriors distorts history, since whites invaded Native American lands, oppressed Native peoples, and even employed and justified a policy of genocide toward them.

Some mascots are especially demeaning to Native Americans. Chief Nok-a-homa of the Atlanta Braves comes out of a teepee after an Atlanta homerun and does a ceremonial dance. Many view this as acceptable. But what if the Atlanta team were the Darkies and after a homerun a person looking like a rural black man would come out of a tarpaper shack and pick cotton? Chances are everyone would consider this depiction of another racial group offensive. So too would naming a team Niggers, Spics, or Gooks. Then there is Chief Wahoo, "the red-faced, big-nosed, grinning, drywall-toothed moron who graces the peak of every Cleveland Indians cap."[15] Is such a caricature appropriate? Clyde Bellecourt, national director of the American Indian Movement (AIM), summarizes the complaints:

> If you look up the word "redskin" in both the Webster's and Random House dictionaries, you'll find the word is defined as being offensive. Can you imagine if they called them the Washington Jews and the team mascot was a rabbi leading them in (the song) *Hava Nagila,* fans in the stands wearing yarmulkes and waving little sponge torahs? The word Indian isn't offensive. Brave isn't offensive, but it's the behavior that accompanies all of this that's offensive. The rubber tomahawks. The chicken-feather headdresses. People wearing war paint and making these ridiculous war whoops with a tomahawk in one hand and a beer in the other. All of these things have significant meaning for us. And the psychological impact it has, especially on our youth, is devastating.[16]

Another problem is the imitation or misuse of symbols that have religious significance to some Native American peoples. Using dances, chants, drummings, and other rituals at sporting events clearly trivializes their meaning. Also problematic is the homogenization of Native American cultures. Native Americans are portrayed uniformly, without regard for the sometimes enormous differences among tribes. Thus, through the use of Native American names of mascots, society defines who Native Americans are instead of allowing Native Americans to determine how society thinks of them.

A few colleges, such as Stanford, Siena, Miami of Ohio, Dartmouth, and St. John's, have taken these objections seriously and have changed their names and mascots. Most high schools and colleges, however, resist such a change. Ironically, they insist on retaining the Native American symbols even though those schools do not have a Native American heritage or significant Native American student representation. The members of these schools and their constituencies insist on retaining their Native American names because they are part of their collective identities. This allegiance to their school symbols seems to have higher priority than sensitivity to the negative consequences produced by inappropriate depictions of Native Americans.

Sexist Names for Women's Teams[17]

Many studies have shown the varied ways in which language acts in the defining, deprecation, and exclusion of women.[18] Names do this, too. Naming women's and men's athletic team is not a neutral process. The names chosen often are badges of femininity and masculinity, hence of inferiority and superiority. To the degree that this occurs, the names of women's and men's athletic teams reinforce a basic element of social structure: gender division and hierarchy. Team names reflect this division as well as the asymmetry that is associated with it. Despite advances made by women in sport since the implementation of Title IX, widespread naming practices continue to mark female athletes as unusual, aberrant, or invisible.

My colleague Maxine Baca Zinn and I examined the names and accompanying logos and mascots of sports teams for women and men at 1,185 coeducational four-year colleges and universities.[19] We identified eight gender-linked practices associated with names/logos that diminish and trivialize women.

First, physical markers. One common naming practice emphasizes the physical appearance of women, such as the Angelo State Rambelles, or the Bellarmine College Belles (the men are the Knights). As Casey Miller and Kate Swift argue, this practice is sexist because the "emphasis on the physical characteristics of women is offensive in contexts where men are described in terms of achievement."[20]

Second, girl or gal. The use of "girl" or "gal" stresses the presumed immaturity and irresponsibility of women, such as the Elon College Golden Girls. "Just as *boy* can be blatantly offensive to minority men, so *girl* can have comparable patronizing and demeaning implications for women."[21]

Third, feminine suffixes. This is a popular form of gender differentiation found in the names of athletic, social, and women's groups. The practice not only marks women but also denotes a feminine derivative by establishing a "female negative trivial category."[22] The devaluation is accomplished by tagging words with feminine suffixes such as "ette." At Dillard University the men's team is the Blue Devils, and the women's team is the Devilettes; at Albany State the men are the Golden Rams and the women are the Rammettes. Another suffix is "esse." At Duquesne University and James Madison University the men are the Dukes and the women the Duchesses.

Fourth, lady. This label has several meanings that demean women as athletes. Lady is used to "evoke a standard of propriety, correct behavior, and elegance,"[23] characteristics that are decidedly unathletic. Similarly, "lady" carries overtones recalling the age of chivalry. "This makes the term seem polite at first, but we must also remember that these implications are perilous: they suggest that a 'lady' is helpless, and cannot do things for herself."[24] The use of "lady" for women's teams is common, for example, the University of Florida Lady Gators or the University of Arkansas Lady Razorbacks. At Kenyon College the men are the Lords and the women the Ladies, and at Washington and Jefferson College the men are Presidents and the women, First Ladies. In both of these instances the names for the women's teams clearly mark their status as inferior to that of the men.

Fifth, male as a false generic. This practice assumes that the masculine in the language, word, or name choice is the norm while ignoring the feminine altogether. Miller and Swift define this procedure as "terms used of a class or group that are not applicable to all members."[25] The use of "mankind" to encompass both sexes has its parallel among men's and women's athletic teams that have the same name, for example, the Rams (Colorado State University), Stags (Concordia College), Norsemen (Luther College), the Tomcats (Thiel College), and the Hokies (a hokie is a castrated turkey; Virginia Tech). Dale Spender has called the practice of treating the masculine as the norm "one of the most pervasive and pernicious rules that has been encoded."[26] Its consequence is to make women invisible as well as secondary to men, since they are robbed of a separate identity.

Sixth, male name with a female modifier. This practice applies the feminine to a name that usually denotes a male, giving females lower status.[27] Examples among sports teams are the Lady Friars of Providence College, the Lady Statesmen of William Penn College, the Lady Penmen of New Hampshire College, the Lady Centaurs of Columbia College, and the Lady Gamecocks of the University of South Carolina (a gamecock is a fighting rooster). Using such oxymorons "reflects role conflict and contributes to the lack of acceptance of women's sport."[28]

Seventh, double gender marking. This occurs when the name of the women's team is a diminutive of the men's team name combined with "belle" or "lady" or other feminine modifier. For example, the men's teams at Mississippi College are the Choctaws, and the women's teams are designated as the Lady Chocs. At the University of Kentucky the men's teams are the Wildcats and the women's teams are the Lady Kats. The men's teams at the University of Colorado are the Buffalos and the women's teams are the Lady Buffs. At Augusta College the women are the Lady Jags, whereas the men are the Jaguars. Similarly, at both the University of Nebraska–Omaha and the University of Texas–Arlington, the men are the Mavericks and the women, the Lady Mavs. Compounding the feminine intensifies women's secondary status. Double gender marking occurs "perhaps to underline the inappropriateness or rarity of the feminine noun or to emphasize its negativity."[29]

Eighth, male/female paired polarity. Women's and men's teams can be assigned names that represent a female/male opposition. When this occurs, the names of the men's teams embody competitiveness and other positive traits associated with sport, whereas the names for women's teams are lighthearted or cute. The essence of sport is competition, and physical skills largely determine outcomes. Successful athletes are believed to embody such traits as courage, bravura, boldness, self-confidence, and aggression. When the names given men's teams imply these traits but the names for women's teams suggest that women are playful and cuddly, then women are trivialized and de-athleticized. For example, the College of Wooster men are the Fighting Scots, and the women are the Scotties; Mercer University men's teams are the Bears and the women are the Teddy Bears; at the Albany College of Pharmacy the men are the Panthers and the women, the Pink Panthers; and at Fort Valley State College the men's teams are named the Wildcats and the women's teams, the Wildkittens.

Another grouping occurs when names that could be included in one of the above categories also incorporate race. This occurs especially with teams using Native American symbols. The men's teams at Southeastern Oklahoma State University are the Savages and the women's teams are the Savagettes, using the diminutive feminine suffix combined with a negative stereotype for the racial category. Similarly, at Montclair State College the men are the Indians and the women are the Squaws. The word "squaw" also refers to a woman's pelvic area and means prostitute in some native languages. Vernon Bellecourt of the American Indian Movement says, "The issue itself is clear. . . . The word 'squaw' has got to go in all its forms. It's demeaning and degrading to Indian women and all women."[30]

Our survey found that approximately three-eighths of U.S. colleges and universities employ sexist names and slightly over half have sexist names and/or logos for their athletic teams. Thus the identity symbols for athletic teams at those schools contribute to the maintenance of male dominance within college sports.

Since the traditional masculine gender role matches most athletic qualities better than the traditional feminine gender role, the images and symbols are male. Women do not fit into this scheme. They are "other" even when they do participate. Their team names and logos tend to perpetuate and strengthen the image of female inferiority by making them secondary, invisible, trivial, or unathletic.

Resistance to Change

It is important to note that many schools do not have team names, mascots, and logos that are racist or sexist. They use race-neutral and gender-neutral names such as Bears, Eagles, Seagulls, Cougars, Wasps, Mustangs, Royals, Saints, Big Green, or Blue Streaks. Schools that currently employ racist or sexist names could change to neutral ones that embody the traits desired in athletic teams such as courage, strength, and aggressiveness.[31] For some, such a change would be relatively easy—dropping the use of "lady" or "ette" as modifiers, for example. Teams with Native American names or male names (stags, rams, hokies, centaurs) must adopt new names to eliminate the racism or sexism inherent in their present names. A few schools have made these changes over the past fifteen years or so. Most schools, however, resist changing names with passion because a name change negates the school's traditions.

The athletic teams at my school, Colorado State University, are called the Rams. Is it appropriate for the women's teams to be called Rams (rams are male sheep)? This question has been raised from time to time by the Faculty Women's Caucus and a few male professors, but strong resistance from journalists, student government leaders, and the Committee on Intercollegiate Athletics, as well as silence by the women athletes and the coaches of women's teams, have worked to maintain the status quo.

The naming issue at Colorado State University reveals a contradiction. Many students, including women student-athletes, express a lack of interest in the issue, yet it evokes strong emotions among others. These responses seem to originate in several sources at Colorado State and, by implication, elsewhere. These arguments parallel resistance to changing sexist language in general.[32]

Tradition, above all, is always a barrier to change. Students, alumni, faculty, and athletes become accustomed to a particular name for their university and its athletic teams, and it seems "natural." This is the argument made on behalf of the many teams that continue to use Native American names and symbols for their teams despite the objections of Native Americans. So too with names that are sexist. But even if a school name has the force of tradition, is it justified to continue using it if it is racist or sexist? If a sexist team name reinforces and socializes sexist thinking, however subtly, then it must be changed. If not, then the institution is publicly sexist.

Many see the naming issue as trivial. However, it is not trivial to the group being demeaned, degraded, and trivialized. Some progressives argue that there are more important issues to address than changing racist or sexist names of athletic teams. This illustrates the contradiction that the naming of teams is at once trivial and important. For African Americans, whether the University of Mississippi fans sing "Dixie" and wave Confederate flags is not as important as ending discrimination and getting good jobs. Similarly, for Native Americans the derogatory use of their heritage surrounding athletic contests is relatively unimportant compared to raising their standard of living. For women, the sexist naming of athletic teams is not as significant as pay equity or breaking the "glass ceiling" or achieving equity with men in athletic departments in resources, scholarships, and media attention. Faced with a choice among these options, the naming issue would be secondary. But this sets up a false choice. We can work to remove all manifestations of racism and sexism on college campuses. Referring to language and relevant to the team names issue as well, the Association for Women in Psychology Ad Hoc Committee on Sexist Language has addressed and refuted the "trivial concern" argument:

> The major objection, often even to *discussing* changing sexist language, is that it is a superficial matter compared with the real physical and economic oppression of women. And indeed, women's total oppression must end; we are not suggesting any diversion of energies from that struggle. We are, however, suggesting that this is an important part of it.[33]

The opposite point—that the naming issue is crucially important—is the third argument. Symbols are extremely compelling in the messages they convey. Their importance is understood when rebellious groups demean or defame symbols of the powerful, such as the flag. Names and other symbols have the power to elevate or "put down" a group. If racist or sexist, they reinforce and therefore maintain the secondary status of African Americans, Native Americans, or women through stereotyping, caricature, derogation, trivialization, diminution, or making them invisible. Most of us, however, fail to see the problem with symbols that demean or defame the powerless because these symbols support the existing power arrangements in society. Despite their apparent triviality, the symbols surrounding sports teams are important because they can (and often do) contribute to patterns of social dominance.

Colleges and universities, for the most part, are making major efforts to diversify their student bodies, faculties, and administrations by race, ethnicity, and gender. This laudable goal is clearly at odds with the existence of racist and sexist names and practices for their athletic teams. The leadership in these schools (boards of regents, chancellors, presidents, and faculty senates) must take a stand against racism and sexism in all its forms and take appropriate action. Removing all racist and sexist symbols such as names, mascots, flags, logos, and songs is an important beginning to this crucial project.

Notes

1. See, for example, Martin Sanchez Jankowski, *Islands in the Street: Gangs and American Urban Society* (Berkeley: University of California Press, 1991).
2. Emile Durkheim, *The Elementary Forms of Religious Life,* trans. Joseph Ward Sivain (New York: Free Press, 1947). This classic was first published in 1915.
3. Janet Lever, *Soccer Madness* (Chicago: University of Chicago Press, 1983), p. 12.
4. See John R. Fuller and Elisabeth Anne Manning, "Violence and Sexism in College Mascots and Symbols: A Typology," *Free Inquiry in Creative Sociology* 15 (1987): 61–64.
5. Margaret Carlisle Duncan, "Representation and the Gun That Points Backwards," *Journal of Sport and Social Issues* 17 (April 1993): 42–46.
6. Dennis Cauchon, "A Slave-Holding Past: Search for Perspective," *USA Today,* March 9, 1998, p. 8A.
7. Brian Britt, "Neo-Confederate Culture," *Z Magazine* 9 (December 1996): 26–30.
8. The following is taken from three sources: William Nack, "Look Away, Dixie Land," *Sports Illustrated,* November 3, 1997, p. 114; Douglas S. Lederman, "Old Times Not Forgotten: A Battle Over Symbols," in *Sport in Contemporary Society,* ed. D. Stanley Eitzen, 5th ed. (New York: St. Martin's, 1996), pp. 128–133; and Paula Edelson, "Just Whistlin' Dixie," *Z Magazine* 4 (November 1991): 72–74.
9. Nack, "Look Away."
10. Lederman, "Old Times Not Forgotten," p. 132.
11. Ibid., p. 133.
12. Ray Franks, *What's in a Nickname? Exploring the Jungle of College Athletic Mascots* (Amarillo, Tex.: Ray Franks, 1982).
13. The names and mascots for schools used in this essay are taken from Ray Franks, *What's in a Nickname?* This comprehensive compilation of information, although dated, is the most current listing. Therefore, some of the schools named in the essay may have subsequently changed the names of their athletic teams.
14. This section is taken primarily from two sources: Laurel Davis, "Protest against the Use of Native American Mascots: A Challenge to Traditional American Identity," *Journal of Sport and Social Issues* 17 (April 1993): 9–22; and Ward Churchill, "Crimes against Humanity," *Sport in Contemporary Society,* ed. D. Stanley Eitzen, 5th ed. (New York: St. Martin's, 1996), pp. 134–141.
15. Rick Telander, "These Nicknames, Symbols Should Offend All Americans," *Chicago Sun-Times,* October 20, 1995, p. 143.
16. Quoted in Bob Kravitz, "Aim of Native Americans' Protest Is True," *Rocky Mountain News,* January 21, 1992, p. 39.
17. This section is based in part on D. Stanley Eitzen and Maxine Baca Zinn, "The De-Athleticization of Women: The Naming and Gender Marking of Collegiate Sport Teams," *Sociology of Sport Journal* 6 (December 1989): 362–370; D. Stanley Eitzen and Maxine Baca Zinn, "The Sexist Naming of Athletic Teams and Resistance to Change," *Journal of Sport and Social Issues* 17 (April 1993): 34–41; D. Stanley Eitzen and Maxine Baca Zinn, "Never Mind the Braves; What about the Lady Rams?" *Baltimore Sun,* November 3, 1991, p. 3D
18. Barrie Thorne, Cheris Kramarae, and Nancy M. Henley, "Language, Gender, and

Society: Opening a Second Decade of Research," in *Language, Gender, and Society,* ed. Barrie Thorne and Nancy M. Henley (Rowley, Mass.: Newbury House, 1985), pp. 7–24; Nancy M. Henley, "This New Species That Seeks a New Language: On Sexism in Language and Language Change," in *Women and Men in Transition,* ed. Joyce Penfield (Albany: State University of New York Press, 1987), pp. 3–27.

19. Eitzen and Baca Zinn, "Sexist Naming of Athletic Teams."

20. Casey Miller and Kate Swift, *The Handbook of Nonsexist Writing* (New York: Lippincott and Crowell, 1980), p. 87.

21. Ibid., p. 71.

22. Casey Miller and Kate Swift, *Words and Women: New Language in New Times* (Garden City, N.Y.: Doubleday-Anchor, 1977), p. 58.

23. Ibid., p. 72.

24. Robin Lakoff, *Language and Woman's Place* (New York: Harper and Row, 1975), p. 25.

25. Miller and Swift, *Handbook of Nonsexist Writing,* p. 9.

26. Dale Spender, *Man Made Language* (London: Routledge and Kegan Paul, 1980), p. 3.

27. Dennis Baron, *Grammar and Gender* (New Haven: Yale University Press, 1986), p. 112.

28. Fuller and Manning, "Violence and Sexism," p. 64.

29. Baron, *Grammar and Gender,* p. 115.

30. Quoted in Lois Tomas, "What's in a Name?" *In These Times,* October 19, 1997, p. 11.

31. Daniel P. Starr, "Unisex Nicknames One Way of Skirting Gender Problem," *NCAA News,* March 20, 1991, p. 4.

32. Maija S. Blaubergs, "An Analysis of Classic Arguments against Changing Sexist Language," *Women's Studies International Quarterly* 3 (1980): 135–147.

33. Association for Women in Psychology Ad Hoc Committee on Sexist Language, "Help Stamp Out Sexism: Change the Language!" *APA Monitor* 6, no. 11 (1975): 16.

Chapter 4

Sport Is Fair, Sport Is Foul

Years ago Dartmouth won a football game with Cornell. A review of the films established that Dartmouth had received a fifth down on its winning drive. Rather than accept an undeserved victory, the Dartmouth president forfeited the win.

In 1990 the University of Colorado scored its winning touchdown against Missouri on a drive that included a fifth down that officials did not notice until after the game. Colorado refused to forfeit and at the conclusion of the season was declared national cochampion. Similarly, in 1994, Stanford and Northwestern played to a 41–41 tie. After reviewing the films, the referees admitted that they had given Stanford an undeserved touchdown, yet Stanford did not forfeit.

We celebrate sport for many good reasons. It excites and inspires us. We identify with athletic teams and our sports heroes. We savor the great moments of sport, when an athlete does the seemingly impossible or when the truly gifted athlete makes the impossible routine. We exult when a team or an athlete overcomes great odds to succeed. We are touched by genuine camaraderie among teammates. We are uplifted by the biographies of athletes who have used sport to get an education that otherwise would have been denied to them because of economic circumstances. Others have used sport to overcome delinquency and drug addiction.

Sport promotes fair play, and a high ethical road is sometimes taken. A month or so after Rockdale County (Georgia) won the state basketball championship

This essay is constructed from a number of sources, including D. Stanley Eitzen, "The Paradox of Sport: The Contradictory Lessons Learned," *The World & I* 11 (July 1996): 307–309, 312–321; D. Stanley Eitzen, "Ethical Dilemmas in American Sport: The Dark Side of Competition," *Vital Speeches of the Day* 62 (January 1996): 182–185; D. Stanley Eitzen, "The Dark Side of Competition in American Society," *Vital Speeches of the Day* 56 (January 1990): 184–187; and D. Stanley Eitzen, "Ethical Problems in American Sport," *Journal of Sport and Social Issues* 12 (Spring 1988): 17–30.

in 1987, the coach, Cleveland Stroud, found that he had unknowingly used an ineligible player. Although the player in question was in the game only a minute or two and had not scored, Stroud notified the authorities of the infraction. As a result, the school forfeited the only state championship it had ever won. Coach Stroud said, "You've got to do what's honest and right. People forget the scores of basketball games; they don't ever forget what you're made of."[1]

Fair play was also exhibited in a Colorado state high school Class A championship basketball game when Agate played Stratton. Because of a mix-up over keys, Agate could not dress in time for the game. The referees called a technical foul, allowing Stratton to begin the game with two free throws. The Stratton coach, feeling that this was unfair to his opponent, told his player to miss the shots. In a similar vein, Andy Herr of Bloomington, Indiana, chose to hold up and finish second in a 10K race in Toledo because the leader had accidentally taken a wrong turn.[2] This unwillingness to accept a tainted victory is found often in professional golf, when players call penalties on themselves, as Greg Norman did when he disqualified himself for a minor rule violation when leading a 1990 tournament. Tom Kite, playing in the 1993 Kemper Open, told his playing partner Grant Waite that Waite was about to commit a rules infraction that would result in a one-stroke penalty. Waite corrected his mistake and went on to beat Kite by one stroke. Kite's sportsmanship cost him about $100,000.[3]

There are countless examples in sport of competitors showing respect for one another. In the 1995 Prefontaine Classic the two-mile competition featured two premier runners, Bob Kennedy and Todd Williams. After a fierce battle (won by Kennedy) the two competitors embraced and then jogged a lap together. Winner Kennedy said, "We're friends but we were both racing to win, and we wound up taking each other to a higher level."[4]

But for all of the honor and integrity found in sport, there is also much about sport that disregards the ideals of fair play. The Colorado State University football team upset Louisiana State University in 1992. On CSU's winning drive there was a fumble. An LSU player fell on the ball, but in the ensuing pileup, a CSU player ended up with the ball illegally. The player, Geoff Grenier, was quoted in the newspaper as saying that he elbowed and kicked a player in the pile to get the ball. The referees did not see this action and awarded the ball to CSU. CSU coach Earle Bruce said, "One player who should get credit for the victory is Geoff Grenier. If we had lost the ball, the game was over. Geoff found a way to get the ball."[5]

The Duality of Sport

A widely held assumption of parents, educators, banquet speakers, and editorial writers is that participating in sport prepares children and youth for success in a competitive society. According to folk wisdom, these young people will take on a number of desirable character traits from sport. They will learn to strive for excellence, to persevere, to sacrifice, to work hard, to follow orders, to work with others, and to be self-disciplined. But are these the lessons that young people actually learn from sport? The answer is complex and paradoxical. Philosopher Charles Banham has observed that many do benefit from the sports experience, but for many others, sport "encourages selfishness, envy, conceit, hostility, and bad temper. Far from ventilating the mind, it stifles it. Good sportsmanship may be a product of sport, but so is bad sportsmanship."[6]

Sport psychologist Terry D. Orlick also points to the contradictory nature of sport:

> For every positive psychological or social outcome in sports, there are possible negative outcomes. For example, sports can offer a child group membership or group exclusion, acceptance or rejection, positive feedback or negative feedback, a sense of accomplishment or a sense of failure, evidence of self-worth or a lack of evidence of self-worth. Likewise, sports can develop cooperation and a concern for others, but they can also develop intense rivalry and a complete lack of concern for others.[7]

Thus there is a fundamental paradox in sport. On the one hand, sport inspires as it fosters the admirable traits of courage, determination, hard work, fairness, respect, sacrifice, selflessness, and loyalty. But sport also promotes rule breaking, selfishness, greed, contempt for opponents, and violence on the field as well as deviant behaviors off the field.

The Dark Side of Sport

Sport has a dark side. Big-time sport has corrupted academe by superseding academics, engaging in recruiting violations, and exploiting athletes (as elaborated in chapter 8). Coaches sometimes engage in outrageous behaviors such as brutalizing and publicly belittling their players. But if they win, they are rewarded handsomely (discussed in chapter 7). The media glorify gratuitous violence. Some athletes take drugs. Some athletes have been convicted of gang rape and spouse abuse. Many athletes cheat to achieve a competitive edge. Sports organizations exploit athletes. Many believe that the problems in sport result from bad people. Others believe that the problems stem from a morally distorted sports world in which winning supersedes all other considerations and moral values have become confused with the bottom line. In this in-your-face, whip-your-butt climate, winning at any price has become the prevailing code of conduct.

Americans demand winners in school, business, politics, and sport.[8] Coaches are fired if they are not successful; teams are booed if they play for ties. Super Bowl losers are defined as *losers,* not as runners-up. A grotesque example of exalting first place and debasing second place is demonstrated by a football team composed of fifth-graders that was undefeated going into the Florida state championship game several years ago. They lost that game in a close contest. At a banquet for these boys following that season, each player was given a plaque on which was inscribed a quote from Vince Lombardi:

> There is no room for second place. I have finished second twice at Green Bay and I never want to finish second again. There is a second place bowl game but it is a game for losers played by losers. It is and always has been an American zeal to be first in anything we do and to win and to win and to win.

The quote from Lombardi told the boys not to accept winning second place. Second is losing. The only permissible placement is first.

If second is unacceptable and all the rewards go to the winners, then some will do whatever it takes to be first. It may require using steroids, trying to injure a competitor, or altering a recruit's transcript so that he or she can play (illegally). These unethical practices are an integral part of sport. This being the case, what lessons are being taught in the sports world? How is the character of athletes being shaped in the process?

The Debasement of Fair Play

The essence of sport is competition. The goal is to win. But to win ethically requires a spirit of fair play. Fairness tends to prevail in certain sports such as golf; in other sports the prevalent mood is to achieve an unfair advantage over an opponent. Getting such a competitive edge unfairly is viewed by many in these sports as "strategy" rather than cheating. Thus some illegal acts are accepted as part of the game. In basketball, for example, it is common for a player to pretend to be fouled in order to receive an unmerited free throw and penalize the opponent with an undeserved foul. Commonly, rebounders nudge or shove their opponents out of position. About Dennis Rodman, the best rebounder in professional basketball, *Sports Illustrated* said, "Like every successful rebounder, Rodman has certain tricks he uses to help him gain advantage. . . . He particularly likes to pin his opponent's arm between his own arm and his body, making it impossible for the opponent to jump. He gets called for this fairly often but not nearly as often as he gets away with it."[9]

Similarly, in soccer, it is common for a player to feign an injury "caused" by an opponent, hoping that an out of position official will award his team an undeserved penalty kick with a relatively high certainty of scoring.

Football players are often coached to use illegal techniques to hold or trip opponents without detection. Some offensive linemen grease their jerseys (an illegal act) so that blockers will have more difficulty holding them (another illegal act). To show how accepted these forms of cheating are, consider the commentary during an NFL game between the Denver Broncos and the Los Angeles Raiders. A replay showed that a Denver offensive lineman grabbed and held a defensive lineman. Upon seeing this blatant infraction of the rules, the sportscaster said, "It's only illegal if he gets caught."[10] Former professional football player Tim Green echoes this sentiment:

> I don't know an NFL cornerback that doesn't consider bumping a receiver beyond the 5-yard chuck rule a matter of survival. And I'll confess that as a player I thought nothing of grabbing an opponent's jersey to complete a pass rush stunt but wasn't called for it once.
>
> You cheat to win, and because you can. Most illegal blocks, pass interference, holding and hands-to-the-face penalties go uncalled. *In football, you're not wrong unless you're caught* [emphasis added].[11]

According to Green, his former coach Jerry Glanville told his team each week, "If you ain't cheatin', you ain't trying."[12]

Pitchers in baseball sometimes achieve an illegal advantage by scuffing the ball or by putting a foreign substance (spit or vaseline) on it so that it drops suddenly when pitched. Catchers sometimes help in this nefarious activity by doctoring the ball for their pitchers, using thumbtacks in their shin guards to rough up a ball or using vaseline that was applied to their forearm. Batters counter by illegally corking their bats.[13] Gaylord Perry, a Hall of Fame pitcher who won 314 games, said, "I became an outlaw in the strictest sense of the word—a man who lives outside the law, in this case the law of baseball. . . . A pitcher who can slick one up effectively has twice the advantage."[14] These vignettes reveal that the culture of some sports is to get a competitive advantage over the opponent even if it means taking an unfair advantage. When this occurs, sport is sending a message that winning is more important than playing fair.

Violence

Another area of concern has to do with normative violence. Many popular sports demand aggressive moves such as body checking, blocking, and tackling, but the culture of these sports sometimes goes beyond what is needed to move or take down an opponent. Players are taught to deliver a blow to the opponent, not just to block or tackle him. They are taught to gang tackle, to make the ball carrier "pay the price." The assumption is that physically punishing the other player increases the probability of the opponent's fumbling, losing his concentration and executing poorly the next time, or being replaced by a less talented substitute.

Coaches sometimes reward athletes for extra hard hits. *Sports Illustrated* noted three types of helmet decals that are awarded. At Florida, a lineman receives a "dead roach" if he knocks his opponent so hard that he lies prone with his legs and arms in the air; at Wisconsin the athlete receives a "decleater" when he stands up to "dee opponent and knocks him off dee cleats"; and at Miami a player is awarded a "slobber knocker" if he hits an opposing player so hard that saliva is expelled from his mouth.[15] In the past the Denver Broncos coaching staff (like other NFL teams yet contrary to league rules) gave monetary awards each week to the players who hit their opponents the hardest. In 1997 a Kansas City Chiefs player said on a radio show that coach Marty Schottenheimer offered to pay off any fines his team incurred for breaking the jaws or knocking down any of Denver's players.[16] Unethical violence is such a part of the game that a Buffalo Bills player in a 1993 playoff game put a splint on the outside of his good leg so that opponents would concentrate on that leg rather than on his bad leg.

This emphasis on intimidating violence is almost universal among football and hockey coaches, players, and fans. The object is not to just hit but to punish and even to injure. Sociologist Michael Smith has argued that violence in hockey, as in war, is a socially rewarded behavior. The players are convinced that aggression (body checking, intimidation, and the like) is vital to winning.[17] As Minnesota Vikings defensive back Joey Browner has put it, "It's not good for business if you care for a second whether blood is bubbling out of a guy's mouth." Sportswriter John Underwood concludes that

> brutality is its own fertilizer. From "get by with what you can" it is a short hop to the deviations that poison sport. . . . But it is not just the acts that border on criminal that are intolerable, it is the permissive atmosphere they spring from. The "lesser" evils that are given tacit approval as "techniques" of the game, even within the rules.[18]

Drugs to Enhance Performance

Some athletes use drugs to increase their intensity, endurance, or strength despite the fact that they are illegal and entail harmful side effects (see chapter 5). The most commonly used drugs are anabolic steroids, which make athletes bigger, stronger, and faster. Various studies have found that 7 percent of high school male athletes and 2.4 percent of high school female athletes use anabolic steroids, as do 15 percent of male college athletes and 6 percent of female college athletes. Former NFL players claim that up to 75 percent of the players in that league use or have used steroids (offensive and defensive lines and linebackers, who play the power positions in professional football, are the most likely to have used them).[19] Elite athletes in weight lifting, body building, and weight throwing (shot put, discus, hammer, javelin) are almost required to take steroids if they want to be successful. Canadian weightlifter Jacques Demers explained why he felt it necessary to use steroids: "To go to international competitions, you have to meet international standards and those are based on what the Russians and Bulgarians do. They are the best weightlifters in the world. . . . and they take steroids. So if I go to the Olympics, I must take steroids."[20]

The use of performance-enhancing drugs corrupts the essence of fair sporting competition—it is cheating. What lessons are being taught when some athletes take drugs, find ways to conceal their actions, and then are honored and rewarded handsomely for winning?

Disrespecting Opponents

Disrespect for opponents takes several forms. One is to humiliate a team by running up the score. Crushing an opponent is clearly evident in big-time college football, since scores affect team rankings, which, in turn, determine participation in bowl games (depending on the prestige of the bowl, teams receive anywhere from $150,000 to $12 million for playing). But humiliation of an opponent occurs at other levels as well. For example, a Laramie, Wyoming, girls junior high school basketball team won a game by a score of 81–1, using a full-court press throughout the game. In 1997 Long Island University, a Division I school, played Medgar Evers College, a Division III school, and won by 117 points (179–62), the largest victory margin in NCAA history. Long Island pressed its hapless opponents for the entire game.[21]

Another part of sport these days, not in golf but clearly in basketball at all levels, is trash talking, wherein one player talks to a player in an excessively boastful or scornful manner. This intimidating form of gamesmanship is tolerated by many coaches and is commonly practiced by players.[22] By definition, this practice does not promote mutual respect among competitors.

Spectators also show disrespect for opponents, even to the point of encouraging violence. They cheer an opponent's injury or engage in bloodlust cheers such as, "Kill! Kill! Hate! Hate! Murder! Murder! Mutilate!"

Sometimes fans try to distract opponents by yelling racial slurs. When Patrick Ewing played at Georgetown, he was confronted by T-shirts that said "Ewing Kant Read Dis," a banner at Providence College that read "Ewing Can't Read," and Villanova fans holding up a bedsheet with the words "Ewing Is an Ape."[23] Several years ago Arizona State fans chanted "P-L-O" at Arizona's Steve Kerr, whose father had been assassinated by terrorists in Beirut.[24]

The Behavior of Coaches

Coaches are important role models for their athletes. Many coaches take this responsibility seriously, insisting on fair play, respect for opponents, and humane treatment of their athletes. Other cheat. Some throw tantrums. Pat Riley, coach of the Miami Heat professional basketball team, fines his players $1,500 if they help an opposing player get off the floor. Some male coaches are sexist and homophobic, calling their male players pussies or fags if they are not aggressive enough. Coach Bobby Knight of Indiana, for example, once put a tampon in the locker of a player as a means of letting him know that Knight thought he was a wimp.[25]

Because winning is so important, some coaches drive their athletes too hard, take them out of the classroom too often, and encourage them to use performance-enhancing drugs. They may also abuse their athletes physically and mentally. Verbal assaults by coaches are routine at all levels of sport (see chapter 7). *Newsweek* carried a mother's description of how one girl was treated by her Little League coach:

> His narrowed eyes burn like hot little coals, and he screams through clenched teeth, his face thrust into hers. . . . She leans back a bit from time to time to avoid the spray of spit he spews as he spells it out for her: she's stupid, lazy and worthless, and if she doesn't shape up someone else will soon be doing her job.[26]

Coaches may encourage violence in their players. Green Bay Packers coach Vince Lombardi once said, "To play this game, you have to have that fire within you, and nothing stokes that fire like hate."[27] Some coaches whip their players into a frenzy that can lead to excessive violence.[28] A North Carolina football coach tried to fire up his squad for their 1939 game with rival Wake Forest by mailing each of his players anonymous threatening letters. Mississippi State football coach Jackie Sherrill had a bull castrated in front of his players at the end of the last practice before they were to play the Texas Longhorns. In a less celebrated case, a high school coach in Iowa playing a team called the Golden Eagles spray painted a chicken gold and had his players stomp it to death in the locker room before the contest. Libertyville, Illinois, football coach Dale Christensen, during a pep talk prior to a state playoff game, tried to break up a fake fight he had arranged between two youths. Shots rang out from a starter pistol that fired blanks and Christensen fell, with fake blood (catsup) spreading across his shirt. Another coach bit off a toad's head in front of his players in an effort to motivate them to be more aggressive.

What lesson is a coach teaching when he openly asks a player to cheat? A few years ago, the Pretty Prairie (Kansas) High School basketball coach had twin boys on his team. One of the twins was injured but suited up for a game in which his brother was in foul trouble at halftime. The coach had the twins change jerseys so that the foul-plagued twin would begin the second half with no fouls charged to the player's number he was now wearing. A high school football coach in Portland sent a player into the game on a very foggy night. The player asked, "Who am I going in for?" "No one," the coach replied, "the fog is so thick the ref will never notice you."[29]

Big-time college coaches are rewarded handsomely when they win. In addition to generous salary raises, successful college coaches receive lucrative contracts from shoe companies, endorsements, media deals, summer camps, speaking engagements, country club memberships, insurance annuities, and the like. With the potential income of college coaches sometimes exceeding $2 million at the highest levels, the temptations are great to offer illegal inducements to prospective athletes or to find illicit ways to keep them eligible (phantom courses, surrogate test takers, altered transcripts). These scandals make a mockery of higher education and also make cynics of the so-called student-athletes (see chapter 8). These athletes know that they are athletes first and students second. They soon realize that winning is the important thing, not how they play the game.

Ethics and Administrative Decisions

College administrators are not always ethical when they hire and fire coaches strictly on their won-lost record. For the most part, school administrators do not fire coaches guilty of shady transgressions if they win.

Immorality is not just a matter of breaking or bending the rules—the rules themselves may be unfair or even immoral. Powerful organizations such as universities, leagues, Little League baseball, and the U.S. Olympic Committee have denied equality to women and have exploited athletes. Until the mid-1970s, Little League, a baseball organization that operates 20,000 leagues for children from eight to twelve years of age, had a males-only policy as part of its federal charter. Similarly, the International Olympic Committee banned women participants early in this century and then relented, allowing them to participate in nonendurance events.

The exploitation of athletes is exemplified by the rules of the NCAA, which are consistently unfair to college athletes. NCAA rules require that athletes commit to a four-year agreement with a school, yet schools make only a year-by-year commitment to athletes. This means that players can lose their scholarships at the whim of their coaches, yet they cannot move to another school without waiting a year before they are eligible to play (two years if the coach does not formally approve of the player's transfer). This rule ties the athlete to the school even if the new recruit has not started school and the coach who signed him has left the school. Full-ride scholarship athletes in the revenue-producing sports of men's basketball and football receive room, board, tuition, and books while generating millions of dollars; their coaches make many hundreds of thousands. The players in big-time programs must wonder about the fairness of such a system.

Disloyalty

One of the traits that sport hopes to transmit to its participants is loyalty—allegiance to teammates, coaches, school, fans, and locality. But loyalty is becoming passé in sport. College coaches often exhibit an absence of loyalty by breaking one contract to coach elsewhere; unlike players who move, they are eligible to coach immediately. A few athletes repeal their commitment to their school by leaving to play at the professional level before their eligibility expires.

Problems with loyalty are even greater at the professional level. With free agency, professional athletes usually follow the money, leaving behind their teammates and fans. As a result, the average major league baseball player changes teams every 3.3 years, Only 13 percent of the players play for the same teams they did four years ago.[30] Greed in sport is more obvious when owners of profitable professional teams move their franchises to other cities for lucrative financial packages (see chapter 10). The Cleveland Browns' move to Baltimore is an especially egregious example of callous disregard for the longtime bond between a team and its fans. What this and other franchise moves, real or threatened, show is the bottom-line mentality in sport that makes loyalty an outmoded concept.

Consequences from the Lessons Learned

Given the contradictions found in sport, the consequences are not uniform for all participants. Sociologist Jay Coakley argues that (1) sports can be constructed in different ways in different situations; (2) people who participate in sports can have a variety of different experiences; and (3) sport experiences take on different meanings, depending on the circumstances and relationships associated with participation. Coakley concludes that "sports do affect the lives of many people in many different ways, but sport participation itself does not automatically lead to the development of particular character traits."[31] With this important caveat in mind, let's examine three areas of concern regarding the effects of sports participation: (1) the behavior of athletes off the field; (2) the moral development of athletes; and (3) the possibility of character building through sport.

Athletes and Off-the-Field Deviance

Research comparing high school athletes with their nonathletic peers shows consistently that athletes are less likely to be adjudicated for delinquency.[32] This finding, however, does *not* prove that sports participation reduces the likelihood of delinquency. There are two major reasons for this. First, delinquency-prone individuals very likely do not try out for athletic teams, or if they do, they are likely to be cut from teams because they do not conform to the coach's orders or team norms. Second, athletes may receive preferential treatment, which keeps them out of the courts when they get in trouble. Thus it is difficult to say whether high school athletes are any more or less deviant than their peers of comparable backgrounds.

Media accounts seem to indicate that college and professional athletes are more prone than nonathletes of the same age and social class to engage in assault, domestic violence, gang rape, recreational drugs, stealing, and other forms of deviance. There is an obvious problem with interpreting these incidents because the deviant behaviors of high-profile athletes are much more likely to be publicized than similar acts by noncelebrities. Nevertheless, a strong case can be made that male athletes in football and basketball are overrepresented in crimes, especially sexual assaults (see chapter 8).[33]

What might account for male athletes being more likely than nonathletes to engage in criminal behaviors? There are several possible explanations. First, male athletes at the highest levels are different from their nonathletic male peers. They are bigger, stronger, and more aggressive because sport, at least the aggressive sports, is the result of a selection process that sorts for aggressive, risk-taking, dominant personalities. They are expected to act aggressively on the field. Can this macho persona be turned off for other social settings? This is especially difficult for athletes when they are verbally abused in bars and other settings (for example, African-American athletes are commonly subjected to racial slurs). Second, like military units, youth gangs, and college fraternities, athletic teams foster a spirit of exclusivity, camaraderie, and solidarity. The result is a prolonged adolescence and an exaggerated male bonding that celebrates male dominance, physical and verbal aggression, and daring behaviors and accords them status.[34]

This male world, epitomized by the locker room, has been studied by sociologist Timothy Jon Curry. He found that the talk among athletes focused on aggression and on women as objects, taking the form of loud, profane performances for other men.[35] As Mariah Burton Nelson has said, "The locker room is a place where men discuss women's bodies in graphic sexual terms, where they boast about 'scoring' and joke about beating women."[36] Thus the athletic subculture that emerges actually legitimizes rape and aggression in general.

Third, the celebrity status of athletes results in preferential and deferential treatment. They receive special treatment that exempts them from the rules that others must follow. This results in a sense of entitlement—a sense that they can take anything they want without asking, including sex. Ken Dryden, Hall of Fame goalie who is now a lawyer, says, "It's really a sense of power that comes from specialness, reputation, money, whether it's an athlete, businessman, or entertainer—anyone who finds himself at the center of the world they're in has a sense of impunity."[37]

According to Jeff Benedict, no fewer than 112 college athletes were charged with sexual assault or incidents of domestic violence during 1995 and 1996. Yet few have been successfully prosecuted, much less jailed for these crimes. According to Benedict, this is how it works:

> Often in packs, like wolves on a deer, college and pro athletes bring down a woman as they would sack a quarterback, play with her, physically hurt her and then toss her away. Should she complain, the college or pro team pays for a lawyer whose

standard ploy is to contrast the popularity and value of the defendant with the con-
temptible star-chasing sexuality of the victim.[38]

Benedict's research led him to conclude that

professional athletes have, as a result of their profession, undergone a socialization process which, in addition to stripping away virtually all off-the-field ac-
countability, churns out an image of women as sexually compliant. Because of the
availability of sex partners and the casualness of their encounters, athletes ultimately have problems distinguishing between force and consent.[39]

Steroid use is a fourth reason for the disproportionate number of athletes involved in cases of sexual aggression. Research shows that aggressiveness and
a heightened sexual drive are among the side effects of anabolic steroid use.[40]
These characteristics are chemically induced, but they also result from the
"steroid culture" that values physicality.

Although athletes are disproportionately guilty of crimes and sexual aggression, only a relatively small number of athletes are involved. Thus sports participation does not cause sexual aggression in the vast majority of athletes. Yet
it seems reasonable that sport does contribute to the aberrant behavior of a few.

Moral Development

The "winning-at-all-costs" philosophy pervades sport at every level and leads
to cheating by coaches and athletes, the dehumanization of athletes, and their
alienation from themselves and their competitors. Under these conditions, it is
not surprising that research reveals consistently that sport stifles moral reasoning and moral development.

From 1987 to the present, physical educators Sharon Stoll and Jennifer
Beller studied over 10,000 athletes from the ninth grade through college. Their
findings include the following:[41]

1. Athletes score lower than their nonathlete peers on moral development.
2. Male athletes score lower than female athletes in moral development.
   However, the average score for female athletes has been declining over
   the past few years.
3. Moral reasoning scores for athletic populations steadily decline from
   the ninth grade through university age, whereas scores for nonathletes
   tend to increase.

This last point is significant: The longer individuals participate in sport, the less
able they are to reason morally. According to Stoll and Beller, "While sport does
build character if defined as loyalty, dedication, sacrifice, and teamwork, it does
not build moral character in the sense of honesty, responsibility, and justice."[42]

Not only is the length of time in sport relevant but so, too, is the level. That is, athletes at the Division I level in college are less ethical than those at Division III. In this regard a recent survey by the Men's and Women's College Basketball Coaches Association produced the following results:[43]

1. In response to the statement "My teammates would expect me to cheat if it meant the difference in winning a game," 46.7 percent of Division I men agreed, compared to 26.6 percent of Division III men.
2. In response to the statement "Trash talking is an acceptable part of being competitive," 45.9 percent of Division I men agreed, compared to 31.4 percent of Division III men.

The unethical practices so common in sport have negative consequences for the participants. Gresham's law would seem to apply to sport—bad morality tends to defeat good morality; unfairness tends to encourage unfairness. Sociologist Melvin Tumin's principle of "least significant morality" also makes this point: "In any social group, the moral behavior of the group as an average will tend to sink to that of the least moral participant, and the least moral participant will, in that sense, control the group unless he is otherwise restrained and/or expelled. . . . Bad money may not always drive out good money, though it almost always does. But 'bad' conduct surely drives out 'good' conduct with predictable vigor and speed."[44]

The irony, as sport psychologists Brenda Jo Bredemeir and David Shields have pointed out, is that many athletes, coaches, and fans believe that "to be good in sports, you have to be bad."[45] You must take unfair advantage and be overly aggressive if you want to win. The implications of this are significant. Moral development theorists agree that the fundamental structure of moral reasoning remains relatively stable from situation to situation. When coaches and athletes corrupt the ideals of fair play in their zeal to succeed, they are likely to employ or condone similar tactics outside sport. They might accept the necessity of dirty tricks in politics, the manipulation of foreign governments for our benefit, and business practices that include using misleading advertising and selling shoddy and/or harmful products. The ultimate goal in politics, business, and sport, after all, is to win. And winning may require moving outside the established rules. Unfortunately, this lesson is learned all too often in sport.

Does Sport Build Character?

Is there proof for the assertion that sports participation builds character? Studies comparing male athletes and male nonathletes (few studies compare women) yield little evidence to support the idea that sport is necessary for complete and adequate socialization or that involvement in sport results in character-building moral development, good citizenship, or valued personality traits. Athletes and nonathletes are comparable on various personality traits and value orientations. Sports participation has no general effect on self-image; it does not reduce prejudice; it is not necessary for leadership development; and it does not enhance social adjustment.[46]

The widespread conclusion by sport sociologists is that when an apparent socialization effect is found, it is actually the result of a selection process that attracts and retains children and youth in sport who already have or are comfortable with the values and behavioral traits that coaches demand and that lead to success in sport.[47] Those without these desired values and traits either show no interest in sport or leave sport voluntarily (i.e., they drop out) or involuntarily (i.e., they are removed by coaches). In other words, young people already having such traits as perseverance, achievement orientation, hard work, and obedience to authority do well in sport when compared to those who are not as strong on these attitudinal and behavioral traits. After studying more than 60,000 athletes at all levels, sports psychologists Thomas Tutko and Bruce Ogilvie concluded:

> We found no empirical support for the tradition that sport builds character. Indeed, there is evidence that athletic competition limits growth in some areas. It seems that the personality of the ideal athlete is not the result of any molding process, but comes out of the ruthless selection process that occurs at all levels of sport. Athletic competition has no more beneficial effects than intense endeavor in any other field. Horatio Alger success—in sport or elsewhere—comes only to those who already are mentally fit, resilient and strong.[48]

In effect, then, sports participation does not build character, discipline, self-esteem, and other achievement-related qualities in young men and women. Rather, it provides an outlet for those already imbued with these positive traits. As this essay points out, the opposite occurs. That is, athletes (not all, but many) learn bad sportsmanship and engage in various forms of cheating to gain an edge over opponents.

Matthew Goodman notes a fundamental contradiction of sport that negatively affects character development:

> The very qualities a society tends to seek in its heroes—selflessness, social consciousness, and the like—are precisely the *opposite* of those needed to transform a talented but otherwise unremarkable neighborhood kid into a Michael Jordan or a Joe Montana. Becoming a star athlete requires a profound and long-term self-absorption, a single-minded attention to the development of a few rather odd physical skills, and an overarching competitive outlook. These qualities may well make a great athlete, but they don't necessarily make a great person.[49]

Ennobling Sport

Sport has the potential to ennoble its participants. Athletes strain, strive, and sacrifice to excel. But if sport is to exalt the human spirit, it must be practiced within a context guided by fairness and humane considerations. Sports competition is great but it can go too far. It has gone too far when a coach fines his players for helping a competitor off the floor. Competition has gone too far when a high school league in Southern California eliminates the mandatory postgame handshake because trash talking in the handshake line leads to shoving and fistfights.[50] Competition has gone too far when the quest to win corrupts organizations, coaches, and players.

Sport teaches and participants learn. But the current sports climate is teaching disrespect for opponents and the use of unfair means to trump those who play by the rules. When moral boundaries are trampled, then sport, instead of achieving its ennobling potential, has the contrary effect. If sport is to achieve its promise, then those involved must be guided by the fundamental premise that to win by going outside the rules and the spirit of fair play is not really to win at all.

Notes

1. Quoted in Rick Reilly, "Too Many Spoilsports: The World Seems Overrun by Athletes, Coaches and Fans Eager to Take the Best Out of Our Games," *Sports Illustrated*, January 1, 1993, p. 68.

2. Ibid.

3. Jeff Thoreson, "The Integrity of Golf," *The World & I* 11 (July 1996): 311.

4. Quoted in *Sports Illustrated*, June 8, 1995, p. 43.

5. Quoted in Jim Benton, "Bruce Says Upset Saved by Grenier," *Rocky Mountain News*, October 2, 1992, p. 3C.

6. Charles Banham, "Man at Play," *Contemporary Review* 207 (August 1965): 62.

7. Terry D. Orlick, "The Sports Environment: A Capacity to Enhance—A Capacity to Destroy" (paper presented at the Canadian Symposium of Psycho-Motor Learning and Sports Psychology, 1974), p. 2.

8. Robert H. Franks and Philip J. Cook, *The Winner-Take-All Society* (New York: Free Press, 1995); William McGowan, "The Hustle-Butt Society," *Business and Society Review* 61 (Spring 1987): 52–54.

9. Phil Taylor, "Tricks of the Trade," *Sports Illustrated*, March 4, 1996, p. 36.

10. NBC Sports broadcast, December 11, 1994.

11. Tim Green, "Cheating to Win Is Rule of Thumb for Teams' Survival," *USA Today*, November 6, 1997, p. 4C.

12. Ibid.

13. See Jim Kaat, "Foul Ball!" *Popular Mechanics*, May 1988, pp. 80–85, 142, 145; Ira Berkow, "The Abundance of Skullduggery in Baseball," *New York Times*, August 23, 1987, p. 20; "Stealing the Edge," *USA Today*, August 14, 1987, p. 10A; Erik Brady, "Craftsmen

Ply Tricks of the Trade," *USA Today,* August 5, 1987, pp. 1C–2C; Murray Chass, "True Confessions: A Pitcher Tells How to Cheat," *New York Times,* July 26, 1987, p. 18; and Rod Beaton, "Pitchers Look for the Edge—by Rules or Not," *USA Today,* May 28, 1987, p. 3C.

14. Quoted in Ira Berkow, "A Spitter, a Hustler and the Hall of Fame," *New York Times,* July 28, 1991, p. 26.

15. *Sports Illustrated,* September 4, 1985, p. 29.

16. Adam Schefter, "Chiefs Players Confirm What the Coach Won't," *Denver Post,* November 22, 1997, p. 7C.

17. Michael D. Smith, *Violence in Sport* (Toronto: Butterworths, 1983).

18. John Underwood, *Spoiled Sport* (Boston: Little, Brown, 1984), p. 85.

19. See Charles B. Cordin et al., "Anabolic Steroids: A Study of High School Athletes," *Pediatric Exercise Sciences* 6 (1994): 149–158; Jeffrey A. Pottieger and Vincent G. Stilger, "Anabolic Steroid Use in the Adolescent Athlete," *Journal of Athletic Training* 29 (1994): 60–64; Skip Rozin, "Steroids: A Spreading Peril: Thousands of Young U.S. Athletes Are Risking Their Health," *Business Week,* June 19, 1995, pp. 138–141; Associated Press, "Steroid Use on Rise with Teenage Girls," *Denver Post,* December 15, 1997, p. 5C; Rick Telander, "In the Aftermath of Steroids," *Sports Illustrated,* January 27, 1992, p. 103; and Scott E. Lucas, *Steroids* (Hillside, N.J.: Enslow, 1994).

20. Quoted in Rozin, "Steroids," p. 177.

21. "179–62 Score Raises Eyebrows," *Denver Post,* November 28, 1997, p. 14C.

22. Phil Taylor, " 'Crackin', Jackin', Woofin' and Smackin'," *Sports Illustrated,* November 23, 1992, pp. 83–85; Mark Starr, "Yakety-Yak: Do Talk Back," *Newsweek,* December 21, 1992; Phil Taylor, "Flash and Trash," *Sports Illustrated,* May 30, 1994, pp. 20–22; and Peter Brewington, "Sportsmanship: Rulesmakers Blow Whistle on Taunting," *USA Today,* March 7, 1995, pp. 1C–2C.

23. Leslie Visser, "Indecencies Ewing Faces Shouldn't Be Tolerated," *Denver Post,* February 14, 1983, p. 5F.

24. Rick Reilly, "Too Many Spoilsports."

25. Rick Telander, "Not a Shining Knight," *Sports Illustrated,* May 9, 1988, p. 122.

26. Rosemary Parker, "Learning by Intimidation?" *Newsweek,* November 8, 1993, p. 14.

27. Quoted in Jerry Kramer, ed., *Lombardi: Winning Is the Only Thing* (New York: Pocket Books, 1970), p. x.

28. These examples are taken from Tom Weir, "Motivators: From Ridiculous to Unrefined," *USA Today,* November 26, 1993, p. 3C; Denise Tom, "Staged Shooting Backfires," *USA Today,* November 26, 1993, p. 10C; and Mike Knobler, "Sherrill's Teaching Tool Causes Flap," *USA Today,* September 15, 1992, p. 2C.

29. John E. Vawter, letter to the editor, *Sports Illustrated,* February 6, 1989, p. 4.

30. Erik Brady, "Big Money, Big Trades Changing Face of the Game," *USA Today,* July 2, 1998, p. 1A.

31. Jay J. Coakley, *Sport in Society: Issues and Controversies,* 5th ed. (St. Louis: Mosby, 1994), p. 93.

32. See, for example, Jeffrey O. Segrave, "Do Organized Sports Programs Deter Delinquency?" *Journal of Physical Education, Recreation and Dance* 57, no. 1 (1986): 16–17.

33. See, for example, Todd W. Crosset, James Ptacek, Mark A. McDonald, and Jeffrey R. Benedict, "Male Student-Athletes and Violence against Women," *Violence against Women* 2 (June 1996): 163–179.

34. John W. Loy, "The Dark Side of Agon: Fratriarchies, Performative Masculinities,

Sport Involvement, and the Phenomenon of Gang Rape," *International Sociology of Sport: Contemporary Issues,* ed. Karl-Heinrich Bette and Alfred Rutten (Stuttgart: Verlag Stephanie Naglschmid, 1995), pp. 263–281; Jill Neimark, "Out of Bounds: The Truth about Athletes and Rape," *Mademoiselle,* May 1991, pp. 196–199, 244–246; David Leon Moore, "Athletes and Rape: Alarming Link," *USA Today,* August 27, 1991, pp. 1C–2C; and Jeff Benedict, *Public Heroes, Private Felons* (Boston: Northeastern University Press, 1997).

35. Timothy Jon Curry, "Fraternal Bonding in the Locker Room: A Profeminist Analysis of Talk about Competition and Women," *Sociology of Sport Journal* 8 (June 1991): 119–135.

36. Mariah Burton Nelson, "Bad Sports," *New York Times,* June 22, 1994, p. 11A. See also Janet Singleton, "Athletes and Abuse: Is Spirit Grown in Locker Room?" *Denver Post,* March 9, 1995, pp. 1E–2E.

37. Quoted in Gerald Eskenazi, "When Athletic Aggression Turns into Sexual Assault," *New York Times,* June 3, 1990, pp. 27, 30.

38. Quoted in Robert Lipsyte, "Violence, Redemption and the Cost of Sports," *New York Times,* October 19, 1997, p. 30Y. See Jeffrey R. Benedict, "Colleges Must Act Decisively When Scholarship Athletes Run Afoul of the Law," *The Chronicle of Higher Education,* May 9, 1997, pp. 6B–7B.

39. Quoted in Robert Lipsyte, "Many Create the Climate for Violence," *New York Times,* June 18, 1995, p. 21.

40. National Institute of Mental Health study reported in Doug Levy, "Steroid Mood Effect 'Dramatic,' " *USA Today,* June 2, 1993, p. 1A; study found in the *Journal of the American Medical Association,* reported in "Teen-Age Steroid Users Likely to Be Aggressive"; Steve Woodward, "Steroids; A Dose of Danger," *USA Today,* April 6, 1989, p. 10C; and John R. Fuller and Marc J. LaFountain, "Performance-Enhancing Drugs in Sport: A Different Form of Drug Abuse," *Adolescence* 22 (1987): 969–976.

41. Jennifer Beller, personal communication with author, April 9, 1993, pp. 1–3. See Jennifer M. Beller and Sharon Kay Stoll, "Sportsmanship: An Antiquated Concept?" *Journal of Physical Education, Recreation and Dance* 64 (August 1993): 74–79.

42. Beller, personal communication, p. 2.

43. Reported in "Attitude," *Sports Illustrated,* May 12, 1997, p. 23.

44. Melvin Tumin, "Business as a Social System," *Behavioral Science* 9, no. 2 (1964): 127.

45. Brenda Jo Bredemeier and David L. Shields, "Values and Violence in Sports Today," *Psychology Today* 19, no. 10 (1985): 22.

46. For a summary, see James H. Frey and D. Stanley Eitzen, "Sport and Society," *Annual Review of Sociology* 17 (1991): 503–522.

47. For summaries by sociologists of the arguments in the character-building debate, see especially George H. Sage, *Power and Ideology in American Sport,* 2d ed. (Champaign, Ill.: Human Kinetics, 1998), chap. 9; and Coakley, *Sport in Society,* chap. 4.

48. Bruce C. Ogilvie and Thomas A. Tutko, "Sport: If You Want to Build Character, Try Something Else," *Psychology Today* 5 (October 1971): 61.

49. Matthew Goodman, "Where Have You Gone, Joe DiMaggio," *Utne Reader* 57 (May–June 1993): 103.

50. E. M. Swift, "Give Young Athletes a Fair Shake: When We Eliminate Postgame Handshakes, We Fail to Teach the Main Lesson of Sports," *Sports Illustrated,* May 2, 1994, p. 76.

Chapter 5

Sport Is Healthy, Sport Is Destructive

The favorite to win, seventeen-year-old Michelle Kwan, skated almost flaw-
lessly but was upset by Tara Lipinsky for the Gold Medal at the 1998 Winter
Olympics. Immediately afterward, during a televised interview, she said "I love
you" to her mom, dad, brothers, and sisters. Then she said, poignantly, "I hope
you still love me."

The exercise required of sports participants is good for them. It promotes coordination, stamina, strength, strong bones, joint flexibility, and heart and
lung capacity. Exercise diminishes the ill effects of diseases such as diabetes.
It reduces hypertension (high blood pressure), lowers bad cholesterol, and
raises good cholesterol. Physical activity is an important part of controlling
weight. Without exercise bones become brittle, muscles atrophy (including
the heart muscle), the efficiency of blood circulation diminishes, plaque in
the arteries builds up rapidly, and the aging process accelerates. *The positive*
effects of physical exercise cannot be denied. The health benefits of exercise
are the motive for requiring physical education and sports programs in
schools, youth sports, community adult recreation, and corporation-spon-
sored sports teams.

As an example of the health benefits of sport, let's examine the consequences
of participation for girls and women. Until recently the commonly held assumption was that certain types of sports participation were harmful to the
health of females. Physical exertion and the encouragement of aggressive behavior were seen as the main culprits. As a result, historically, women were not
permitted to run, swim, or cycle long distances. Girls' basketball teams were
divided into offensive players and defensive players, who played one end of the
court only and were limited to no more than two dribbles at a time to minimize
physical effort. The title of an article chronicling the history of women's sport
captures the reason for not permitting girls and women to engage in strenuous
activities: "Nice Girls Don't Sweat."[1]

Young girls were channeled into sports that emphasized graceful movement (diving, gymnastics, and ice skating) and limited physical contact with opponents. The most popular women's sports often separated the athletes by a net (tennis, badminton, volleyball). According to sociologist Nancy Theberge, "Women have been discouraged or prevented from participating in sport by a complementary set of exclusionary practices and cultural ideals that viewed them as fragile and unsuited to strenuous physical activity."[2]

Since the 1970s these barriers to participation in all types of sports have weakened. The numbers of women participants in high school sports, college sports, and adult running and fitness activities have risen dramatically. From the 1970s to the 1990s, the participation of girls in high school sports increased from one in twenty-seven to one in three. Along with this dramatic increase in sports participation has come important health benefits for girls and women.

Traditionally, it was widely assumed that women do not have the mental toughness for athletic competition and that such activities damage them psychologically. Research shows this belief to be a myth, however. Sociologist Don Sabo has summarized the deymthologizing findings.[3] Compared to nonathletes, female athletes are more achievement-motivated, independent, poised, and inner-controlled. They have higher self-confidence, higher energy levels, better health, and a general well-being. They have more positive attitudes toward life, more positive psychological well-being (in good spirits, satisfied with life, happy), and a more positive body image. In addition, current research shows that regular and strenuous exercise results in a lower lifelong risk of breast cancer.

Research also shows that when teenage girls involved in sport are compared with teenage nonathletes, the athletes are less likely to drop out of school, smoke cigarettes, and use illicit drugs, and more likely to be virgins. If sexually active, they are more likely to have begun intercourse at a later age, to engage in sex less often, and to have fewer sex partners, as well as being less likely to become pregnant.[4] A likely explanation for these differences is that sport may provide girls with the self-esteem necessary to ward off peer pressure to have sex and to use illicit drugs.[5]

It is true that running, jumping, lifting, throwing, swimming, skiing, skating, cycling, rowing, and calisthenics enhance the physical and emotional health of female and male participants. But athletes can also be injured during these sporting activities. Behind the popular myth is the reality that many aspects of sport are unhealthy—physical injuries, mental abuse from coaches or parents, drugs, eating disorders, overtraining, and even the sexual abuse of athletes by authorities. These latent tragedies of sport are its dark side, often hidden from view. Because they usually do not make the headlines of the sports section, they are emphasized here. Let's begin with injuries that occur in the normal course of engaging in a sport, followed by drug use, dietary dangers, emotional damage to child athletes, and the sexual abuse of girls and women.

Physical Injuries from Sports Participation

Football is a collision sport. The average National Football League player will take 130,000 full-speed hits over a seven-year period.[6] "I hate to say it," says Barry Sanders, the Detroit Lions' superb—and relatively durable—running back, "but one of the first things you notice in this league is how steadily people step in and out of the lineup because of injuries. After a while you hardly notice it anymore. You just go on."[7] During the 1992 season, 482 NFL players were hurt seriously enough to miss at least one game because of injury—an average of seventeen players per team.[8] The sprains, muscle tears, broken bones, and concussions that the players endure may have lasting physical consequences. A 1990 study commissioned by the NFL Players Association surveyed 645 ex-players and found that nearly two-thirds had a permanent disability from football.[9]

Team doctors and trainers may compound the injury problem. Prescribing painkillers that allow players to participate before they are physically ready can lead to a greater likelihood of permanent damage. Yet athletes may insist on this because they (1) are socialized to accept pain and injury as part of the game and to "play hurt"; (2) fear losing a starting position or even a place on the team; (3) want to keep their careers going as long as possible; (4) feel the pressure of teammates or coaches to play; or (5) want to sacrifice themselves for the good of the team. Team doctors may also inject painkillers such as Novocaine, cortisone, or anti-inflammatories because their primary task is to keep players on the field, not in the training room. These doctors and trainers are in a bind between doing what is medically appropriate for a player and doing what benefits their employer.[10] Hall of Fame linebacker Dick Butkis was given cortisone and other drugs by the Chicago Bears team doctor during the last two years of his career to deaden the pain in his knees. Butkis argued that the doctor had put the short-term needs of the team over his long-term health. He sued for $1.6 million and received $600,000 in an out-of-court settlement.

Sports injuries are not limited to contact sports (football, rugby, hockey, wrestling, and boxing). Sociologist Howard Nixon surveyed nearly two hundred male and female athletes in eighteen varsity sports at an NCAA Division I school. Nixon found that over 75 percent reported sustaining significant injuries, and nearly all of those had played hurt. Also, over 45 percent experienced long-term effects from these injuries.[11]

Sport poses special dangers to young bodies, including Little League elbow, tennis elbow, gymnast's back, and swimmer's shoulder. The collisions in tackle football and ice hockey are especially dangerous to preadolescents. According to the U.S. Consumer Product Safety Commission, an estimated 2 million children under age fifteen experienced sports injuries in 1996, 750,000 of whom required a visit to the hospital emergency room.[12] At greatest risk are young people striving for elite sport status. Their ambition leads to accelerated training regimens that can include more than one workout a day, cumulative daily workouts of six hours a day, six days a week, year-round.

Of concern to all athletes, especially young athletes, are the so-called overuse injuries (stress fractures, tendinitis, and bursitis) that result from overdoing a certain action without given the body sufficient time to recover. Swimmer's shoulder, for example, is caused by a repetition of shoulder strokes than can reach 400,000 for a typical male over a ten-month training season, and 660,000 for females.[13] Lyle Michel, director of sports medicine at Boston Children's Hospital, argues that sports injuries are especially serious for children:

> Sports injuries in children are serious. Growing children are predisposed to overuse injuries because of the softness of their growing bones, and the relative tightness of their ligaments, tendons and muscles during growth spurts. And because overuse injuries develop slowly and insidiously, unlike sprains or fractures, which happen all of a sudden, they often go undetected. The damage to a growing child's hard and soft tissues caused by an unreported or undetected overuse injury can be permanent. Evidence suggests that overuse injuries sustained in childhood may continue to cause problems in later life—arthritis, for instance.[14]

Athletes of any age who train seriously every day year-round engage in what sport sociologists call "positive deviance." This concept refers to "cases of conformity that are so intense, extensive, or extreme that they go beyond the conventional boundaries of behavior. They are cases of *over*conformity rather than *counter*conformity, but they are deviant because of their extreme nature."[15] Positive deviants in sport take the sport ethic to the extreme—subordinating other interests for the sake of sport, being dedicated to becoming number one, accepting risk and playing through pain, and believing that there are no limits for someone who is dedicated enough.[16] Athletes who aspire to stardom as swimmers, distance runners, bodybuilders, cyclists, and triathletes often are positive deviants. They follow this ethic without question to the point of risking their own safety and well-being. This may lead to self-injurious overtraining, eating disorders, rigid training schedules, uncritical commitment to playing through pain and injury, and problems in family relationships, school, and work responsibilities.

Intensive sports training has detrimental effects for both males and females, but it creates some special health dangers for women. The most prominent is amenorrhea (cessation of menstrual function without menopause). This condition occurs when rigorous training causes the body to stop producing the hormones that make estrogen. Without the normal amount of estrogen, irregularities in the menstrual cycle occur, which results in a lack of bone density and, if left untreated, osteoporosis and a relatively high susceptibility to fractures.[17]

Drugs

Athletes use restorative drugs such as painkillers, anti-inflammatories, and muscle relaxers to help them overcome injuries. Used properly, with adequate time to restore health before vigorous exercise, these drugs are helpful. They may, however, as noted before, be used to return athletes to play before their bodies are healthy, leading to long-term health problems. Athletes may use other drugs such as alcohol, marijuana, and cocaine to mask pain or to help them deal with anxiety and stress. According to a *New York Times* study in 1997, some 60 to 70 percent of the players in the National Basketball Association smoked marijuana and drank excessively (the NBA Players Association is opposed to testing for these drugs and the league does not do so).[18] There are dangers in using these drugs, among them drug dependency. Also, these drugs can lead to problems with the criminal justice system (underage drinking, possession, and, perhaps, the marketing of a banned substance), jail time, and a criminal record.

A more important drug issue is athletes' use of additive drugs—drugs that improve performance. Some examples are beta blockers (used by golfers, archers, and marksmen), which slow down the heart, steady the nerves, and calm performance anxiety, and so-called brake drugs such as cyproterone acetate that delay puberty (female gymnasts and ice skaters). Human growth hormones increase strength and size (weight lifters, football linemen); amphetamines get players fired up and keep them stimulated and aggressive (football and rugby players). Prescription drugs are also misused. Approximately 10 percent of the population has some degree of asthma, but 60 percent of Olympic athletes use a prescription drug for asthma, presumably not because they have asthma but because it increases the lung capacity for endurance athletes.[19] The hormone erythropoietin (EPO) is the current drug of choice for distance runners and cyclists because it stimulates the production of red blood cells, thereby increasing the oxygen-carrying capacity of the blood.[20] Anabolic steroids, along with human growth hormones, constitute the most commonly abused performance-enhancing drugs used by athletes.

There are also dangerous practices that increase athletic performance. Female endurance athletes, for example, can get pregnant in order to have an abortion to benefit from the natural increase in certain hormones. Wrestlers and boxers use diuretics for weight loss to compete at lower weight classes, and drug-using athletes often use diuretics to minimize detection of other drugs by diluting the urine. Blood doping (removing a pint of blood, allowing the blood volume to return to normal, and then transfusing the blood back into the blood supply in order to enhance the body's oxygen-carrying capacity) is thought to increase fitness by as much as 20 percent. In a fit, elite athlete blood doping appears to add 1 to 3 percent, which translates into running the 1,500 meters three seconds faster than would be the case without the extra oxygen-carrying blood.

There are legal nutritional supplements that increase performance. The current supplement of choice for athletes is creatine, a muscle-building compound.[21] This popular drug is sold under at least thirteen different brand names and is a $100 million product (about 10 percent of the sports nutrition business). Creatine is a synthetic version of the nitrogenous compound that the body makes in the pancreas and liver to give power to muscles. Its negative effects are unknown. A survey of professional sports teams by *USA Today* found that twenty-one teams explicitly disapproved of creatine, whereas sixteen approved of its use. The remaining thirty-four teams took no formal position, leaving the decision up to individual players. Among athletes who have used creatine are Mark McGuire of the St. Louis Cardinals, Mike Piazza of the New York Mets, Brady Anderson of the Baltimore Orioles, Dante Bichette of the Colorado Rockies, over half of the 1998 Super Bowl champion Denver Broncos (including John Elway), about half of the seven hundred male and female athletes at the University of Nebraska, and two-thirds of the football squad of Arvada West High School (the 1997 Colorado state championship team). Although there are no known immediate negative effects of using creatine, there are worries about prolonged use and, especially, use by young athletes:[22]

> When it comes to teenagers, many doctors, nutritionists, coaches and some prep players themselves wonder whether taking sports supplements now will haunt them later, perhaps in the form of damaged kidneys or malfunctioning livers. They worry that the products could mess up an adolescent's churning hormones. They fear that gung-ho, young body-builders will assume that if one daily dose is good, five is even better. And with creatine, there's no research to see how the supplement affects the turbulent teenage body now or in the future.[23]

The most common illegal drugs used to enhance sports performance are anabolic steroids, a group of compounds that are related to the male hormone testosterone. The adjective "anabolic" refers to protein building, since the steroids promote dramatic increases in muscle bulk, strength, and power. Synthetic steroids were first developed in 1935, and weight lifters began using them in the early 1950s. The practice spread rapidly among athletes whose performance was improved by increased size and strength. An unofficial poll taken by a U.S. athlete at the 1972 Munich Olympics revealed that over two-thirds of the track and field athletes used some form of steroids in preparing for the games.[24] Some governments, as a matter of public policy, used performance-enhancing drugs as building blocks to international sports success (indirectly demonstrating the superiority of their culture). After the breakup of the Soviet empire and the fall of East Germany, documents were found showing that 1,000 to 1,500 scientists, physicians, and trainers ran controlled experiments on East German athletes in an effort to boost athletic performance while avoiding detection. This was confirmed by twenty former East German coaches who admitted that anabolic steroids had been used for over two decades as East German women dominated international swimming.[25] Chinese athletes have been disqualified repeatedly for illicit drug use. In 1994, seven swimmers, two canoeists, a cyclist, and a hurdler (all Chinese) failed drug tests before and during the Asian Games. Other Chinese athletes were banished again in the 1997 Asian Games. In the 1998 Tour de France, one cycling team was banished for allegedly using banned substances, and six other teams withdrew in protest. During the same week, two U.S. track stars, sprinter Dennis Mitchell and shot-putter Randy Barnes, were banned from competition for failing drug tests.

Many U.S. athletes take these drugs by choice, not as a matter of state policy. They want to be bigger, stronger, and faster, which may lead to a college scholarship, all-star status, a professional career, or success in international sports. Boys and girls as young as ten take illegal steroids to perform better in sports.[26] Various studies have found that 7 percent of high school male athletes and 2.4 percent of high school female athletes use anabolic steroids, as have 15 percent of male college athletes and 6 percent of female college athletes. As many as 75 percent of NFL players use or have used steroids.[27] Elite athletes in weight lifting, bodybuilding, and weight throwing are almost required to take steroids if they are to compete successfully internationally.

The use of anabolic steroids has serious health consequences.[28] Prolonged use can damage the liver. It increases total cholesterol and decreases good forms of cholesterol, thus increasing the risk of coronary heart disease. It causes the body to retain sodium, potassium, and water, which increases the chances of congestive heart failure. Anabolic steroids cause testicular atrophy and breast enlargement in males and menstrual cycle difficulties, deepening of the voice, and increased body hair growth in women. Acne is common in both sexes. Mood swings and an increase in aggressive behavior are also byproducts of steroid use.[29] A study of fifty steroid-using weight lifters revealed that one common side effect was sexual aggression.[30]

Consider what happened to University of South Carolina lineman Tommy Chaiken when he first took anabolic steroids:

I went from about 210 pounds to a lean 235 in eight weeks. My bench press went from the upper 300s to 420 and my squat from 400 to 520. I watched my diet and I was really cut—big arms, chest and legs, great definition. . . . Besides the muscle growth, there were other things happening to me. I got real bad acne on my back, my hair started to come out. I was having trouble sleeping, and my testicles began to shrink—all the side effects you hear about. But my mind was set. I didn't care about the other stuff. . . . In fact, my sex drive during the cycle was phenomenal, especially when I was charged up from all the testosterone I was taking. I also had this strange, edgy feeling—I could drink all night, sleep two hours and then go work out. In certain ways I was becoming an animal. And I was developing an aggressiveness that was scary.[31]

Chaiken ended up with tumors and clinical depression that nearly drove him to suicide. There are other extreme examples of the apparent consequences of prolonged steroid use. Steve Courson, an NFL player who used steroids for eleven years, needed a heart transplant.[32] Aside from the side effects from steroids, their use increases the chances for injury. The increased aggression ("roid rage") contributes to excessive violence on and off the field, including sexual assault.[33]

During the 1998 season the average Denver Bronco offensive linemen weighed 296 pounds; Denver was the only team in the NFL with offensive linemen averaging *under* 300 pounds. By contrast, the linemen on the Green Bay Packers team that won Super Bowl I in 1966 weighed on average 245 pounds. The extra weight of contemporary football players is probably not only the consequence of better diet and weight training but of steroid or other drug use. When players put on more weight than their frames were meant to hold, this puts extra stress on ligaments and joints, leading to more sprains, strains, and ligament tears. The additional bulk without loss of speed makes collisions all the more violent, leading to an increase in the number and severity of injuries.

Despite the many dangers associated with performance-enhancing chemicals, their use continues and even increases. The motive is obvious—an extreme desire to excel. A 1995 poll of sprinters, swimmers, power lifters, and other U.S. Olympians or aspiring Olympians asked:

> You are offered a banned performance-enhancing substance, with two guarantees: 1) You will not be caught. 2) You will win. Would you take the substance?
> One hundred and ninety-five athletes said yes; three said no.
> Scenario II: You are offered a banned performance-enhancing substance that comes with two guarantees: 1) You will not be caught. 2) You will win every competition you enter for the next five years, and then you will die from the side effects of the substance. Would you take it?
> More than half the athletes said yes.[34]

Dietary Dangers

Women and girls in certain sports (figure skating, gymnastics, tennis, swimming, diving, and distance running) are advantaged if they are slim. Thus by choice or by coercion from parents or coaches, many severely limit their diets. The extreme forms of this are anorexia nervosa (self-imposed starvation) and bulimia (cyclical binging and purging).[35] An NCAA study estimated that 58 percent of women in college sports are at risk of developing an eating disorder.[36] A 1992 University of Washington study of 182 female college athletes found that 32 percent practiced some radical form of weight control (vomiting and using laxatives, diuretics, or diet pills). Among college gymnasts, the rate was 62 percent.[37]

World-class gymnast Christy Heinrich is an extreme example of a self-imposed eating disorder in an athlete.[38] In 1989 Christy was fifteen, standing four feet, eleven inches, and weighing ninety pounds. A judge told her that she had to lose weight or she would never make the Olympic team. She knew that a small, lean, limber body was necessary (at the 1992 Olympics the average U.S. female gymnast weighed 83 pounds). A perfectionist, she took this advice seriously, increasing her training beyond the nine-hours-a-day regimen she was already following and severely restricting her diet. Food became her enemy. By the time she was eighteen, she weighed less than eighty pounds and became too weak to continue as a gymnast. She retired from the sport but could not stop the extreme dieting. After five years of virtual starvation, Christy died of multiple organ failure, weighing less than fifty pounds.

In some women's sports, such as gymnastics, figure skating, and diving, the athlete's appearance is a significant part of the judging. As a result, coaches insist on their athletes being thin. Bela Karolyi, the most famous women's gymnastics coach in the United States, is a fanatic about his gymnasts' weight. His 1992 Olympic squad members were limited to a thousand calories to fuel their bodies through their eight-hour-a-day workouts. Their food intake was monitored by assistant coaches and their belongings were searched for contraband food.[39] "Karolyi draws the most criticism of any gymnastics coach for mistreating his athletes. Perhaps it's because he's the most famous coach and thus the easiest target. Or perhaps it's because his track record for producing gymnasts with eating disorders is stunning."[40]

For males, eating disorders are most prevalent among wrestlers and boxers, athletes who need to make a weight category to compete. Since there are more amateur wrestlers than boxers (e.g., high school), they make up the largest pool of athletes using extreme measures to lose weight. The problem stems from the practice of competing at a weight level below one's natural weight. They may also lose weight to make the team, that is, they may not be able to beat their teammate at the 130-pound level or the 125-pound level, but they can defeat the 119 guy. If they can get down to 119 pounds, then they can wrestle in meets and get a letter. Otherwise, they stay on the sidelines.

Dangerous weight loss has long been the norm in wrestling. To meet lower weight requirements, wrestlers limit calories and engage in a number of questionable activities such as minimizing liquid intake; using diuretics, laxatives, and saunas; and exercising in rubber suits in overheated rooms to promote rapid weight loss. Wrestler Jeff Reese died after shedding seventeen pounds in two days. He spent his last two hours of life wearing a plastic suit and riding a stationary bike in a room that had been heated to ninety-two degrees.[41]

Serious problems occur with excessive dehydration, especially when it is combined with substances such as creatine. During a thirty-three-day span in late 1997, three college wrestlers died while trying to sweat off pounds. Since no college wrestler had died in the previous fifteen years, some experts wonder if the addition of this new supplement was responsible, since it can contribute to dehydration.[42]

The drastic methods used to lose weight in wrestling have been widely accepted by athletes, coaches, and sports organizations. Worse yet, these practices have gone unregulated. However, the deaths of the three college wrestlers stunned NCAA officials, who quickly announced rule changes. First, rubber suits, saunas, and diuretics were banned from competition preparation. Second, official weigh-in times were moved from twenty-four hours before matches to no more than two hours before (thus making it much more difficult to recover from rapid weight loss). Third, for the rest of the season, a seven-pound weight allowance was added to all classes. These changes will be reviewed and amended if necessary by the NCAA's wrestling committee.[43] Although the NCAA's quick action was commendable, it is akin to locking the barn door after the horse is gone, since the NCAA was negligent in allowing unhealthy practices to flourish unhindered until three athletes died of them.

At the other end of the weight continuum, some sports require heaviness. Sumo wrestlers in Japan eat enormous amounts of foods and supplements to achieve a weight of four hundred pounds or more. The prevailing view is that football linemen are more effective if heavy. Tom Cable, the offensive line coach at the University of Colorado, asked his top seven linemen to report to the first practice in the fall weighing more than three hundred pounds.[44] It is not uncommon for high school football players to weigh in excess of 240 pounds. But what is the impact of such corpulence on the heart, blood pressure, circulation, and weight-bearing joints?

Emotional Damage to Child Athletes

Most children engage in organized sport at some time during their lives. About 47 million six- to eighteen-year-olds participate in agency-sponsored programs like Little League, community recreation programs, interscholastic or intramural sports, or club or other paid programs.[45] Although these numbers are inflated because young people often participate in more than one sport and for several different organizations, it is obvious that there is widespread participation in organized, adult-sponsored sports. These youth sports programs are beneficial in many important ways. The exercise is healthy. Team sports emphasize cooperation and teamwork. Individual sports foster self-reliance. Playing under adult supervision helps children stay out of trouble. And children gain acceptance from their peers for their accomplishments and contributions to the team.[46]

There is also a downside to youth sports. Unlike pickup games organized by the players, adult-structured sport limits the creativity of the participants.[47] In peer play, the players adapt to the field conditions, available playing equipment, and number of players. Everyone plays, and if one side is too dominant, changes are made to equalize the teams. During the play itself, the players do their own officiating and negotiate over rules. Although children's informal games should not be romanticized (there can be a lot of bickering, the bigger children may exploit the smaller ones), there is much to be said in favor of informal, child-run sport. Adult-run, organized sport for children, which dominates contemporary youth sport, is more problematic. It leaves children out of the decision making. It is rule centered rather than action centered. Adults divide players into teams and assign them to major and minor leagues. The play is serious, with the outcome being more important than the process.

A major problem with formal youth sport is the intrusion of adults into the play of children. Some parents and coaches are too demanding, making sport work instead of fun—something to be dreaded rather than enjoyed. Kids are pressured by parents who live vicariously through their children's accomplishments (the "achievement-by-proxy" syndrome).[48] This may manifest itself in starting the children in sport too soon, forcing them to train or play when injured, and being too critical of their performances. At the extreme it can result in programming a child to become a star athlete. Consider the case of Todd Marinovich and his father, Marv.[49] Todd's training began before he was born: His mother ate nothing but natural foods during her pregnancy. When Todd was two weeks old, Marv, a former pro football player, forced daily stretching and flexibility exercises on him. As an infant Todd was given only natural foods. He was encouraged to crawl as long as possible because crawling improves hand-eye coordination. Throughout his youth Todd was never allowed to eat white sugar, white flour, or processed foods. He drank only fruit juices, bottled water, and raw skim milk. During Todd's formative years, Marv hired experts to work on every phase of Todd's physical condition—speed, agility, endurance, strength, and peripheral vision. For most of his young life, Todd worked out seven days a week. On his fourth birthday, he ran four miles at an eight-minute pace. He was never punished for failure, only for not trying. Once, when he was in the sixth grade, Marv felt that Todd had slacked off in basketball practice and had him run home—a distance of five miles. In high school, Todd switched schools three times because of what Marv viewed as inept coaching.

Was Marv Marinovich's experiment a success? Todd became a star high school quarterback and later a starting quarterback for the University of Southern California. He was drafted by the Oakland Raiders but lasted only two years. Since then, Todd has tried his hand at art and music. He has been busted several times for possession of illegal drugs and was once sentenced to six months in jail. Marv's next project is Todd's half-brother Mikhail, who is undergoing the same serious physical regime to become a star athlete.

Bruce Ogilvie, a noted sports psychologist, has responded to Marv Marinovich's parenting:

My goodness, what a distortion of love. When you love someone, you extend them total freedom in what they want to be. You must remain a guest in your child's life. Emotional distance is essential. When parents begin vicariously to live through their children, there is the inherent danger of stunting their children's growth. The parent starts failing to discriminate as to when the child's life begins and ends.[50]

What consequences ensue for a child who fails to live up to parental expectations after the parent has made such an investment? Todd Marinovich was an athletic success but failed to meet the goals his father set for him. What emotional scars does that failure leave? What does it do to the parent-child relationship?

Most parents, of course, do not go the extremes of a Marv Marinovich to make sports stars of their children. But they may do other things that put excessive pressure on their children to succeed. They may send their child to a tennis academy for year-round training. Nick Bollettieri's camp costs range from a no-frills $25,000 to $50,000 for hands-on coaching by Bollettieri. The two hundred or so children who aspire to professional tennis careers put in daily workouts of four to five hours. Most, however, fail to achieve professional status. "Youths who are deposited at academies to live out their parents' vicarious dreams don't last long. Competition is too fierce, and only the fittest survive."[51] And, lest we forget, Bollettieri's Tennis Academy is only one of more than three hundred such camps in the United States. The chances of success are extremely thin even for talented players.

The situation is the same for aspiring young gymnasts. About 2,500 U.S. female gymnasts train seriously, with about two hundred competing on the elite level and only twenty making the national team. Bela Karolyi has coached the most Olympic gymnastics champions in history, including Nadia Comaneci and Mary Lou Retton. He selects fifty of the most promising for his camp. The financial cost to their parents is high. The workouts are grueling. The competition at the camp is intense. The coaches are incredibly demanding. The athletes in such a setting work extremely hard, even when in pain, for fear of losing.[52] But most of them do lose, that is, they do not become champions. At least forty-four of those excellent gymnasts at Karolyi's camp, and all the others at other camps, do not make the Olympic team, since there is only room for six on that elite squad. The successes are ecstatic, but what of the "losers"? They have sacrificed their childhoods, their homes, their parents' financial resources, and their bodies without meeting expectations. Some, of course, handle failure with little trauma. Others experience depression and low self-esteem. Still others become antisocial and rebellious.[53] Even the successes may experience a downside. Tennis stars Tracy Austin and Jennifer Capriati, for example, turned professional and made the cover of *Sports Illustrated* at thirteen. By age seventeen, however, both were out of the sport, experiencing severe burnout. Austin suffered physical injuries, and Capriati assumed an alternative lifestyle that included the use of illicit drugs.

At a less intense but nonetheless serious level, many parents push their children to win college scholarships and become champions. They start their children at an early age, specialize in one sport, hire trainers and coaches, and send their children to summer camps for skills improvement. As a result, some children start as young as three in competitive swimming. Boxing can start as young as five. There are football, soccer, and other sports leagues for five-year-olds. Some children at that age compete in marathons and triathlons. Many specialize, with a passion:

> Joseph [Lorenzetti] recently turned 12. With his slender limbs and unblemished skin, he looks like a boy. But he is really a hockey machine, one as dedicated to the sport as any man-sized player. When he started playing at 3 1/2, he was so small he couldn't hold a stick. He now trains 300 days a year, attends seven summer hockey camps, and travels 4,500 miles a year to compete, while his parents spend $6,000 a year on equipment, ice time, and hotels.[54]

Or consider the dedication of fourteen-year-old James Johnson, an aspiring basketball player:

> At 6 a.m. he is at Pro Club in Bellevue, Washington, shooting for an hour and a half. After school, he goes back to Pro Club, gets instruction, works on ball-handling, scrimmages and lift weights until 6 p.m. Then he has eighth grade AAU practice until 8:30 p.m. At home, he does homework, shoots on the immaculate backyard court ($38,000 to build) and goes to bed early. Every weekend, he travels to tournaments, playing at least three games. [His father says] "In today's world, if you want to be a college basketball player, you have to make a commitment at his age."[55]

These two young men (and their parents, through their children) are pursuing the American Dream. Their efforts can be characterized positively as dedicated and achievement oriented, or negatively as fanatical and one-dimensional. In either case, the children are giving up the chance to develop a wide range of skills from a variety of sports, music, and other activities. They are also missing out on a normal childhood, a time that includes periods of unstructured freedom, free from the demands of parents and other adults. Their monomaniacal devotion to achieving success may lead them to use performance-enhancing drugs or otherwise cheat. Moreover, most of these children are also being set up to fail. Even when they achieve success, will it be good enough for them (or their parents)? And what if they do not get a college scholarship, let alone become a professional athlete?

Consider the case of Kristie Phillips. Her mother entered her in a beauty pageant when she was a year old, enrolled her in modeling classes at eighteen months and dance school at two.[56] By the time she was five, Kristie was training at gymnastics four hours a day. At fourteen she was training with Bela Karolyi and was featured on the cover of *Sports Illustrated* with the headline "The Next Mary Lou." Her parents spent $180,000 over six years for Kristie to train under Karolyi. She competed while hurt and used laxatives to control her weight. In the 1988 Olympic trials she finished in eighth place, one spot short of being named an alternate.

> The road she had followed since she was four years old did not lead to the Olympics after all, but back home to Baton Rouge, where she had not lived since she was eight. Now she was sixteen and saw herself as a complete failure. A zero. Without gymnastics she felt she was nothing—less than nothing because she had disappointed everyone who had believed in her. Her parents were never going to see a payoff for all the money they had invested in her. She hated gymnastics, she hated herself, she hated Karolyi. She refused to watch the Olympics on television.[57]

The Sexual Abuse of Girls and Women

Athletes, male and female, are sometimes targets for sexual abuse from persons in authority, usually coaches. I shall focus on women, especially young girls, since they are victimized most frequently. This emphasis should not obscure the fact that some young male athletes are also sexually abused.[58] The social conditions that make female athletes vulnerable to sexual harassment and abuse are just as real for male athletes. These factors include the close bonds that form between coaches and athletes.[59]

In college and high school sports, harassment by the coach might be tolerated more easily than in other social spheres, since the athletes accept the coach as the authority figure who gives orders that extend into the private sphere of their lives. This includes control over medical treatment, nutrition, injuries, social activities, use of alcohol and cigarettes, and sexual behavior. Individual rights in athletes often take a backseat to the notion of "winning" and the "good of the team." Lenskyj[60] claims that "even the most assertive and independent women rarely question the coach's authority, nor do they challenge psychologically manipulative or abusive behavior on the part of coaches." In many sports there is a lot of hands-on instruction, for example, in gymnastics and wrestling. Close physical contact between the coach and the athlete occurs during practice and is part of the sporting experience. However, this also creates possibilities for inappropriate touching, harassment, and abuse. This potential is intensified by the physical, technical, and social power that coaches have over athletes.[61]

Coaches, most of whom are men, have enormous power over athletes. The coaches decide who makes the team, who gets to play, who gets scholarships, and who gets to remain on the team. To say no to this all-powerful person places the athlete's career in jeopardy. Athletes have been socialized to obey their coaches, even if they disagree with their demands. Joan Ryan says that "the very traits that make young girls good gymnasts or figure skaters—obedience, reticence, pliability, naivete—also make them prime targets for sexual abuse."[62]

The perceived and actual separation from "normal" life inside sport increases the reliance on support systems, especially coaches. Athletes spend most of their time with other athletes and coaches, practicing, eating, and playing. Athletes do not have time to build relationships outside the sports sphere. Many athletes, some as young as ten, are separated from their parents, removing the parents as protectors and confidants. Their team becomes their surrogate family. A survivor of sexual abuse by a coach called his actions incest. "I consider it incest—that's what this is all about. Because of time spent, the demands, the friendship, the opportunity. . . . they are giving you something no-one else can. They're brother, uncle, father. . . . the child feels safe and will do anything. That's why it's incest."[63]

Another factor increasing the likelihood of sexual abuse (in this case, the abuse of young athletes) is that they are under a coach's control when they begin to mature sexually. The onset of puberty is a crucial time for a young athlete. Referring to males, sociologist Mike Messner says that "the athlete's relationship with his coach takes place during boyhood and young adulthood, when the young male's masculine identity is being formed, when he is most insecure about his public status, about his relationships, his sexuality, his manhood."[64] The problem is even more acute for girls because they reach puberty at a younger age than boys. Their earlier sexual development makes them targets for sexual abuse at an earlier and more vulnerable age. Moreover, girls can achieve elite sports status much earlier, chronologically, than boys. Girls, for example, in swimming, ice skating, and gymnastics can be world-class at fourteen, whereas boys must wait until their late teens or early twenties to attain a similar rating. This means that young girl athletes, more so than young boys, are going to live away from home and be coached by someone with a world-class reputation, making them vulnerable to a sexual predator.

A final variable leading to a higher risk of sexual abuse is their level of performance, the highest risk occurring when the athlete has the most at stake. Celia Brackenridge and Sandra Kirby's research reveals that athletes who have reached a high standard of performance but are just below the elite level (the "stage of imminent achievement," SIA) are most vulnerable.[65] Novices can drop out or change coaches rather easily because they have invested less time, effort, money, and family sacrifice. Elite athletes have a proven record of success and may be less dependent on their coaches for continued achievement. These established athletes are also more likely to have high self-esteem and personal confidence, which provides them with the personal resources to operate independently of coaches. Athletes on the verge of stardom, however, are more likely than novices or elite athletes to be dependent on a coach. Brackenridge and Kirby claim that athletes whose SIA coincides with or precedes their age of sexual maturity are at greatest risk of sexual abuse in sport. This hypothesis, if true, means that prepubescent girls are the most likely victims of sexual abuse.

Conclusion

Sport encapsulates a fundamental duality—it is healthy yet unhealthy. Some sports are inherently dangerous. In others overtraining may lead to injury. The nature of sport is such that to be good requires commitment and dedication. Sometimes this dedication to achieving a goal leads to ethical distortions such as taking dangerous drugs, engaging in unsafe practices such as taking diuretics, perhaps even trying to hurt an opponent. To achieve success by unethical means is hallow, cheap, and undeserved. Should not youth sports organizations and schools be guided by the principle that the ends do not justify the means? Putting this principle into practice requires sponsoring organizations to monitor coaches for abusive behaviors or other demands with unhealthy consequences for their athletes. Athletes, coaches, and parents must be educated about the unhealthy consequences of taking performance-enhancing drugs. There must be random drug testing and zero tolerance for violators if sport is to a healthy activity.

Although sport can never be entirely free of injury, it needs to be structured to enhance the safety of the participants. Schools, communities, organizations, and parents need to put youth sport programs in perspective. To maximize the health of the athletes, one operating principle should prevail—the outcome of the athlete (physically and emotionally) is infinitely more important than the outcome of the game.

Notes

1. William H. Beezley and Joseph P. Hobbs, "Nice Girls Don't Sweat: Women in American Sport," *Journal of Popular Culture* 16 (Spring 1983): 42–53.

2. Nancy Theberge, "Women's Athletics and the Myth of Female Frailty," in *Women: A Feminist Perspective,* ed. Jo Freeman, 4th ed. (Mountain View, Calif.: Mayfield, 1989), p. 507.

3. Ibid., pp. 334–335.

4. Reported in Steven S. Woo, "Teen Girl Athletes Less Sexually Active," *Rocky Mountain News,* May 14, 1998, p. 36A; *USA Today,* "Sports Lower Teen Pregnancy," July 13, 1998, p. 1C; and Women's Sports Foundation, "Sport and Teen Pregnancy: Executive Summary," July 9, 1998.

5. Although these findings show consistently positive effects in athletic participation for women, there is a methodological problem in studies that compare athletes with nonathletes (female and male). We do not know whether (1) participation in sport causes the differences or (2) there is a selectivity bias. In short, people who are physically and psychologically healthier are more likely than the less favored to participate in sports or to stay in sports longer than those who do not participate, drop out, or are pushed out at an early age.

6. Mark Kram, "If You Think Pro Football Is All Broken Noses and Shattered Knees, You're Wrong. It's Worse. No Pain, No Game," *Esquire,* January 1992, p. 75.

7. Cited in Peter King, "The Unfortunate 500," *Sports Illustrated,* December 7, 1992, p. 23.

8. Ibid.

9. Cited in a four-part series on injuries by Brian Hewitt, *Chicago Sun-Times,* September 19–22, 1993.

10. Joseph Nocera, "Bitter Medicine," *Sports Illustrated,* November 6, 1995, pp. 74–88. See also Gerald Eskenazi, "Team Doctors: Operating in a Quandary," *New York Times,* April 15, 1987, p. 44.

11. Howard L. Nixon II, "Accepting the Risks of Pain and Injury in Sport: Mediated Cultural Influences on Playing Hurt," *Sociology of Sport Journal* 10 (1993): 183–196.

12. Reported in Larry Tye, "Injured at an Early Age," *Boston Globe,* September 30, 1997, p. 18A.

13. Ibid.

14. Lyle J. Micheli, "Children and Sports," *Newsweek,* October 29, 1990, p. 12.

15. Howard L. Nixon II and James H. Frey, *A Sociology of Sport* (Belmont, Calif.: Wadsworth, 1996), p. 103.

16. Robert Hughes and Jay J. Coakley, "Positive Deviance among Athletes: The Implications of Overconformity to the Sport Ethic," *Sociology of Sport Journal* 8, no. 4 (1991): 307–325. See also Jay J. Coakley, *Sport in Society: Issues and Controversies,* 5th ed. (St. Louis: Mosby, 1994), pp. 139–144.

17. D. Stanley Eitzen and George H. Sage, *Sociology of North American Sport,* 6th ed. (Madison, Wis.: Brown and Benchmark, 1997), pp. 287–288; and Dylan B. Tomlinson, "Too Much of a Good Thing," *Denver Post,* February 24, 1998, p. 10D.

18. Selena Roberts, "N.B.A.'s Uncontrolled Substance," *New York Times,* October 26, 1997, pp. 25, 28.

19. *CBS Evening News,* February 22, 1994.

20. "Is *Everybody* Doing It?" *Sports Illustrated,* August 3, 1998, p. 30; Tim Layden, "Distance Thunder," *Sports Illustrated,* July 20, 1998, pp. 35–37.

21. The following is dependent on Gary Strauss and Gary Mihoces, "Jury Still Out on Creatine Use," *USA Today,* June 4, 1998, pp. 1C–2C; Bill Briggs, "Sports Supplements Pervasive in Schools," *Denver Post,* May 17, 1998, pp. 1A, 14A.

22. Kim A. McDonald, "Scientists Debate the Benefits and Hazards of a Seemingly Magical Powder," *Chronicle of Higher Education,* June 26, 1998, pp. 15A–16A.

23. Briggs, "Sports Supplements," p. 14A.

24. Terry Todd, "Anabolic Steroids: The Gremlins of Sport," in *Sport in America: From Wicked Amusement to National Obsession,* ed. David K. Wiggins (Champaign, Ill.: Human Kinetics, 1994), pp. 285–300.

25. Michael Janofsky, "Women Swimmers Used Steroids, 20 German Coaches Acknowledge," *New York Times,* December 3, 1991, p. 1B; Associated Press, "Magazine: Athletes Treated Like Lab Animals," February 9, 1992.

26. Mike Robinson, "Fifth-graders Using Steroids, Survey Finds," *Denver Post,* May 5, 1998, p. 17A.

27. See Charles B. Cordin et al., "Anabolic Steroids: A Study of High School Athletes," *Pediatric Exercise Sciences* 6 (1994): 149–158; Jeffrey A. Pottieger and Vincent G. Stilger, "Anabolic Steroid Use in the Adolescent Athlete," *Journal of Athletic Training* 29 (1994): 60–64; Skip Rozin, "Steroids: A Spreading Peril: Thousands of Young U.S. Athletes Are Risking Their Health," *Business Week,* June 19, 1995, pp. 138–141;

Associated Press, "Steroid Use on Rise with Teenage Girls," *Denver Post,* December 15, 1997, p. 5C; Rick Telander, "In the Aftermath of Steroids," *Sports Illustrated,* January 27, 1992, p. 103; and Scott E. Lucas, *Steroids* (Hillside, N.J.: Enslow, 1994).

28. The following information on steroids and their consequences is from R. H. Barry Sample, "An Overview of Anabolic/Androgenic Steroids," *NCAA Sport Sciences,* Spring 1992, pp. 3–4.

29. William Nack, "Muscle Murders," *Sports Illustrated,* May 18, 1998, pp. 96–106.

30. John R. Fuller and Marc J. LaFountain, "Illegal Steroid Use among Fifty Weightlifters," *Sociology and Social Research* 73 (October 1988): 19–21; and John R. Fuller and Marc J. LaFountain, "Performance-Enhancing Drugs in Sport: A Different Form of Drug Abuse," *Adolescence* 22 (Winter 1987): 969–976.

31. Tommy Chaikin with Rick Telander, "The Nightmare of Steroids," *Sports Illustrated,* October 24, 1988, p. 90.

32. Steve Courson and Lee R. Schreiber, *False Glory* (New York: Longmeadow, 1992).

33. Skip Rozin, "Steroids: A Spreading Peril," *Business Week,* June 19, 1995, pp. 138–141.

34. Reported in Michael Bamberger and Don Yaeger, "Over the Edge: Aware That Drug Testing Is a Sham, Athletes Seem to Rely More Than Ever on Banned Performance Enhancers," *Sports Illustrated,* April 14, 1997, p. 62.

35. For two sociological analyses of this phenomenon, see Diane E. Taub and Rose Ann Benson, "Weight Concerns, Weight Control Techniques, and Eating Disorders among Adolescent Competitive Swimmers: The Effect of Gender," *Sociology of Sport Journal* 9 (March 1992): 76–86; and David Johns, "Fasting and Feasting: Paradoxes of the Sport Ethic," *Sociology of Sport Journal* 15, no. 1 (1998): 41–63.

36. Jack McCallum and Kastya Kennedy, "Small Steps for a Big Problem," *Sports Illustrated,* January 22, 1996, pp. 21–22. See also Herbert A. Haupt, "Substance Abuse by the Athletic Female," in *The Athletic Female,* ed. Arthur J. Pearl (Champaign, Ill.: Human Kinetics, 1993), pp. 125–140.

37. The studies are noted in Joan Ryan, *Little Girls in Pretty Boxes: The Making and Breaking of Elite Gymnasts and Figure Skaters* (New York: Warner Books, 1995), pp. 63–64.

38. The following is from Ryan, *Little Girls,* pp. 55–95.

39. Ibid., p. 72.

40. Ibid.

41. David Fleming, "Wrestling's Dirty Secret," *Sports Illustrated,* January 5, 1998, p. 134.

42. Karen Springer and Marc Peyser, "The New Muscle Candy," *Newsweek,* January 12, 1998, p. 68.

43. "The Right Mat Moves," *Sports Illustrated,* January 26, 1998, p. 33.

44. Quoted in B. G. Brooks, "More Than Bragging Rights on Line," *Rocky Mountain News,* August 2, 1998, p. 23C.

45. Larry Tye, "Playing under Pressure," *Boston Globe,* September 28, 1997, 30A.

46. Eric A. Margenau, *Sports without Pressure* (New York: Gardner, 1990).

47. The following is from Jay J. Coakley, *Sport in Society: Issues and Controversies,* 5th ed. (St. Louis: Mosby, 1994), pp. 106–114.

48. Ronald L. Kamm, "Out of Williamsport, into the Parent Trap," *New York Times,* June 29, 1997, p. 19.

49. The following is from Mark Christensen, "Robo Quarterback," *California Magazine,* January 1988, pp. 69–77; Douglas S. Looney, "Bred to Be a Superstar," *Sports Illustrated,* February 22, 1988, pp. 56–58; Malcolm Moran, "Raising a Quarterback with a Game Plan," *New York Times,* August 24, 1990, pp. 11B–12B; and Denise Tom, "The Marinovich Plan Reaches Its Goal," *USA Today,* April 30, 1991, p. 9C.

50. Quoted in Tom, "Marinovich Plan."

51. Robin Finn, "Camp Is a Career for Tennis Prodigies," *New York Times,* November 21, 1991, p. 8B.

52. Ryan, *Little Girls.*

53. Elizabeth Gleick, "Every Kid a Star," *Time,* April 22, 1996, pp. 39–40.

54. Tye, "Playing under Pressure," p. 1A.

55. "All Hoops, No Chores," *USA Today,* June 2, 1997, p. 3C.

56. The following is from Ryan, *Little Girls,* pp. 109–120.

57. Ibid., p. 116.

58. M. Ann Hall, "Review of Crossing the Line," *International Review for the Sociology of Sport* 32 (September 1997): 307–309. See also Merrill J. Melnick, "Male Athletes and Sexual Assault," *Journal of Health, Physical Education and Recreation* 63 (1992): 32–35.

59. The following is taken primarily from Celia H. Brackenridge, "Fair Play or Fair Game? Child Sexual Abuse in Sport Organizations," *International Review for the Sociology of Sport* 29 (1994): 287–299; Celia Brackenridge, "He Owned Me Basically: Women's Experience of Sexual Abuse in Sport," *International Review for the Sociology of Sport* 32 (June 1997): 115–130; and Celia Brackenridge and Sandra Kirby, "Playing Safe: Assessing the Risk of Sexual Abuse to Elite Child Athletes," *International Review for the Sociology of Sport* 32 (December 1997): 407–418.

60. Helen Lenskyj, "Unsafe at Home Base: Women's Experience of Sexual Harassment in University Sport and Physical Education," *Women in Sport and Physical Activity Journal* 1 (1992): 19–33.

61. Karin A. E. Volkwein et al., "Sexual Harassment in Sport: Perceptions and Experiences of American Female Student-Athletes," *International Review for the Sociology of Sport* 32 (September 1997): 285.

62. Ryan, *Little Girls,* pp. 168–169.

63. Brackenridge, "He Owned Me," p. 118.

64. Michael A. Messner, *Power at Play: Sports and the Problem of Masculinity* (Boston: Beacon, 1992), p. 105.

65. Brackenridge and Kirby, "Playing Safe," pp. 413–414.

Chapter 6

Sport Is Expressive, Sport Is Controlled

In April 1998, at his first team meeting as the newly appointed head basketball coach at the University of Texas, Rick Barnes set down the rules for the team, including no facial hair, no earrings, no hats in buildings, and no headphones on campus. Anyone who was late to a team meeting or workout would cause the entire team to run. There would be mandatory team breakfasts throughout the season every day, not just game day.[1]

The play element that characterizes all sport involves enjoyment, self-expression, and creativity. Unorganized peer-centered play is spontaneous, informal, and fun. But as sport becomes more organized, these playful elements are replaced by rules, external decision making, specialization, hierarchy, and nonsport concerns such as making money and public relations. In short, as we move from the playground to Little League, from Little League to school sports, and from school sports to professional sports, the added layer of controls at each level removes the fun, spontaneity, and joyous abandon that should be the foundation of sports participation.[2]

Understanding Social Control

Control is essential for social order. Without it, social organizations (e.g., societies, communities, churches, prisons, hospitals, schools, corporations, families, athletic teams, or sports leagues) would be chaotic, fragmented,

Adapted from D. Stanley Eitzen, *Social Control: Handbook of Sport and Society*, ed. Eric Dunning and Jay J. Coakley (London: Sage, in press). Also incorporated in this essay are D. Stanley Eitzen, "Sport Unites, Sport Divides: Sport in a Multicultural World" (speech presented at North Central College, Naperville, Ill., October 17, 1995); D. Stanley Eitzen and Maxine Baca Zinn, *In Conflict and Order: Understanding Society*, 8th ed. (Boston: Allyn and Bacon, 1998), pp. 131–153; and D. Stanley Eitzen and George H. Sage, *Sociology of North American Sport*, 6th ed. (Dubuque: Brown and Benchmark, 1997), pp. 174–186.

uncoordinated, unpredictable, and fragile. Sport serves control functions for society, and social control is an integral part of sport.

Social control is based on concepts such as social order, norms, and deviance. Every human group attempts to achieve conformity to the norms (the standards of right and wrong). If a social organization succeeds in controlling its members, then deviant behavior is minimized and order is sustained. But attempts to achieve conformity in groups often meet with noncompliance, resistance, or outright rebellion.[3] Social control is never perfect, as evidenced, for example, by the boycott of the 1968 Olympics by many African Americans. Some black athletes who participated did so but took the occasion to symbolize their solidarity with the boycotters. Other black athletes, most notably boxer George Foreman, opposed the boycott. These variations show that some athletes were part of the mainstream while others challenged the dominant ideology. In this regard sport is a "dynamic social space where dominant . . . ideologies are perpetuated as well as challenged and contested."[4]

All social groups have mechanisms to ensure conformity that can be thought of in two dimensions: ideological control and direct intervention. Ideological control manipulates the ideas and perceptions—the consciousness—of individuals so that they accept the ruling ideology and ignore or resist competing ideologies. It persuades members to follow the rules and to accept without question the existing distribution of power and rewards. Ideological social control works through the socialization of new members, or cultural control, because the individual is given authoritative definitions of what should and should not be done. To many group members there appears to be no choice. Leaders or their representatives also employ frontal attacks on competing ideologies or propaganda efforts to persuade the members what actions are moral, who the enemies are, and why certain courses of action are required. Ideological control is more effective than overt social control measures—strictures on actual behavior—because individuals impose controls on themselves.[5] Through socialization people learn and internalize not only the rules of an organization but also the supporting ideology. When socialization works well, individuals are not forced to conform; they *want* to conform. As sociologist Peter Berger observed, "Most of the time we ourselves desire just that which society expects of us. We *want* to obey the rules."[6] But the efficiency of ideological control does not render useless direct social controls that reward those who conform and punish or neutralize those who deviate or rebel.

Sport as Ideological Control

Sport, as an institution, is conservative. Sport promotes traditional values and societal arrangements and employs social control mechanisms to foster the status quo. Three representative areas in which it exercises this function are the transmission of societal values, traditional gender roles, and compulsory heterosexuality.

Sport and the Transmission of Values

In the United States, sport, through the influence of coaches, parents, and peers, transmits certain values—success in competition, hard work, perseverance, discipline, teamwork, and obedience to authority—to participants and observers. This is the explicit reason given for the existence of children's sports programs such as Little League baseball and the tremendous emphasis on sports in American schools.

Coaches commonly believe that they should not only teach sports skills but should also promote values. Coaches often place signs in locker rooms to inspire traits in their athletes such as hard work, perseverance, and teamwork. Sociologist Eldon Snyder provides some examples of these messages: "The will to win is the will to work." "By failing to prepare yourself you are preparing to fail." "Never be willing to be second best." "Winners never quit and quitters never win." "United we stand, divided we fall." "Win by as many points as possible."[7] Roy Williams, the highly successful University of Kansas basketball coach, provides his players with a different inspirational quote each day during the season that *they must memorize.* Why does Coach Williams have his players spend time thinking about an aphorism instead of basketball fundamentals or game strategy?

Whether sport actually transmits these values is a good question. But organized sport clearly makes the effort. According to sociologist David Matza, "The substance of athletics contains within itself—in its rules, procedures, training, and sentiments—a paradigm of adult expectations for youth."[8]

Sport and Traditional Gender Roles

Sport in its organization, procedures, and operation serves to promote traditional gender roles, thus keeping order (order, however, is not always positive). Sport advances male hegemony in practice and ideology by legitimating a certain dominant version of social reality. From early childhood games to professional sports, the sports experience is "gendered." Boys are expected to participate in sports, to be aggressive, to be physically tough, to take risks, and to accept pain. Thus sport, especially aggressive physical contact sport, is expected for boys and men but not for girls and women. These expectations reproduce male domination in society.

Lois Bryson has argued that sport reproduces patriarchal relations through four minimalizing processes: definition, direct control, ignoring, and trivialization.[9] By definition, "dominant forms of sport in most cultures are played and organized in ways that work to the advantage of most men and to the disadvantage of women."[10] Male standards are applied to female performance, ensuring female inferiority and even deviance. As sport sociologist Paul Willis has observed, "[The ideal description of sport] is a *male* description concerning males. Where women become at all visible, then the terms of reference change. There is a very important thread in popular consciousness which sees the very presence of women in sport as bizarre."[11]

Sports participation is expected for men. Sport is strongly associated with male identity and popularity. For women, though, the situation is entirely different. As Willis has stated, "Instead of confirming her identity, [sports] success can threaten her with a foreign male identity. . . . The female athlete lives through a severe contradiction. To succeed as an athlete can be to fail as a woman, because she has, in certain profound symbolic ways, become a man."[12] Superior women athletes are suspect because strength and athletic skill are accepted as "masculine" traits.

Women's sport is minimized when it is controlled by men. This is demonstrated in the gender composition of leadership positions in the International Olympic Committee, various international and national sports bodies, the National Collegiate Athletic Association, and the administrative and coaching roles in schools and professional leagues.[13]

Women in sport are minimized (and men maximized) when women's activities are ignored. The mass media in the United States have tended to overlook women's sports. When they are reported, the stories, photographs, and commentary tend to reinforce gender role stereotypes. Studies of television coverage indicate that men's sports receive about 92 percent of air time. Moreover, 97 percent of the athletic figures employed in television commercials are males.[14]

Women's sports are also ignored when cities and schools disproportionately spend enormous amounts on men's sports. As writer Mariah Burton Nelson has noted,

> We live in a country in which the manly sports culture is so pervasive we may fail to recognize the symbolic messages we all receive about men, women, love, sex, and power. We need to take sports seriously—not the scores or the statistics, but the process. Not to focus on who wins, but on who's losing. Who loses when a community spends millions of dollars in tax revenue to construct a new stadium and only men get to play in it, and only men get to work there? Who loses when football and baseball so dominate the public discourse that they eclipse all mention of female volleyball players, gymnasts, basketball players, and swimmers?[15]

Women are also minimized when they are trivialized in sport. As I noted, the media framing of the female athlete reinforces gender stereotypes. Considering photographs of women and men athletes, scholar Margaret Carlisle Duncan[16] found that these images emphasized gender differences: (1) female athletes who are sexy and glamorous are most common; (2) female athletes are often photographed in sexual poses; (3) in the framing of photos, male athletes are more likely to be photographed in dominant positions and female athletes in submissive positions; (4) camera angles typically focus up to male athletes and focus down on female athletes; and (5) female athletes are more likely to be shown displaying emotions. As Michael A. Messner has argued, "The choices, the filtering, the entire mediation of the sporting event, is based upon invisible, taken-for-granted assumptions and values of dominant social groups, as such the presentation of the event tends to support corporate, white, and male-dominant ideologies."[17]

Another example of the trivialization of women's sports activities is the naming of their teams. A study comparing the unifying symbols of women's and men's teams found that more than half of colleges and universities in the United States employ names, mascots, and/or logos that demean and derogate women's teams.[18] As elaborated in chapter 3, some schools name their men's teams the Wildcats and their women's teams the Wildkittens. Or the men are the Rams and the women, the Lady Rams (a oxymoron if there every was one). Thus the naming of women's teams tends to define women athletes and women's athletic programs as second-class and trivial.

The secondary treatment of women in sport that defines and characterizes them as inferior also defines them, by extension, as less capable than men in many other areas of life. Scholar Lois Bryson asserts that "each cultural message about sport is a dual one, celebrating the dominant at the same time as inferiorizing the 'other,' "[19] in this case, celebrating the masculine and inferiorizing the feminine.

Although this dominant ideology is perpetuated in many ways, it is also challenged and contested with some success in all institutional areas, including sport.[20] Pioneering women have broken down the "men only" rules in such traditionally unlikely areas as automobile racing (Janet Guthrie became the first woman to race in the Indianapolis 500 in 1977), men's locker rooms (women sportswriters now routinely conduct interviews there), high school wrestling against boys (in 1997 there were 1,629 girls wrestling at the high school level in twenty-four states[21]), and refereeing men's games (in 1997 the NBA hired two women, Dee Kantner and Violet Palmer, as referees, the first women to officiate in a major professional all-male sports league).

The traditional conception of femininity as passive and helpless is challenged today by the fit, athletic, and even muscular appearance of women athletes. Women now engage in pumping iron to sculpt their bodies toward a new standard of femininity that combines beauty with taut, developed muscles. Similarly, women are now rejecting traditional notions of femininity by pushing the limits in endurance events in running, cycling, swimming, and mountain climbing and by engaging freely in strength sports such as bodybuilding, weight lifting, and throwing weights.

Sport and Sexuality

Sport has been socially constructed as a masculine activity. Young boys are inducted into a fiercely heterosexual world of male toughness and competitiveness that embodies a fear of the effeminate and subordinates gay men.[22] In the United States boys learn to play football and thereby develop both a social and a personal identity that is consistent with the hegemonic conception of masculinity.[23] This is the common pattern in other societies as well.[24] If boys in the United States do not meet these cultural expectations, they are called sissies. Once labeled, they typically are teased and excluded from peer group relationships and activities. Because they do not participate in "manly" sports, they are socially marginalized by their peers. Older boys and young men in the United States who do not fit the dominant behavior patterns of masculinity often face serious questions about their sexual orientation, with labels such as "fag," "gay," and "queer" being used to describe them.[25] A common motivational ploy by some coaches is to question a male athlete's heterosexuality (calling him a "pussy" or a "fag" or placing Kotex in his locker) if he does not play as aggressively as the coach demands. Indiana basketball coach Bob Knight once stopped the videotape of a game to say to one of his players:

> Daryl, look at that. You don't even run back down the floor hard. That's all I need to know about you, Daryl. All you want to be out there is comfortable. You don't work, you don't sprint back. Look at that! You never push yourself. You know what you are Daryl? You are the worst f——pussy I've ever seen play basketball at this school. The absolute worst pussy ever. You have more goddamn ability than 95 percent of the players we've had here but you are a pussy from the top of your head to the bottom of your feet. An absolute f——pussy.[26]

Sociologist Timothy Jon Curry's[27] research on the male bonding in athletic locker rooms found that the talk there focused on affirmations of traditional masculinity, homophobia, and misogynistic slurs. Curry found that locker room talk by males was decidedly heterosexual and absolutely intolerant of homosexuality. Curry reasons that athletes do not want to be singled out as unmasculine in any way. Thus the "expression of dislike for femaleness or homosexuality demonstrates to oneself and others that one is separate from it and therefore must be masculine."[28] Needless to say, gay males are not welcome in the masculine sports world.

Female athletes, just as other women who enter traditional male domains, especially sports domains that require strength, endurance, and aggression, face the social control mechanism of slander concerning their sexuality. "Slander against female athletes usually takes the form of describing them as mannish, butch, musclebound, unpretty, unnatural, and otherwise unfeminine. It contains two related messages: one, that to be a female athlete is to be a lesbian (or at least in danger of becoming one), and two, that to be a lesbian is wrong."[29]

Women in sport, more than men, endure intense scrutiny about their sexual identity. A common fear among many men and women is that women in sport transgress gender lines, which disrupts the social order. "The lesbian label is used to define the boundaries of acceptable female behavior in a patriarchal culture: When a woman is called a lesbian, she knows she is out of bounds."[30]

Lesbians in sport are considered deviants and are stereotyped by the media.[31] Women (whether lesbian or not) sometimes face discrimination as they compete against men for coaching or sports administration jobs because of the assumption of homosexuality. In 1991 Penn State basketball coach Rene Portland told the *New York Times* that she did not allow lesbians on her team (she was not fired or forced to change her policy by the authorities at Penn State, although she was asked to take a sensitivity course).[32] Highly successful athletes (e.g., Martina Navratilova) have lost millions of dollars in endorsement money after acknowledging their homosexuality. The Ladies Professional Golf Association has faced allegations, epithets, and innuendo that its athletes were disproportionately lesbian, which has damaged women's professional golf through loss of sponsorship, television coverage, and fan support. CBS golf commentator Ben Wright was fired in 1996 when he told another reporter that "lesbians hurt the game of golf."

The result is that many lesbian athletes and coaches stay closeted. Some may act in an exaggeratedly "ladylike" way by using certain personal effects (such as bows, ribbons, makeup, dresses, heels) and by talking about eventually settling down and having children.[33] Others develop a lesbian identity.[34] Still others resist and work with heterosexuals to overcome homophobia, heterosexism, and sexism in sport.[35] The larger consequence of homophobia in sport is that compulsory heterosexuality remains the norm. And, as with gender roles, the mechanisms of social control in sport have sustained "compulsory heterosexuality [as] part of a system of domination that perpetuates patriarchal relations and the wielding of power over other sexualities."[36]

Direct Social Control in Sport

Athletes engaged in sport beyond the informal play stage are subject to various forms of social control aimed at shaping their behaviors. Control obviously comes from powerful sports organizations, which determine eligibility, scheduling, and rules for games. The National Collegiate Athletic Association (NCAA) sanctions schools and players for rules violations. The Olympic Committee decides what nations are eligible to compete, ruling, for example, that the Union of South Africa was banned from Olympic competition from 1964 to 1991 because of its racist policies.

In 1972 the U.S. Congress imposed its will on school sports by instituting Title IX to encourage gender equity in sports and other school programs.

National leaders may also decide to prohibit their athletes from participating in an international event (e.g., 34 Islamic nations prohibited their women from competing in the 1996 Olympics because participating violated Muslim rules for appropriate women's dress).

The gatekeeping function of sports organizations, although necessary, has been used historically to exclude or limit participation by athletes from certain social categories. The notion of "amateurism" was used, for example, by the affluent to exclude members of the working class from their athletic activities. "Amateurism" has also been used as an exploitative ideology whereby colleges and universities use "amateur" athletes to generate considerable income for coaches, schools, leagues, the NCAA, and bowl/tournament organizers.[37] The highest paid college coaches, for instance, make as much as $2 million annually, while their athletes receive room, board, tuition, and books. African Americans were excluded from participation in mainstream U.S. college and professional leagues, with rare exceptions, from World War I until the years after World War II. This exclusion was a consequence of tradition, Jim Crow laws, institutional racism, and even explicit rules in the bylaws of certain sports (e.g., professional baseball, golf, and bowling).[38] Girls were excluded from Little League baseball until the "boys-only" clause was dropped as a result of a court case in the 1970s. Women were kept from competing in Olympic track and field events until 1928 by the men running the International Olympic Committee. Slowly and reluctantly, women's events have been added to the Olympics, with women finally allowed to run a marathon in the 1984 Olympics (overcoming the traditional belief that women were too fragile for endurance events).

Sports organizations tend to control the athletes' behavior on the field. These bodies vary in their rules and enforcement zeal, but they all attempt to control excessive violence, combat the use of banned substances to enhance performance, and oppose point shaving. They also sanction negatively, again with considerable variation, off-the-field behaviors by athletes, such as criminal acts, use of recreational drugs, and, most especially, gambling on sports events.

Each sports social organization includes authoritative positions that exert control over others. Coaches have the formal task of teaching and training athletes to maximize their athletic performance and devising game strategies that maximize the chances of winning. Most important, the coach-player relationship is an asymmetrical power relationship. Coaches decide who makes the team, who plays, and when they play. They create the procedures for determining and enforcing team rules. Coaches determine training schedules. They sanction player behaviors that they deem detrimental to team goals.

Coach-centered power over athletes varies widely. A few coaches are open and democratic, allowing their athletes to make and enforce rules and involving them in strategy decisions. Abe Lemons is one of the few antiauthoritarian coaches. Once when he was head basketball coach at Oklahoma City University, his team arrived in Las Vegas two days before they were to play. Coach

Lemons, unlike almost any coach in America, told his players that they were on their own until meeting a few hours before game time forty-eight hours later. At the opposite extreme, some coaches are tyrants, demanding total control over virtually all aspects of their players' lives. They have rules about how to dress, when to go to bed, and what to eat. Most coaches are either paternalistic or authoritarian in their methods. With few exceptions, coaches impose their will on athletes. Often they violate the privacy rights of athletes, deny their individual rights, and, in extreme cases, subject athletes to oppression, brutality, and terror. When Sark Arslanian was football coach at Colorado State University, he ruled that his players must wear a coat and tie on road trips. When the players arrived to board the bus for the airport for a game, he found that his star defensive back was not wearing a tie. Coach Arslanian sent the player home. Why would a coach do this? Will his action cause the player to play harder next time? Or is the issue one of control—bending the players to the will of the coach? Coach Bob Knight of Indiana holds a practice (sometimes two practices) on Christmas Day. Occasionally he does not inform his players when the next practice will be, forcing them to stay in near their phones until an assistant informs them—clearly a control technique. Knight's basic coaching philosophy has been summarized as follows:

> His fundamental approach to motivation has never changed: fear is his number one weapon. He believes that if the players are afraid of getting screamed at or of landing in the doghouse, they will play better. And, if they fear him more than the opponent, they are likely to play better.[39]

Another coach who uses intimidation, humiliation, and even physical aggression is legendary Notre Dame football coach Lou Holtz. After Chet Lacheta made several mistakes in practice, "[Holtz] started yelling at me. He said that I was a coward. He said that I should find a different sport to play and that I shouldn't come back in the fall. He was pretty rough. . . . First he grabbed me by my face mask and shook it. Then he spit on me."[40]

Why are so many coaches so demanding, inhumane, and autocratic? It has been suggested that the coaching profession attracts inflexible and manipulative personalities, but empirical research does not support this contention.[41] The key to understanding the tendency toward autocratic coaching behavior lies in the role of coach and the unique demands that coaches face. First, the limits on coaching behaviors are set by communities and societies. Within the United States, for example, there is wide approval for demanding, autocratic coaches. Most players accept their subordination to higher authority.[42] Ironically, a democratic society permits, even demands, undemocratic coaches. I elaborate on this paradox in chapter 7.

A second and crucial reason for authoritarian coaches is the uniqueness of the coaching role. Coaches face distinctive pressures not present in other occupations. They are held totally accountable for game outcomes. The games are unpredictable and highly visible, and the outcomes are objectively measured. Coaches react to their pressured situations in three characteristic ways. First, they seek public support by demanding that their athletes behave according to community norms (in dress, demeanor, patriotism, and religiosity). Moreover, they generate community support by showing an absolute confidence in their methods and strategies. As coaches are fond of saying, "It's my way or the highway." The other tactic is to control as much as possible. Thus most coaches control on- and off-the-field behaviors, determine game strategy, and make all decisions during games.

Second, coaches themselves are subject to social control. Coaches are employed by clubs, schools, and professional teams. When their behaviors go too far, they are subject to sanctions by those who hold authority over them. Coaches engage in such outrageous behaviors as physical abuse of players, gambling, point shaving, drug and alcohol abuse, and insubordination. On rare occasions, coaches have been sanctioned because of the initiatives of aggrieved players who complained to authorities, threatened boycotts, and brought grievances to the civil courts. Although some coaches clearly get away with maltreating their players, on relatively rare occasions they do not. In 1993 Lou Campanelli lost his job as basketball coach at the University of California–Berkeley because players complained about the vulgar and personally degrading attacks that he directed against them. The athletic director, Robert Bockrath, said that Campanelli had crossed the line. Sportswriter Bryan Burwell commented on this unusually courageous act by the athletic director:

> Does it matter if [the coach] treats his players like indentured servants? It matters. Someone needs to point out to all these power-tripping task masters that there is a very distinct line between merely cursing at a player to scold or motivate and launching these pointless, humiliating, derogatory personal attacks that far too many coaches think is an acceptable practice. . . . The end doesn't justify the means. Times have changed. Athletes shouldn't have to deal with this abuse, and if the coach can't understand that, then there ought to be more administrators with the guts to make them get IT.[43]

Social control is not limited to the powerful supervising and managing those below them in a social organization. Most significantly, social control emerges from interactions among peers within the informal social order. Sociological research from such diverse settings as workplaces and urban street corners have found that social norms, sanctions, and roles emerge in informal interaction, resulting in social order. This social phenomenon has also been observed in sport settings. Regulars participate as individuals with others whom they see during the activity but exchange few words with. Sociologist Howard Nixon found, for example, that the regular participants in swimming constructed and maintained social order in that setting.[44] This order involved an informal code of behavior, enforcement of rules, and role differentiation. Social control mechanisms used by the participants included nonverbal cues, polite verbal prods, and even aggressive retaliation.

Loic Wacquant's ethnographic study of a boxing gym[45] located in a Chicago ghetto portrays the informal but elaborate social order maintained by the participants:

> The first thing trainers always stress is what you are *not* supposed to do in the gym. Stoneland's coach-in-second offers the following compressed enumeration of the gym's don'ts: "Cursin' Smokin' Loud talkin'. Disrespect for the women, disrespect for the coaches, disrespect for each other. No animosity, no bragging." To which could be added a host of smaller, often implicit rules forming a tightly-woven web of restrictions that converge to *pacify* behavior in the gym: It is forbidden to bring food or drinks in the club, to talk during training, to rest leaning on the sides of tables, to alter the sequence of drills (for instance), to start a session by skipping rope instead of loosening up and shadow-boxing. It is mandatory to wear a jockstrap under one's towel when coming out of the shower and dry clothes when out of the gym. There is no using the equipment in an unconventional fashion, throwing punches against objects, sparring if one is not fully equipped for it, or worse, starting or even simply faking a fight outside of the ring. . . . Most of the implicit "internal regulations" of the club are visible only in the conduct and demeanor of the regulars who have progressively internalized them, and they are brought to explicit attention only when violated. Those who do not manage to assimilate this unwritten code of conduct are promptly dismissed or advised . . . to transfer to another gym.[46]

Children at play also exert control over each other. Peers may mock behaviors that go beyond their norms, such as boys not being aggressive or girls who are tomboys. Thus behaviors are channeled in approved ways and gender is socially constructed.[47] Male locker rooms, as I have noted, constitute a sports setting in which the informal norms promote aggression, homophobia, and sexism. Peer group dynamics encourage such talk, since avoiding it calls an individual's masculinity into question.[48]

Ethnographic studies of sport subcultures (e.g., bodybuilders, surfers, climbers, gymnasts) reveal that new members engage in the deliberate act of identity construction. They adopt the attitudes, style of dress, speech patterns, and behaviors of the established members of the subculture.[49] In short, the behavior of these neophyte members is controlled even *before* they become full members in the subculture through a process called "anticipatory socialization."

I emphasize in this book the centrality of social control in sport. Observers of this ubiquitous phenomenon can interpret it in two contradictory ways. One interpretation of social control is that it has positive functions, leading to consensus and cooperation among members, everyone pulling together for a common goal, and stability in the social organization. The opposite view is that the status quo is not necessarily good for all members of the group. From this perspective, certain categories benefit while others do not from the normal ways in which the group is structured. The irony is that the power of social control is so great and so thoroughly constructed into the culture of sports that many who are oppressed do not recognize their oppression.

Notes

1. "Texas Coach Lays Down the Law," *Rocky Mountain News,* April 14, 1998, p. 16C.

2. My thanks to George Sage for highlighting this paradox in his review of the manuscript.

3. John Walton, *Sociology and Critical Inquiry: The Work, Tradition, and Purpose,* 2d ed. (Belmont, Calif.: Wadsworth, 1990), pp. 343–361.

4. Michael A. Messner, "Sports and Male Domination: The Female Athlete as Contested Ideological Terrain," *Sociology of Sport Journal* 5 (September 1988): 198.

5. Randall Collins, *Sociological Insight: An Introduction to Non-Obvious Sociology,* 2d ed. (New York: Oxford University Press, 1992), pp. 63–85.

6. Paul L. Berger, *Invitation to Sociology: A Humanistic Perspective* (Garden City, N.Y.: Doubleday-Anchor), p. 93.

7. Eldon E. Snyder, "Athletic Dressing Room Slogans and Folklore," *International Review of Sport Sociology* 7 (1972): 89–102.

8. David Matza, "Position and Behavior Patterns of Youth," in *Handbook of Modern Sociology,* ed. Robert E. L. Faris (Chicago: Rand McNally, 1964), p. 207.

9. Lois Bryson, "Sport and the Maintenance of Masculine Hegemony," *Women's Studies International Forum* 10 (1987): 349–360.

10. Jay J. Coakley, *Sport in Society: Issues and Controversies,* 5th ed. (St. Louis: Mosby, 1994), p. 225.

11. Paul Willis, "Women in Sport Ideology," in *Sport, Culture and Ideology,* ed. Jennifer Hargreaves (London: Routledge and Kegan Paul, 1982), p. 121.

12. Ibid., p. 123.

13. R. Vivian Acosta and Linda J. Carpenter, "Women in Intercollegiate Sport: A Longitudinal Study—Seventeen Years Update, 1977–1994" (manuscript, Department of Physical Education, Brooklyn College, 1994).

14. Edward Turner et al., "Television Consumer Advertising and the Sports Figure," *Sport Marketing Quarterly* 4 (March 1995): 27–33.

15. Mariah Burton Nelson, *The Stronger Women Get, the More Men Love Football: Sexism and the American Culture of Sports* (New York: Harcourt Brace, 1994), p. 8.

16. Margaret Carlisle Duncan, "Sports Photographs and Sexual Difference: Images of Women and Men in the 1984 and 1988 Olympic Games," *Sociology of Sport Journal* 7 (March 1990): 22–43.

17. Messner, "Sports and Male Domination," pp. 204–205.

18. D. Stanley Eitzen and Maxine Baca Zinn, "The De-athleticization of Women: The Naming and Gender Marking of Collegiate Sport Teams," *Sociology of Sport Journal* 6 (1989): 362–370.

19. Bryson, "Sport," p. 349-360.

20. Messner, "Sports and Male Domination."

21. Jeffrey Blackwell, "Girls Grapple with Breaking Tradition," *USA Today,* February 14, 1997, p. 9C; Dylan B. Tomlinson, "Grappling with a Dilemma," *Denver Post,* June 16, 1998, p. 8D.

22. Jennifer Hargreaves, *Sporting Females: Critical Issues in the History and Sociology of Women's Sport* (London: Routledge, 1994); see also Douglas E. Foley, "The Great American Football Ritual: Reproducing Race, Class, and Gender Inequality," *Sociology of Sport Journal* 7 (June 1990): 111–135; Michael A. Messner and Donald F. Sabo, eds., *Sport, Men, and the Gender Order: Critical Feminist Perspectives* (Champaign, Ill.: Human Kinetics, 1990); and Brian Pronger, *The Arena of Masculinity: Sports, Homosexuality, and the Meaning of Sex* (London: GMP Publishers, 1990).

23. Donald F. Sabo, "The Football Coach as Officiant in Patriarchal Society: Conformity and Resistance in the Social Reproduction of Masculinity" (paper presented at the annual meeting of the North American Society for the Sociology of Sport, Edmonton, Alberta, November 1987).

24. Lois Bryson, "Challenges to Male Hegemony in Sport," in *Sport, Men, and the Gender Order: Critical Feminist Perspectives,* ed. Michael A. Messner and Donald F. Sabo (Champaign, Ill.: Human Kinetics, 1990), p. 175.

25. Jay J. Coakley, *Sport in Society: Issues and Controversies,* 6th ed. (New York: McGraw-Hill, 1998), p. 238.

26. Quoted in John Feinstein, *A Season on the Brink: A Year with Bob Knight and the Indiana Hoosiers* (New York: Macmillan, 1986), p. 7.

27. Timothy Jon Curry, "Fraternal Bonding in the Locker Room: A Profeminist Analysis of Talk about Competition and Women," *Sociology of Sport Journal* 8 (June 1991): 119–135.

28. Ibid., p. 128.

29. Gail Whitaker, "Social Control Mechanisms: Ties That Bind—and Chafe," *Perspectives* (1982): 83.

30. Pat Griffin, "Changing the Game: Homophobia, Sexism, and Lesbians in Sport," *Quest* 44, no. 2 (1992): 252.

31. Angela Burroughs, Liz Ashburn, and Leonie Seebohm, "'Add Sex and Stir': Homophobic Coverage of Women's Cricket in Australia," *Journal of Sport and Social Issues* 19 (August 1995): 266–284.

32. Dylan B. Tomlinson, "Fear and Loathing," *Denver Post,* April 28, 1998, p. 10D.

33. Coakley, *Sport in Society.*

34. Birgit Palzkill, "Between Gymshoes and High-Heels: The Development of a Lesbian Identity and Existence in Top Class Sport," *International Review for the Sociology of Sport* 25, no. 3 (1990): 221–234.

35. Griffin, "Changing the Game."

36. Hargreaves, *Sporting Females,* p. 261.

37. See D. Stanley Eitzen, "The Sociology of Amateur Sport: An Overview," *International Review for the Sociology of Sport* 24, no. 2 (1989): 95–105; and Walter Byers with Charles Hammer, *Unsportsmanlike Conduct: Exploiting College Athletes* (Ann Arbor: University of Michigan Press, 1995).

38. Ocania Chalk, *Pioneers of Black Sport* (New York: Dodd, Mead, 1975).

39. Feinstein, *Season on the Brink,* p. 86.

40. Quoted in Don Yaeger and Douglas S. Looney, *Under the Tarnished Dome: How Notre Dame Betrayed Its Ideals for Football Glory* (New York: Simon and Schuster, 1993), pp. 22–23.

41. The following relies on Coakley, *Sport in Society,* pp. 191–198.

42. Robert Hughes and Jay Coakley, "Positive Deviance among Athletes: The Implications of Overconformity to the Sport Ethic," *Sociology of Sport Journal* 8 (December 1991): 307–325.

43. Bryan Burwell, "Cal Lesson: Coaches Better Not Cross Line," *USA Today,* February 19, 1993, p. 3C.

44. Howard L. Nixon II, "Social Order in a Leisure Setting: The Case of Recreational Swimmers in a Pool," *Sociology of Sport Journal* 3 (December 1986): 320–332.

45. Loic J. D. Wacquant, "The Logic of Boxing in Black Chicago: Toward a Sociology of Pugilism," *Sociology of Sport Journal* 9 (September 1992): 221–254.

46. Ibid., pp. 235–236.

47. See Barrie Thorne, *Gender Play: Girls and Boys in School* (New Brunswick, N.J.: Rutgers University Press, 1993); and Monica A. Kunesh, Cynthia A. Hasbrook, and Rebecca Lewthwaite, "Physical Activity Socialization: Peer Interactions and Affective Responses among a Sample of Sixth Grade Girls," *Sociology of Sport Journal* 9 (December 1992): 385–396.

48. Curry, "Fraternal Bonding."

49. Peter Donnelly and Kevin Young, "The Construction and Confirmation of Identity in Sport Subcultures," *Sociology of Sport Journal* 5 (September 1988): 223–240.

Chapter 7

The Democratic Ideal and School Sport

In the movie Crimson Tide *the commander of a U.S. nuclear submarine (played by Gene Hackman) says to his crew, "We are here to preserve democracy, not to practice it."*

Democracy is learned through practice. Young people do not learn democracy when their leaders are tyrants. They do not learn democracy when they are spied on, demeaned, and degraded by authorities. They do not learn democracy when their lives are regimented from above. They do not learn the qualities of democratic citizenship from verbal and physical punishments imposed arbitrarily. Nor do they learn democracy when they are denied fundamental human freedoms. In short, if young people are to believe in democracy, they must live in a democracy.

—D. Stanley Eitzen

When the old communist empire collapsed in 1990, ending the Cold War, the United States characterized this development as a victory: capitalism defeating communism; freedom winning over authoritarian control; and democracy overcoming a system ruled by an elite.

This claim of victory for the American "way of life" over the "evil empire" presents us with a fundamental paradox. Although Americans claim to be democratic, American institutions, whether they be families, armies, corporations, churches, or schools, are not especially democratic. In short, there is a fundamental contradiction in what Americans claim to be and what Americans are.

The antidemocratic nature of schools is especially interesting, since schools

This essay is a revised and updated version of D. Stanley Eitzen, "Sports and Ideological Contradictions: Learning from the Cultural Framing of Soviet Values," *Journal of Sport and Social Issues* 16 (December 1992): 144–149. Portions are also taken from D. Stanley Eitzen and George H. Sage, *Sociology of North American Sport,* 6th ed. (Madison, Wis.: Brown and Benchmark, 1997), chaps. 5–6.

formally cherish and nourish the values and traditions of society and inculcate them into each succeeding generation. But what actually happens in our schools? Many school procedures and activities produce social control more than they educate. Rules are determined and enforced by administrators with no input from teachers or students. Policies are determined by school boards and administrators. School boards are elected, but how well do they represent the community? The middle and upper classes are always represented, but the working and lower classes usually are not. Minority racial groups are typically underrepresented on school boards, if they are represented at all. Is democracy viable when teachers are autocratic? Students elect student councils and officers, but these are "toy" governments with little or no power. How does the ideal mesh with the real in our schools when it comes to democracy? And what are the consequences of incongruity and hypocrisy? If the schools are undemocratic, is it not possible that their products will be undemocratic or authoritarian as well?

Clearly, the most undemocratic part of schools is team sports. In this chapter I argue that there is a more fundamental problem in sport than the frequent scandals we hear so much about. My seemingly outrageous proposition is that team sports as they are practiced in the high schools and colleges of the United States bear a remarkable resemblance to the way communism was practiced in the former Soviet Union and its satellites. The values that we have learned to associate with the Soviets and to hate are actually present in our own social system. In making this comparison, I intend to advocate change, not merely criticize. I draw here on the approach of immanent critique followed by sociologist Robert Antonio and other critical theorists: "Immanent critique is a means of detecting the societal contradictions which offer the most determinate possibilities for emancipatory social change."[1] By examining such a fundamental paradox as authoritarianism in a democracy, we can begin to achieve consistency with the lofty goal of democracy.

Parallels between School Team Sports and the Soviet System

In many cases there are striking parallels between the Soviet regime that Americans found so abhorrent and American school team sports. And beyond sport, parallels with the Soviet system could be drawn in regard to other American institutions as well.[2] Before elaborating on the parallels, I want to acknowledge and clarify my position. I am not naive about team sports. Team members must strive for excellence. They must pull together to achieve common goals. They must sacrifice to improve. They must strive for excellence as individuals and as a team. Effective leadership and teaching are essential. But must these necessary requirements for success be imposed in an authoritarian way? Or is there a better way?

The End Justifies the Means

According to Western observers, the Soviet Union was unprincipled, willing to do anything to achieve the goal of spreading communism and keeping the elite in power. However, this "will to win," the notion of doing whatever it takes, is the very foundation of competitive sport. Coaches, boosters, and others often break the rules to secure the services of athletes.[3] Coaches sometimes exploit the athletic skills of their players while not helping them move toward graduation. Athletes may be taught to cheat (e.g., how to hold an opponent without being caught by an official), or they may be encouraged to intimidate their opponents with overly aggressive hitting and verbal taunts.

Leveling of Economic Differences

One objective of communism was to reduce economic inequality. This goal is antithetical to capitalism, which sees economic advantages as the primary means to motivate individuals to achieve. In school sport, however, all athletes are treated the same—as amateurs—as defined by the codes determined by administrative bodies. All college athletes on scholarship, for example, receive identical benefits—tuition, books, food, and lodging—as decreed by the National Collegiate Athletic Association (NCAA). First teamers and benchwarmers have the same benefits, although star players may receive generous rewards, including monetary ones, that are outside the rules. All-Americans and also-rans are subject to the same economic limitations. The economic value of the athletes is inconsequential to their remuneration. As an extreme example, basketball star Patrick Ewing brought more than $12 million to Georgetown University during his four years there (a tripling of attendance, increased television revenues, and qualifying for the NCAA tournament each year). The cost to Georgetown for Ewing's talents and drawing power totaled $48,600.[4]

Despite the avowed goal of the communist "classless" society, vast differences in material wealth developed between leaders of the Communist Party and the masses. A contradiction developed between official communist dogma and reality as the members of the ruling elite acquired luxuries, homes, cars, and incomes that were many times greater than what the workers had. This also occurs in U.S. sport. College athletes in the revenue-producing sports raise millions for their schools (Notre Dame, for example, has a five-year deal with NBC for $45 million, allowing it exclusive television rights to Notre Dame football games), conferences, the NCAA, and the television networks. Yet they receive subsistence wages. The athletes cannot capitalize on their fame until they leave school. When a football team plays in a bowl game, the players practice an extra month and receive nothing. Their coaches, on the other hand, receive bonuses for the team's success and, of course, the school receives the added money from participating in the bowl game. Similarly, the school may spend over $1 million sending the team and the band, as well as administrators and their spouses, to the bowl game, yet the parents of the athletes must attend at their own expense. Most egregious, high-profile coaches make as much as $2 million annually from salaries, shoe contracts, summer camps, and radio and television, whereas the athletes they depend on for success receive the "minimum wage": room, board, tuition, and books.

Invasion of Privacy

Another contradiction between values and actions involves the violation of the privacy rights of individuals. Americans frowned on the KGB and other organizations in the Soviet Union for clandestinely monitoring citizens for possible "deviant" behaviors. Ideally, this type of monitoring is intolerable in a free society, yet it occurs in the government as the police may have wiretaps with court orders and the FBI and CIA use electronic surveillance with or without court orders.[5] Some employers require prospective employees to take drug and psychological tests. Workers using telephones and computers may find their work watched, measured, and analyzed in detail by supervisors. Employers can peruse employees' e-mail, tap their work telephones, and examine confidential medical information. They can even film them secretly in the restroom.[6] In schools, students' lockers are subject to searches by administrators and teachers.

In school sport the privacy of athletes is invaded routinely. College athletes (but not their coaches, teachers, administrators, or other students) are subject to mandatory drug testing. Personnel from the athletic department watch athletes in their dorms and locker rooms, either in person or on closed-circuit television, for "deviant" behaviors. Bed checks are not uncommon. Sometimes there are "spies" who watch and report on behaviors of athletes in local bars and other places of amusement.

No Freedom of Choice

In the former Soviet Union freedoms were severely limited. Travel outside the country was refused to many. Religious freedom was denied. People were shifted by the authorities from job to job as needed. Workers on collective farms were told what to do, what to plant, when to harvest, and so on. In U.S. sport, decisions are also made for the athletes. They may be red-shirted (i.e., held from play for a year so they will be more mature) without consent. They may have little or no choice in what position they play. They may be told to gain or lose weight, with penalties for noncompliance. Off-season weight lifting and conditioning are typically mandatory. And most interesting of all, college athletes can leave to play for another school only if they do not play for a year (two years if their former coach does not release them).

Bureaucratic Authoritarianism

A basic flaw in the Soviet system was the centralization of authority. This seemingly rational organizational tool had a detrimental effect because the rules were inflexible and creativity was stifled. Initiative went unrewarded or was even punished. College sport for men and women (except for the very smallest schools) is controlled by a single organization, the NCAA, which has problems with flexibility, authoritarianism, an emphasis on revenues, and rules and punishments that hurt players more than coaches and institutions.[7] Vaclav Havel, a Czechoslovakian playwright who later became president of the Czech Republic, in an interview with the *London Times* characterized the communist system in his country as follows:

> In the system we live in . . . [one encounters] something that George Orwell saw.
> . . . From morning to night, everything every ordinary citizen does is in some way
> interfered with by the system. The regime leaves its mark on everything. . . . You
> can even see this manipulation in apparently trivial things.[8]

To which college sport critic Dick DeVenzio stated,

> Like not being able to have a job during the school year [the NCAA has relented
> on this in principle but as of this writing has not determined how much athletes
> can work and earn and still retain their eligibility], or do a commercial, or borrow
> a car or accept a free hamburger, or take the course schedule that is best for you.[9]

The United States criticized the Soviet system for being run from the top down and for party leaders who made binding decisions without guidance from citizens. Coaches, with very few exceptions, are autocratic. They impose their will on team rules, discipline, personnel decisions, and strategy. Team captains look to the sidelines for guidance on whether to accept a penaltys. Quarterbacks receive orders on what plays to call. The operant principle is that coaches lead and players follow. As coaches are fond of declaring, "It's my way or the highway."

Lack of Individualism

In the Soviet Union freedom of expression in art, in literature, and in the universities was stifled. In U.S. sport, obedience to authority allows coaches to demand mandatory study halls. Some high school coaches have rules prohibiting players from holding hands with their love interests during school hours. Some athletic departments have the final say on athletes' choice of majors and the courses that they take. Some coaches insist that their athletes avoid political protest. When I was teaching at the University of Kansas, two well-known advocates of the the "athletic revolution" (a late 1960s, early 1970s movement for athletes' rights)—Jack Scott and Dave Meggysey—were scheduled to speak in the school auditorium. Athletes were told not to attend, and assistant coaches were stationed at each entrance to enforce this ban.

Soviet citizens were expected to submerge their individual needs to the goals of the society. Similarly, athletes in team sports are expected to put team goals above their own (hence the common coaches' sayings, "There is no *I* in team"; "there is no *U* in team"). Famed economist John Kenneth Galbraith once wrote that

> [in team sports] the individual is taught from the earliest age to surrender himself or herself to the team. Nothing is more sternly rebuked than self-assertion at the expense of group achievement. No one is more praised than the good team player; none is more reviled than the individual who pursues his own goals, seeks to enhance his own reputation, at the expense of the group.[10]

For these reasons coaches often demand dress codes and organize leisure-time activities that everyone will attend, from church services to movies. Typically, big-time college football and basketball teams stay in a hotel the night before games (including home games). This is done to facilitate team meetings and eating schedules, but it also is done to control the athletes, keeping them away from romantic trysts, drinking, and staying up too late. University of Colorado basketball coach Ricardo Patton, in his first two years as head coach, included the following mandatory team activities: touring a prison, attending church services, sleeping together on cots in the gym for a week, and practicing at six in the morning. Another example of the expectation to put team first is the negative characterization given to college players who consider leaving a team before their eligibility is up to become professionals. They are considered traitors for elevating their needs above those of their schools, coaches, and teammates.

Lack of Human Rights

Americans saw the Soviet Union as particularly flawed because it had no equivalent to the Bill of Rights. Their lack of free speech and press, as well as their lack of the rights to assemble and to have a fair trial, inspired an ideological assault against their system. But a similar situation is tolerated in regard to U.S. athletes. Athletes who challenge the athletic power structure lose their scholarships and eligibility. Athletes who have a grievance are on their own. They have no union, no arbitration board, and rarely do they have representatives on campus athletic committees.

Oppression, Brutality, and Terror

Instances of brutality and terror in the Soviet Union were often framed by U.S. government officials as attempts by the powerful to command loyalty and obedience in an "evil empire." But coaches of athletic teams in the United States often degrade their athletes without being criticized. The athletes are subject to being cursed, belittled, and even struck by their coaches. University of California–Berkeley athletic director Robert Bockrath fired his basketball coach, Lou Campanelli, in 1993 because of the coach's verbal abuse. Bockrath characterized the situation this way:

> The words that were used were "losers," "cowards," "no guts." So many four-letter words you couldn't believe it. Now I know that is somewhat standard fare in sports today, but it's one thing to say "WE didn't play well" . . . or "WE played like a bunch of bleepin' losers." But when it becomes "YOU are a bunch of bleepin' losers," "JOHN SMITH is a bleepin' worthless coward," . . . a line has been crossed and it can't be tolerated. He destroyed their confidence. He stripped them psychologically. They were beaten mentally.[11]

How many athletic directors would fire a coach for such behavior if he was winning games? Bockrath, to his credit, fired a winning coach who had crossed the line. Others, most notably the athletic director and president of Indiana University, whose basketball coach Bob Knight has a long history of outrageous behaviors that include demeaning his players,[12] lack the courage to fire a winning coach who abuses his players.

On the return trip from a road game coaches may punish their players by having the bus driver let them off several miles from the school. Another tactic is to schedule practices at inconvenient times such as 2 A.M. or on holidays. These acts of control are similar to those used by the military to train recruits. As sociologist Philip Slater has commented,

> Exposure to random punishment, stress, fatigue, personal degradation and abuse, irrational authority, and constant assertions of one's worthlessness as a human being—all tried-and-true techniques of "reeducation" used by totalitarian regimes—are in most cases effective in creating and maintaining an obedient killing machine.[13]

These boot camp tactics are common among coaches. The question is, Are such behaviors appropriate in an educational setting that purports to train citizens for living in a democracy?

Just as the masses in the Soviet Union rarely resisted the authoritarian regime, most athletes are passive politically. Sport sociologist George Sage explains why:

> A question may be raised about the lack of protest from intercollegiate athletes about the prevailing conditions under which they labor. In one way it can be expected that the athletes would not find anything to question; they have been thoroughly conditioned by many years of organized sport involvement to obey athletic authorities. Indeed, most college athletes are faithful servants and spokespersons for the system of college sport. They tend to take the existing order for granted,

not questioning the status quo because they are preoccupied with their own jobs of making the team and perhaps gaining national recognition. As a group, athletes tend to be politically passive and apathetic, resigned to domination from above because, at least partly, the institutional structure of athletics is essentially hostile to independence of mind. Hence, athletes are willing victims whose self-worth and self-esteem have largely become synonymous with their athletic prowess. Their main impulse is to mind their own business while striving to be successful as athletes.[14]

This interpretation is especially damning of school sport, since it shows how athletic participation tends to generate political passivity, clearly not what is required of citizens in a democracy.

Why, then, do parents, school administrators, teachers, and community members permit these authoritarian practices that are antithetical to what we believe? The reason may be, first, that young people need structure; without activities that are supervised and controlled by adults, youth with be aimless and disorganized. Second, regimentation, obedience to authority, and working together for common goals are what adults want of children, so that they will fit easily into their adult roles and society's niches. And, third, just as adults believe that military discipline is good for the development of young people, so too is the top-down discipline of sport good for their development (building character, leadership). These rationales are dubious at best. Might there be a better way, a way more congruent with society's stated goals, to achieve the desired results?

Alternatives

These parallels between our society's interpretation of the authoritarian and oppressive Soviet regime and the organization of team sports in U.S. schools point to a glaring contradiction between the official ideology of the United States and its actual practice. If we truly believe in democracy, then we must democratize our institutions, including sport.

The West was excited when the Soviet Union instituted *perestroika* (restructuring) and *glasnost* (openness). These were the initial steps that brought democracy to that country. Can the same be done in sport in our own society?

Starting Points for Change

For starters, hire humanistic coaches who are democratic, open, and just. Second, make coaches part of the faculty so that they are part of the educational enterprise and not separate from it. Third, there must be mechanisms to ensure players' rights, perhaps a campus ombudsman or a committee separate from the athletic department with student representation. And, fourth, the goal of the coaches and their schools must be to build autonomous, self-reliant, self-disciplined individuals. This goal can be achieved in sport by having athletes share decision making in areas such as team rules, discipline, starting lineups, strategy, play calling, and game plans. Of course, leadership by the coaches is essential, but players can be groomed to accept more and more responsibility as they move up in class rank and experience. Jay Coakley has suggested a way to restructure sport along these lines:

> Why should adult coaches make all the decisions on student sport teams? Ideally, the goal should be to prepare the team to be self-coached. In fact, some leagues should require that for the last two or three games of the season, coaches must sit in the stands and watch while the players coach themselves. This would be real leadership training.[15]

Although rare, some experiments promoting athlete involvement in decision making have taken place. One radical experiment with democracy in football was used by George Davis, a football coach at several California high schools and a junior college. At St. Helena High School, his teams won forty-five consecutive games. The Davis coaching system was unique. His players voted on who should be in the starting lineup; they decided what positions they wanted to play; and they established the guidelines for discipline. In other words, Davis's revolutionary system was democratic. Some critics in Willits, a community in which Davis wanted to establish this system, were upset with it. They accused Davis of shirking responsibility, promoting disunity, and aiding communist agitators. The irony is that these evils were the presumed consequences of a democratic system. As sociologists Howard Nixon and James Frey commented,

> The adult doubts are ironic because George Davis was a genuine educator who tried to translate the American Dream and the Dominant Sport Creed into reality for his athletes. The fact that his teams won makes resistance to his approach even more curious. . . . Davis's willingness to give up some of his control to his players enabled him to teach a basic civics lesson about participatory democracy, and in doing so he did not have to give up winning. The primary cost of his experiment was the backlash from community members and some athletes who apparently did not believe that adolescents could handle the responsibility of making team decisions or, perhaps, that democracy belonged in sport.[16]

Davis, on the other hand, believed that his system would (1) increase confidence between players and coaches; (2) promote team cohesion; (3) teach responsibility, leadership, and decision making, thereby fostering maturity rather than immaturity and independence rather than dependence; (4) increase player motivation so that instead of being driven by fear, harassment, and physical abuse by the coach, the players would have to impress their peers; (5) free the coach to teach skills, techniques, and strategies; and (6) allow the players to experience the benefits of democracy. Davis summed up his system this way:

What does the vote achieve? It takes the problems of discipline and responsibility and puts them where they belong, with the players. The coach becomes a teacher, what he is being paid to do, a resource unit. My job is to teach, to help athletes reach a level of independence. At any level this is how democracy works and why it succeeds.[17]

A variant of this system is currently being used by basketball coach Lee Mc-Kinney at Fontbonne College in St. Louis, a Division III school. The team has compiled a successful 34–17 record in the two seasons since the one-man, one-vote system was instituted.[18]

Leaders in school sport have two choices. They can continue walking the undemocratic path, which espouses character building and leadership training but practices tyranny. This is the path of least resistance because, although hypocritical, it is accepted, even encouraged, by almost everyone—school administrators, coaches, community members, influential friends of the schools, parents, and even players. The tougher alternative path is to organize sport so that there is a close fit between the democratic ideals we cherish and the way sport is organized. If we choose the former, then our athletes may suffer the ills we attributed to the former Soviet strategy, becoming an intimidated mass of people who are afraid to speak their minds, who do what they are told, and who are denied their fundamental freedoms. The second path affirms our twin values of democracy and freedom.

Is such fundamental change possible? But then a few years ago, who dared to imagine that the Soviet Union and its empire would be broken up without a war? Who believed that these peoples would turn to the values of the West? If those momentous changes are possible, then it may also be possible to change team sports in schools to make them congruent, rather than contradictory, to our own ideals. Since sport reflects society, it cannot achieve democracy without simultaneous and parallel changes in the other institutions of society.

Notes

1. Robert J. Antonio, "Immanent Critique as the Core of Critical Theory: Its Origins and Developments in Hegel, Marx, and Contemporary Thought," *British Journal of Sociology* 32 (1981): 330.

2. See Noam Chomsky, *Deterring Democracy* (London: Verso, 1991); Michael Parenti, *Democracy for the Few*, 6th ed. (New York: St. Martin's, 1995); and Philip Slater, *A Dream Deferred: America's Discontent and the Search for a New Democratic Ideal* (Boston: Beacon, 1991).

3. See Alexander Wolff and Kostya Kennedy, "Winning Ugly," *Sports Illustrated*, September 1995, p. 14; David Whitfkord, *A Payroll to Meet: A Story of Greed, Corruption, and Football at SMU* (New York: Macmillan, 1989); Charles Thompson and Allan Sonnenschein, *Down and Dirty: The Life and Crimes of Oklahoma Football* (New York:

Carroll and Graf, 1990); Francis X. Dealy Jr., *Win at Any Cost: The Sell Out of College Athletics* (New York: Carol Publishing, 1990); John R. Thelin, *Games Colleges Play: Scandal and Reform in Intercollegiate Athletics* (Baltimore: Johns Hopkins University Press, 1994); and James H. Frey, "Deviance of Organizational Subunits: The Case of College Athletic Departments," *Journal of Sport and Social Issues* 18 (May 1994): 110–122.

4. Gregg Leslie, "Pick-and-Bankroll," *Regardie's,* January 1986, p. 17.

5. See Mike Rothmiller and Ivan Goldman, *L.A. Secret Police* (New York: Pocket Books, 1992); Frank Donner, *Protectors of Privilege, Red Squads and Police Repression in Urban America* (Berkeley: University of California Press, 1991); and Parenti, *Democracy,* pp. 149–162.

6. Lee Smith, "What the Boss Knows about You," *Fortune,* August 9, 1993, pp. 88–93.

7. For critiques of the NCAA, see Walter Byers with Charles Hammer, *Unsportsmanlike Conduct: Exploiting College Athletes* (Ann Arbor: University of Michigan Press, 1995); George H. Sage, "Blaming the Victim: NCAA Responses to Calls for Reform in Major College Sports," *Arena Review* 11 (November 1987): 1–11; Timothy Davis, "A Model of Institutional Governance for Intercollegiate Athletics," *Wisconsin Law Review* 599 (1995): 599–645; Murray Sperber, *College Sport, Inc.: The Athletic Department vs. the University* (New York: Holt, 1990); and Tom McMillen with Paul Coggins, *Out of Control: How the American Sports Establishment Is Being Driven by Greed and Hypocrisy—And What Needs to Be Done about It* (New York: Simon and Schuster, 1992).

8. Quoted in Dick DeVenzio, "NCAA: National Communists against Athletes," *Revenue-Producing Major College Student-Athletes Newsletter* (Charlotte, N.C., n.d.), p. 2.

9. Ibid.

10. John Kenneth Galbraith, "Baseball: Socialist as Apple Pie," *New York Times,* August 7, 1988, p. 23E.

11. Quoted in Bryan Burwell, "Cal Lesson: Coaches Better Not Cross Line," *USA Today,* February 19, 1993, p. 3C.

12. See John Feinstein, *A Season on the Brink: A Year with Bob Knight of the Indiana Hoosiers* (New York: Macmillian, 1986); Rick Telander, "Not a Shining Knight," *Sports Illustrated,* May 9, 1988, p. 122; Ron Fimrite, "These Guys Are Leaders? Those in Charge in Sports Don't Control Themselves," *Sports Illustrated,* May 23, 1988, p. 102; Tim Franklin, " 'General' Corrupts Essence of Leadership," *Chicago Tribune,* March 23, 1997, sec. 3, p. 13.

13. Slater, *Dream Deferred,* pp. 47–48.

14. George H. Sage, *Power and Ideology in American Sport: A Critical Perspective* (Champaign, Ill.: Human Kinetics, 1990), p. 187.

15. Jay J. Coakley, *Sport in Society: Issues and Controversies,* 5th ed. (St. Louis: Mosby, 1994), p. 412.

16. Howard L. Nixon II and James H. Frey, *A Sociology of Sport* (Belmont, Calif.: Wadsworth, 1996), pp. 132–133.

17. Quoted in Neil Amdur, *The Fifth Down: Democracy and the Football Revolution* (New York: Delta, 1972), p. 218.

18. "Franchise Players," *Sports Illustrated,* April 14, 1997, pp. 22–23.

Chapter 8

The Contradictions of Big-Time College Sport

A few years ago, after Duke was eliminated from the NCAA Division I men's basketball tournament, its highly successful and esteemed coach, Mike Krzyzewski, made an emotional speech. Coach K, as he is affectionately known, extolled the virtues of big-time college sport—the camaraderie, the shared sacrifice, the commitment to excellence, collective responsibility, and integrity. He said, "All this stuff where people talk about college sports and things as bad, you have no idea. I want to whack everybody who says that. College sports are great. They're O.K. when you yell at each other, when you hug each other, when you live."[1]

This essay is a revised and expanded version of D. Stanley Eitzen, "Big-Time College Sports: Contradictions, Crises, and Consequences," *Vital Speeches of the Day* 64 (December 1997): 122–126; it also draws on my observations from other sources: D. Stanley Eitzen and George H. Sage, *Sociology of North American Sport*, 6th ed. (Dubuque: Brown and Benchmark, 1997), 101–121; D. Stanley Eitzen, "Racism in Big-Time College Sport: Prospects for the Year 2020 and Proposals for Change," in *Racism in College Athletics: The African American Experience*, ed. Dana D. Brooks and Ronald C. Althouse, 2d ed. (Morgantown, W.Va.: Fitness Information Technology, in press); D. Stanley Eitzen, "Reforms Don't Fix Commercialization of College Sports," *Baltimore Sun*, March 17, 1991, p. 4N; D. Stanley Eitzen, "Athletes in Big-Time College Programs: No Rights, No Voice, No Power," *Denver Post*, December 12, 1992, p. 11B; D. Stanley Eitzen, "Students First and Athletes Second?" in *Points of View on American Higher Education*, vol. 2, ed. Stephen H. Barnes (Lewiston, N.Y.: Mellen, 1990), pp. 71–77; D. Stanley Eitzen, "Academic Preparation and Success of College Athletes" (paper presented to the Amateur Athletic Foundation of Los Angeles, May 15–16, 1987); D. Stanley Eitzen, "How We Can Clean Up Big-Time College Sports," *Chronicle of Higher Education*, February 12, 1986, p. 96; and D. Stanley Eitzen, "Athletics and Higher Education: A Conflict Perspective," *Sport and Social Theory*, ed. C. Roger Rees and Andrew W. Miracle (Champaign, Ill.: Human Kinetics, 1986), pp. 227–237.

Contrast Coach Krzyzewski's statement with sportswriter Mike Littwin's comment: "It's a dirty business, big-time college sports. The best way to watch is with blinders and to pretend what you're seeing smells like school spirit."[2]

I love sports. As sportswriter John Feinstein says, "As in life, [sport] is really about competition and teamwork and succeeding—or failing—after a worthy struggle."[3] College sport intensifies those feelings for me. Although I truly love college sport, I believe that big-time college sport compromises the values of higher education. I am one of those critics that Coach K wants to "whack." Coach K acknowledges that there are abuses in college sports—cheating and other unethical practices. In his view, these are behaviors by bad people "who have lost sight of the true purpose of college sport and let the pursuit of winning override the pursuit of teaching."[4] I do not question Coach K's genuine affection for his players or his sincerity about the glories of big-time college sport. I do question his perception and analysis. Coach K takes an individualistic perspective, which means that he does not see—and this is the crucial sociological point—the wrongs that occur because of the way big-time college sport is organized.

Is big-time college sport compatible with higher education? Clearly, it has entertainment value, unites supporters of a given school, provides free publicity for the schools, gives good athletes from economically disadvantaged backgrounds the chance for a college education, and serves as a training ground for the relatively few future professional athletes. But does big-time college sport[5] complement or promote the educational goals of colleges and universities? Put another way, are the athletic programs at big-time schools consistent with the educational mission of U.S. colleges and universities? To answer this question, I shall, as is my sociological inclination, examine the dark side of big-time college sport as well as the "big picture."

A brief survey of the history of college sport shows that aspects of commercialization, sham students, and "tramp" athletes were there at the start. In 1852 the first intercollegiate sports contest occurred as the crews from Harvard and Yale raced against each other. The expenses of both teams were funded by the Boston, Concord, and Montreal Railroad, which saw the event as a commercial venture. In 1867 the first college football game was played between Princeton and Rutgers, with several players taking the field who could have been ruled academically ineligible. Later, some schools used players who had no connection to their institutions. These early contests, for the most part, were organized by students. Faculties, administrators, friends of the school, and alumni were not involved. Alas, the students soon lost their control over their sports. Leagues were formed and a national organization, later called the National Collegiate Athletic Association (NCAA), was organized in 1905 to standardize rules and address problems associated with college sport (questions concerning the eligibility of athletes, the high rate of injuries, cheating, and the like).

The popularity of college sport was rather localized during the first half of the twentieth century. There were occasional scandals that involved cheating in recruitment and gambling. Around 1970 the advent of televised athletics transformed college sport. Television focused on a few schools and funneled ever greater amounts of money to them. This was the true beginning of big-time college sports, which became hugely popular, national in scope, and increasingly commercial. With the new source of funds flowing into a few schools, university athletic departments became quasi-separate entities, some boosters wielded extraordinary influence over athletic departments, and players were often abused and exploited—a far cry from the beginning of intercollegiate sport.

What was once a student-run activity has been transformed, and now students have virtually no voice in athletic policies, control being vested in coaches, boosters, school administrators, leagues, national organizations, corporations, and television. In the process, college sport changed from an activity primarily for the participants to full-scale commercial entertainment with large monetary payouts. This transformation of intercollegiate sport saw scandals increase in number and gravity. These scandals stem from intense pressure to win and to succeed financially. Again I ask, Is the current state of big-time college sport appropriate to institutions of higher learning?

Education and Big-Time College Sport

Ironically, athletes who are recruited for reasons *other* than their cognitive abilities receive about $600 million in full or partial athletic scholarships. Many schools award more merit-based scholarship money to athletes than to all other scholarship students combined.[6] Not only that, but many of these athletic scholarships are given to athletes who have little chance of making it academically or even to those who do not care about receiving a college education. One egregious example from the past involves North Carolina State. Whereas the average SAT score for the student body was 1030 at the time, the school admitted a basketball player, Chris Washburn, who had an SAT of 470 and an IQ of 86. Especially telling about this example is that over one hundred universities offered Chris Washburn a full scholarship. Chris Washburn would not receive a scholarship and would not even be eligible to play under current NCAA rules. There is a higher SAT requirement (900 for a high school GPA of 2.0 in 13 core courses and 820 if the high school GPA is 2.5), and athletes must have passed certain core courses in high school. Nevertheless, athletes who are marginal students continue to be admitted. Football and men's basketball players in big-time sports programs are more than six times as likely as other students to receive special treatment in the admissions process, that is, they are admitted *below* the standard requirements for their universities.

Many argue that special admissions criteria should be targeted to assist underprivileged minority students. This is a legitimate argument because many young people live in a "third world" of grinding poverty, violent neighborhoods, inadequately financed schools, and few successful role models. However, I argue that these exceptions for admission should be granted to those who have the potential for academic success, not, as is the case now, for athletic success.[7] Although affirmative action is frowned on by many as favoritism, there is a comprehensive, well-financed, and widely supported form of affirmative action for athletes, especially African-American athletes. Coaches, scouts, and sports recruiters nurture disadvantaged athletes, identifying talented athletes and finding ways to enhance their talents. No similar infrastructure exists to coach minority youngsters with nonathletic talents.

What is troubling about this imbalance is not that athletes are undeserving or that helping them is wrong. The problem is that an opportunity to provide an education for academically talented minorities is missed. Their talents are not developed, which limits them and society. African Americans constitute 12.6 percent of the population but account for only 3.7 percent of all physicians, 3.4 percent of all lawyers, and 6.9 percent of all managers and professionals in the United States.[8] On the other hand, African Americans are overrepresented as professional athletes. They make up 80 percent of the players in professional basketball, 60 percent in professional football, and 18 percent in professional baseball. Some argue that the disproportionately high number of African Americans in professional sport is an appropriate rationale for giving them scholarships to college—going to college allows them to hone their skills for a professional sports career. But only a small proportion of college athletes make it at the professional level. More than 17,600 young men play Division I-A football and basketball, and each year only 150 to 200 (about 1 percent) reach the big leagues, and even fewer last more than a year. When schools overrecruit minorities for their athletic skills and underrecruit minorities for their academic skills, they contradict the fundamental purpose of education in a democratic society. Moreover, recruiting African Americans mostly for their physical skills reinforces the negative stereotype that African Americans are endowed with special physical attributes but lack the necessary mental attributes.

The fact is that college athletes in big-time programs are recruited to be part of a commercial entertainment organization that has nothing to do with the educational mission of schools. As president of the University of Chicago, Robert Hutchins dropped the football program, saying, "A college racing stable makes as much sense as college football. The jockey could carry the college colors; the students could cheer; the alumni could bet; and the horse wouldn't have to pass a history test."[9] Murray Sperber, an Indiana professor, makes a similar point:

Athletes are the only group of students recruited for entertainment—not acade-mic—purposes, and they are the only students who go through school on grants based not on educational aptitude, but on their talent and potential as commercial entertainers.

If colleges searched for and gave scholarships to up-and-coming rock stars so that they could entertain the university community and earn money for their schools through concerts and tours, educational authorities and the public would call this "a perversion of academic values." Yet every year, American institutions of higher education hand out over a hundred thousand full or partial scholarships, worth at least $500 million [now $600 million], for reasons similar to the hypothetical grants to rock performers.[10]

The Education of Athletes

The education of inadequately prepared athletes is a daunting task. The latest data show that athletes in big-time programs are more than two hundred points behind the average student on the SAT. At Clemson the average SAT score of the football squad trails the average of all students at that university by 271 points; at Duke, 304 points; at Colorado, 216 points; at Rice, 382 points; at Michigan, 364 points; at UCLA, 229 points; at Stanford, 298 points; at Arizona, 213 points; and at Florida, 319 points.[11] How do the schools deal with these discrepancies? The athletic departments hire tutors for their athletes. Typically, there are mandatory study sessions for freshmen and for nonfreshmen whose grades are in jeopardy. That's the good news. The bad news is that the athletic role, in the eyes of many coaches and athletes, supersedes the student role. A statement by the late Paul "Bear" Bryant, legendary football coach at the University of Alabama, illustrates a fundamental contradiction that big-time sport brings to academe:

> I used to go along with the idea that football players on scholarship were "student-athletes," which is what the NCAA calls them. Meaning a student first, an athlete second. We were kidding ourselves, trying to make it more palatable to the aca-demicians. We don't have to say that and we shouldn't. At the level we play, the boy is really an athlete first and a student second.[12]

Coaches who concur with this sentiment, coupled with the pressure to win, tend to diminish the student role by counseling their students to take easy courses, to choose easy majors, and to sign up for courses from cooperative faculty members who are willing to give athletes "special" considerations in the classroom. Or they may steer them toward correspondence courses with few or no requirements. To accentuate the athlete role, the coaches demand incredible amounts of time (practices, meetings, travel, studying videotape and play books). Athletes are required to lift weights and engage in other forms of conditioning as well as "informal" practices during the off-season. The NCAA has attempted to control the excesses of these demands but has met with little success.

In addition to the time constraints of big-time college sport, the athletes most also cope with physical exhaustion, mental fatigue, media attention, and demanding coaches. Athletes in these commercialized, professionalized programs have trouble reconciling the roles associated with their dual status of athlete and student. This problem is especially acute for those who were poorly prepared for higher education. Academically challenged athletes, research has shown, are most likely to take easy courses, cheat on exams, hire surrogate test takers, take phantom courses, and otherwise do the minimum.[13] A study of one basketball program by sociologists Patricia and Peter Adler found that the pressures of big-time sport and academic demands resulted in the gradual disengagement of the athletes from their academic roles.[14] The researchers found that most athletes entered the university feeling idealistic about the academic side of their college performance. This idealism lasted about one year and was replaced by disappointment and a growing cynicism as they realized how difficult it was to keep up with their schoolwork. The athletic role came to dominate all facets of their existence. The athletes received greater positive reinforcement for their athletic performance than for their academic performance. They became increasingly isolated from the student body as a result of segregated living arrangements, and their racial and socioeconomic differences isolated them culturally from the rest of the students. They were even isolated socially from other students by their physical size, which many found intimidating. They interacted primarily with other athletes, and these peers tended to put down academics. First-year athletes took courses from "sympathetic" professors, but this changed as they moved through the university curriculum. The athletes were unprepared for escalating academic expectations. The typical response of these athletes was role distancing, that is, they distanced themselves from the student role. The Adlers say that for these athletes, "it was better not to try than to try and not succeed."[15] This attitude was reinforced by the peer subculture. Thus the structure of big-time programs works to maximize the athlete role and minimize the academic role—clearly opposite the goals of higher education.

Poor preparation for college and depreciation of the role of student result in a lower graduation rate for big-time college athletes compared to their nonathlete peers. This is contrary to the NCAA media spin. Its 1997 report on graduation rates noted that 58 percent of the more than 13,000 scholarship athletes who entered Division I schools as freshmen in 1990 had earned degrees by the summer of 1996. That exceeds the 56 percent graduation rate for the general student body at the same schools. This relatively high rate of 58 percent is attributable to female athletes' graduating at a much higher rate (68 percent) than male athletes (53 percent). Race is also an important variable to consider, since African Americans are overrepresented in the revenue-producing sports. The graduation rate for white athletes in football was 61 percent and in men's basketball, 45 percent. For African-American athletes, the graduation rate in football was 53 percent and in men's basketball, 39 percent.

Although some schools have superior graduation rates for their athletes, many of the top athletic programs have low rates. Consider, for example, the top men's basketball programs. In 1996, seven of the season's final top ten teams had four-year graduation rates below the Division I average, including first-ranked Arizona (25 percent), second-ranked Kentucky (27 percent), and third-ranked Minnesota (29 percent). Cincinnati had a 0 percent graduation rate and Louisville had a 15 percent rate.[16]

There are at least three probable explanations for these low rates among basketball powers. First, the best programs have the best athletes, some of whom leave their schools prior to graduation to become professionals. Second, the most successful programs may recruit academically marginal players to stay on top, and, third, about 50 percent of the players in Division I men's basketball are African Americans, and they are much more likely than whites to come from economically and educationally deprived backgrounds.

In every study African Americans, when compared to their white counterparts, are less prepared for college. They enter as marginal students and, in general, leave that way. Sociologist Harry Edwards, an African American, has argued that the black "dumb jock" is a social creation. "Dumb jocks are not born; they are systematically created."[17] This social construction results from several factors. First, African American athlete-students must contend with two negative labels: the dumb athlete caricature and the dumb black stereotype. This double negative tends to result in a self-fulfilling prophecy as professors, fellow students, and the athletes themselves assume low academic performance.

Moreover, as soon as African-American youngsters are labeled as potential athletic superstars, many teachers, administrators, and parents lower their academic demands, believing that athletic stardom will be the ticket out of the ghetto. In junior high school and high school little is demanded of them academically. The reduced academic expectations continue in college (or in community college if they do not qualify for college). With professors who "give" grades, occasional altered transcripts, surrogate test takers, and phantom courses, there is, as Harry Edwards has said, "little wonder that so many black scholarship student-athletes manage to go through four years of college enrollment virtually unscathed by education."[18]

The inescapable conclusion is that providing a free education to athletes while expecting more from them as athletes than as students, as well as creating a situation that moves them away from academic pursuits, is contrary to the lofty goals of higher education.

College Sport as Big Business

Big-time college sport is organized in such a way that separating the business aspects from the play on the field is impossible. The intrusion of money into collegiate sport is evident in the following representative examples:

1. Some university athletic budgets are now as much as $33 million.
2. Each school in the 1999 Rose Bowl received $12.6 million, which it divided with other schools in its conference.
3. A number of bowls have corporate tie-ins. For example, for an annual contribution of $2 million, USF&G sponsors the Sugar Bowl. At the university level, a school such as San Diego State has corporate sponsors that pay, collectively, $2 million a year to the athletic department. Coors Brewing Company paid $5 million to the University of Colorado when the university agreed to name the new field house Coors Events Center.
4. Notre Dame has a $45 million contract with . . . to televise its football games for several years. The sale of Notre Dame merchandise brings the school another $1 million in royalties, and an appearance in a bowl game raises more millions.
5. An estimated $2.5 billion a year in college merchandise is sold under license, generating about $100 million to the schools in royalties. The University of Michigan receives the most income from this source— about $6 million annually. After Kentucky won the NCAA men's basketball tournament in 1996, it received about $3 million in royalties from the sale of basketball-related merchandise.[19]
6. The University of Colorado will receive $5.6 million (in shoes, apparel, and cash) over six years from Nike. In addition, CU will receive a $100,000 bonus from Nike if its football team ends the season with a number-one ranking (only $5,000 for a number-five ranking). If CU wins the NCAA men's basketball tournament, it receives $200,000 in bonuses ($50,000 for a Final Four appearance).[20] Nike has similar contracts with other top programs, including Florida State, Ohio State, Penn State, Miami, Michigan, North Carolina, and Southern California. Nike's competitor, Reebok, has contracts with four major schools: Georgia Tech, UCLA, Texas, and Wisconsin. Wisconsin, for example, has a five-year contract with Reebok worth $9.1 million.[21]
7. Each school in the Big Twelve receives $4.25 million annually from the conference distribution of television, bowl money, and basketball tournament payoffs.
8. In 1994 CBS agreed to pay the NCAA $1.725 billion ($215.6 million a year) for the rights to televise the men's basketball tournament through 2002.

9. When Kentucky basketball coach Rick Pitino was being sought by the pros in 1996, he was offered a $3 million deal to stay (three times more than any other college basketball coach at the time). But he turned the offer down, and his replacement, Tubby Smith, signed a deal worth $1.2 million. The highest-paid college football coach is Steve Spurrier of Florida, who has a contract through the 2002 season that averages $2 million a season in salary, bonuses, and extras.

These illustrations have serious implications for institutions of higher education. First, the system creates economic imperatives that lead college administrators, athletic directors, and coaches to make business decisions that supersede educational considerations. Tulane law professor Gary Roberts argues that this emphasis results in what he calls an "athletic arms race" among the schools:

> The careers of key policy-makers [in sport] depend on the program's ability to produce and sell an entertainment product that will be attractive to consumers only if it spends enough money to be consistently competitive with other institutions that are constantly increasing their expenditures. So the desperate pressure to generate increasingly large amounts of revenue inevitably leads to business, not academic decisions.
>
> What else could explain why schools have special admits for the most unprepared students, go to all great lengths to keep them eligible, schedule as many games as allowed and play them at absurd times of the week and night to accommodate television? Division I programs are, first and foremost, market-driven revenue producers, and their professed commitment to academics and the welfare of the student-athlete must be accommodated within and compromised by the limits that each institution's minimum-revenue requirements dictate.[22]

Thus to make money, an athletic department must spend money on, for example, increasing the recruiting budget, hiring more fund raisers, improving practice facilities, adding new seating in the stadiums and arenas (especially skyboxes), purchasing the latest equipment, and building expensive new sports annexes with state-of-the-art locker rooms, weight rooms, training rooms, meeting rooms, and offices for the coaches and athletic administrators.

Nevertheless, except for a few schools, athletic programs lose money. About fifty out of the NCAA's eight hundred member institutions make more money on their athletic programs than they spend. The losses are covered by their schools' general revenue funds.[23] It is commonly believed that men's basketball and especially football bring in the funds that pay for the rest of the athletic budget. But, for the most part, this is a fiction. The NCAA reported that only 17 percent of its member institutions made money on their football programs in 1995, with a majority of Division I programs reporting a deficit and 45 percent losing an average of $628,000 in 1995.[24] These deficits would be much greater, however, if the accounting procedures were more appropriate.

That is, the football teams play in stadiums paid for by taxpayers, contributors, and, more typically, bonds being paid off by students *at no expense to the athletic departments*. As John Silber, president of Boston University, said of his former employer, the University of Texas: "They've got a $50 million to $60 million capital investment in their football plant at U.T. Try amortizing that at 5 or 6 percent and you will see the program is actually losing money."[25] Moreover, a large proportion of student fees are automatically turned over to the athletic departments, as are subsidies from state legislatures and school administrators to pay for the athletes' scholarships. Using the University of Colorado as an example, the 1995 athletic budget included $900,000 in presidential support, $1,064,331 in chancellor's support, and $1,254,000 in support from mandatory student fees.[26] These student fees and university subsidies (in the case of Colorado totaling $3.218 million) artificially inflate athletic department income. At Colorado State University (a school with a budget $13 million below that of the University of Colorado), more than one-third of the budget comes from within the university—university support and student fees.[27]

These subsidies also show how universities make business decisions concerning athletics that override educational considerations. In 1996 Tulane's governing board announced that it would increase its subsidy to the athletic department sixfold, from $550,000 to $3.4 million. This action by the board occurred just as it approved trimming $8.5 million from the university's budget while raising the tuition by 4 percent, freezing most faculty and staff salaries for one year, cutting fifty staff positions, and reducing funds for undergraduate student financial aid and graduate student stipends.[28] Clearly, in this situation moneys are being transferred from the educational function of the universities to the entertainment function—a questionable transfer of wealth to say the least.

Successful programs (mostly in football) do generate donations to the university but almost exclusively to the athletic programs rather than to the general operating budget of the university.[29] And if an athletic department happens to generate a surplus, the money almost always stays with it and is not distributed to the academic budgets. There are several reasons for the red ink generated by big-time athletic departments. I have already mentioned the continuing perception that programs must be upgraded with costly improvements to stay even or ahead of competitors. Another reason is that employees in athletic departments tend to be better paid than other university employees. Travel budgets for the teams and recruiters are generous. A common practice, for example, is for the football team and coaches to stay in a local hotel the night before *home* games. Deficits are also generated by the costs associated with pregame football parties given by the athletic departments for influential alumni, boosters, and legislators. At the University of Colorado the annual cost of brunches and game tickets for important supporters of the athletic program is about $100,000.

A third consequence of an athletic department's quest for money is that decision making tends to leave the university and flow toward the sources of revenue. Television money dictates schedules. Booster organizations that supply funds may influence the hiring and firing of coaches. At the University of Colorado twenty-five boosters pledged $40,000 each toward the purchase of a new house for football coach Rick Neuheisel.[30] What kind of power will these twenty-five big spenders have over the University of Colorado's athletic program? Similarly, who has the power when a football coach makes over eight times more money than the university president (as is the case at the University of Florida) and when the coach has a powerful constituency outside the university? On numerous occasions public opinion, governors, and boards of regents have sided with the coach when the university president and a popular coach clashed.[31] For example, John DiBiaggio resigned as president of Michigan State University when its board of trustees twice circumvented his authority, extending the contract of the head football coach and then making that coach, George Perles, interim director of athletics. The point of these examples is that the athletic "tail" is wagging the university "dog." As Murray Sperber says, these practices "undermine one of the fundamental tenets of colleges and universities—their independence."[32]

Another consequence of the athletic money chase is that students are, for the most part, left out. The irony is that students, who typically help the athletic department through their fees (which total more than $1 million annually at most big-time programs), have no influence over how their money is spent. Of all the categories of contributors to athletics, only students are left out of the power equation. Over 25,000 students at the University of Colorado give more than $1.2 million annually to the athletic budget. Twenty-five boosters gave $40,000 each (a total of $1 million) to help the football coach buy an expensive home. Which group do you suppose has more influence over athletic department policy?

Students are also left out in the distribution of the relatively scarce seats available in the arenas of successful teams. These seats go to big-spending boosters, depriving some students of the chance to watch their teams play. The University of Louisville, for example, allots 10 percent of seats at basketball games to students. The University of Arizona holds a lottery to choose the students who may attend basketball games. The situation worsens during tournament time, when schools are allotted relatively few tickets. These scarce tickets, typically, are given to the greatest benefactors of the athletic department rather than to students. This common practice raises a serious question: Should not *school* sports be primarily for the enjoyment of *students?*

Winning begets money, which increases the pressure to win, which, when the pressure becomes too great, may result in cheating. Cheating takes several forms. Most common is the offer of special inducements outside the rules by coaches and/or boosters to lure athletes to the school and to keep them there.

Cheating may also involve unethical means to ensure the scholastic eligibility of the athletes. According to a recent expose by *Sports Illustrated,* test fraud on the SAT examination is common, promoted by recruiters, high school coaches, middlemen, agents, and college coaches.[33] Scandals also involve altering transcripts, fraudulent courses from diploma mills, the use of surrogate test takers, and the like. In one celebrated case, a federal jury indicted Baylor University's head basketball coach and three of his assistants, two junior college coaches, and two junior college administrators on charges of violating federal mail fraud, wire fraud, and conspiracy statutes. In effect, Baylor had faxed a term paper to a junior college player it was recruiting so that the player could use that paper in an English composition class he was taking at Westark Community College. Moreover, another Baylor recruit was instructed to take a correspondence course on the Old Testament from Southeastern College of the Assemblies of God because the Baylor coaches had a copy of the final exam for this course and others.[34] Finally, an athlete wanting to enroll at Baylor was provided with a fraudulent transcript by two administrators at his school, Shelton State Community College.[35]

There are many examples of scandal in big-time programs. In most instances school administrators, students, and supporters do not demand that guilty coaches be fired for their transgressions—if they win. As *Sports Illustrated* writer John Underwood has characterized the situation, "We've told them that it doesn't matter how clean they keep their programs. It doesn't matter what percentage of their athletes graduate or take a useful place in society. It doesn't even matter how well the coaches teach their sports. All that matters are the flashing scoreboard lights."[36]

The pursuit of money has prostituted the university, demeaning the education of the athletes and fostering immorality. In this milieu winning and the money that is generated by winning are paramount. Thus the evil that results is not due to the malevolent personalities of coaches but to a perverse system. In this regard Philip Taubman has said:

> [Big-time college sport] has become a big business, completely disconnected from the fundamental purposes of academic institutions. The goal of college ball is no longer for young men to test and strengthen their bodies, to learn about teamwork, and to have a good time. All that matters is winning, moving up in the national rankings, and grabbing a bigger share of the TV dollar. . . . To achieve these aims, schools and coaches not only bend and break the National Collegiate Athletic Association (NCAA) rules governing college football but, far more destructively, violate the intellectual integrity and principles of the American university system.[37]

Finally, there are always schools that seek to be in the big-time category, despite the problems associated with big-time college sports, including the long odds against financial success. This desire creates major fiscal problems for them. They must upgrade their facilities. They have to launch special fund-raising campaigns that may siphon money that might otherwise be do-nated to the academic side of the university. They need increased subsidies from the university administration. They also need to take more money from student fees. They may also seek subsidies from various levels of govern-ment. As an example, *Sports Illustrated* noted that "in Birmingham, where 25 percent of the population lives in poverty and 11 percent has less than an eighth-grade education, the city council has voted to give the University of Alabama at Birmingham $2.2 million in public funds to start a Division I-A football program."[38]

These schools typically schedule away games with established powers for big payouts. On the surface, this is a win-win situation for the two schools. The big-time school adds a win to its record, fills the arena, and keeps its place in the polls while the school on the make gets money to float its program. The downside for the would-be big-time school is that it might be humiliated on the field, and some of its players might be injured by the superior team. Surely this practice of deliberately scheduling mismatches for money is a form of prosti-tution.

The Dominance of Male Elite Sport

Title IX, which Congress passed in 1972, mandated gender equity in school sports programs. Women's intercollegiate sports programs have made tremen-dous strides toward that goal in the intervening years. Participation in intercol-legiate sports has risen from 30,000 women in 1971 to more than 116,272 (43,712 in Division I) in 1996. In 1971 only about 7 percent of the athletic bud-get went to women, whereas now it is 27 percent. Athletic scholarships for women were virtually unknown in 1972, whereas now women athletes receive 35 percent of the athletic scholarship money that is distributed. These increases in a generation represent the good news concerning gender equity in collegiate sport. The bad news, however, is quite significant. An assessment of the situa-tion at big-time schools for 1995–1996 discloses the following disparities by gender:

1. Head coaches of women's teams were paid 63 cents for every dollar earned by coaches of men's teams[39] (not including the many more ex-tras the coaches of men's teams receive).
2. Only seven schools met the proportionality test for equity (if the per-centage of women athletes in a school is within 5 percent of the pro-portion of women undergraduates enrolled, the school meets the pro-portionality test). The average negative gap was 16 percent between the numbers of women participating in sports with the numbers of women enrolled.

3. The average athletic department had 292 male athletes and 163 female athletes[40] (65 percent male and 35 percent female), with a similarly disproportionate distribution of scholarships.
4. Spending for recruiting was skewed 76 percent to 24 percent in favor of males.

Operational expenditures were distributed even more unevenly at 78 percent to 22 percent in favor of males.[41] And, most telling, it was not uncommon for a school with a big-time football program to spend *twice as much on its football team as it spent on all women's sports.* In 1993, for example, 85 Division I-A schools spent an average of $4 million on men's football while spending an average of $1.8 million on *all* women's sports.[42]

Clearly, gender equity is not part of big-time college sports programs. To move from its current 65 percent–35 percent split toward gender balance, athletic administrations have three choices: spend more on women's sports, reduce or eliminate nonrevenue men's sports, or constrict football. If recent history is a guide, athletic departments will continue to add low-cost women's sports such as soccer and crew and cut low-profile men's sports such as wrestling, gymnastics, and baseball. Adding women's sports increases their participation, but it does not move them much closer to gender parity in scholarships or in other forms of economic assistance. Cutting men's programs is unfair to men because it reduces their participation and opportunities in the so-called minor sports. College sport, it seems to me, should enhance opportunities for participation, not limit them. Athletic departments achieve high male participation, but they do this with disproportionate participation opportunities for men in football. Division I-A programs are allowed to have 85 scholarship players, and squads include as many as 130 players. Thus football is a huge drain on the athletic budget and forms the basis for gender inequality in college athletics.

The rationale advanced to justify this unequal largesse to one sport is that football underwrites women's sport. *This is a myth.* Only about one-third of Division I-A football programs make a profit; one-third of them run an annual deficit that averages more than $1 million.[43] The truth is that at most schools students pay for football through mandatory student fees and university subsidies.

Another myth is that football has already been cut to the bone. The NCAA a few years back did institute some cost-cutting reforms for football, such as reducing the number of scholarships to eighty-five and limiting the number of coaches. But some incredibly spendthrift practices remain, such as quartering entire squads in off-campus hotels on the night before home games, buying out the lucrative contracts for coaches no longer in favor and replacing them with even more expensive coaches, and building ever more palatial football annexes and arenas.[44]

The law requires that women receive the same opportunities to play sports as men. Football, "the overfed sacred cow of college sports," stands in the way of gender equity, however. Football does bring in more money than any other sport and generates a profit for a relatively few schools. Football and men's basketball do bring in the deals from shoe and apparel companies that provide a good share of the equipment for athletes in all sports, but only at the most successful programs. But with football considered sacred, men's so-called minor sports have been cut and women's sports underfunded. The answer, I believe, is to reduce the outlay for football without reducing the quality of the product. This can be easily achieved by reducing football squads to sixty scholarship athletes (the pros have squads of fifty without sacrificing quality). This reduction in numbers decreases the cost of scholarships, equipment, training supplies, and the like. Accompanying this reduction would be a proportionate decrease in the number of coaches. Does a football team really need an interior offensive line coach or an outside linebacker coach? Such a plan cannot be enacted unilaterally and must be accomplished by the NCAA. This plan can also bring more balance to big-time football, as it would prevent the major powers from stockpiling talented benchwarmers.[45]

Another solution to the gender equity bind is for women's sports to generate more revenue. In 1995–1996 men's sports teams generated $13 for every $1 from women's sports at the Division I level.[46] Women's sports programs are at a disadvantage in producing significant revenues for several reasons:

1. Men's intercollegiate sport had a hundred-year head start in building tradition and fan support.
2. It takes money to make money, and women's sports programs have not been given anything approaching parity in resource allocation.
3. Women's sports are relatively ignored by university sports publicity and promotion staff, local and national newspapers, magazines, and television.
4. Women's sports continue to be trivialized by the schools in the naming of their teams (e.g., Wildkittens),[47] as well as by the emphasis on the looks and nonathletic side of women athletes rather than their performance.

Granted, some of these obstacles to gender equity are changing slowly, with more television time being devoted to women's play, better promotions by the athletic departments, and the success of U.S. women athletes in international competition. Some women's basketball programs are profitable (the national champion Connecticut women's basketball team showed a profit of nearly a half million dollars in 1995–1996). But with success, women's budgets increase just as men's do. For example, Pat Summitt, coach of the women's basketball team at Tennessee (1997 NCAA champions) received about $400,000 in base salary and extras for the 1997–1998 season. The problem with women's programs focusing on revenue is that in time they are likely to replicate all of the problems that money has brought to men's collegiate programs. Women's programs need more money, but at what point will money taint the women's game?

Finally, with regard to gender, universities must address the following question: Is it appropriate for a college or university to deny women the opportunities that it provides men? Shouldn't our daughters have the same opportunities that our sons have in all aspects of higher education? Women represent slightly more than half of the undergraduates in U.S. higher education. They receive half of all master's degrees. Should they be second-class participants in any aspect of the university's activities? The present unequal state of affairs in sport is not inevitable. Choices made in the past have given men an advantage in university sports. As Duke law professor John Weistart has put it, "Just as the existing tensions between genders in sport are the product of choice, they can be unchosen."[48] University administrators could implement true gender equity if they wished. Why do they continue to drag their collective feet on gender equity?

"Shamateurism"

Although many athletic programs lose money, they are nevertheless pursuing a commercial activity. Some coaches make millions. Universities invite corporations to advertise in their arenas for large sums. Schools sell sweatshirts, beer mugs, sculpture, and other memorabilia emblazoned with university sports logos for profit. Big-time college sport is clearly market driven. Ironically, though, athletic departments engage in these moneymaking activities while exploiting their labor under the guise of amateurism. Although the athletes generate the millions, they receive only room, board, tuition, and books. As "amateurs," athletes cannot use their celebrity for income—although their employers can use the players' celebrity for commercial purposes. They cannot sell the tickets allotted to them. They cannot be reimbursed for trips home. Nor can their parents be compensated with a complimentary trip to a game, although university administrators, coaches, and their spouses can attend with all expenses paid.

Defining the labor force as amateurs serves at least four purposes. First, it maximizes profits for the schools, the leagues, and the NCAA. Second, as "amateurs," the athletes are not considered employees and therefore are not subject to workmen's compensation and other benefits. Third, by clinging to the myth that athletes are amateurs, the activity is viewed as part of the educational program of the universities. This means that none of the money generated by the athletic departments and the NCAA is taxable. "All taxpayers help pay for football because colleges and universities are tax-exempt and every football booster gets a tax deduction for their donation."[49] And, fourth, if the athletes were

then the NCAA would likely come under federal
siness cartel.[50]
dministrators are using the ideal of amateurism as an
This is clearly hypocritical, to say the least. We go
; sportswriter Mike Littwin argues, we want to pretend
rst. We don't want the athletes to be professionals. We
kids on the playing field are students. We want to de-

Deviant Athletes

sturbing issue concerning big-time college sport is that
;rams are disproportionately involved in assaults, rapes,
nes. In the late 1980s, for example, over a thirty-two-
ere twenty incidents involving University of Colorado
criminal charges. Arizona State in one year had four-
teen of its football and men's basketball players involved in arrests, charges,
plea bargains, probation, or jail time. The *Los Angeles Times* reported that in
1995, some 220 college athletes faced criminal proceedings.[53] In 1995, *Sports
Illustrated* wrote an open letter to the president of the University of Miami ar-
guing that he should eliminate the football program to salvage his school's reputation. Included in that letter was a rationale for doing so:

> During the past decade your school enrolled and suited up at least one player who
> had scored a 200 on his verbal SAT—the number you get for spelling your name
> correctly. An on-campus disturbance, involving some 40 members of the football
> team, required 14 squad cars and a police dog to quell. Fifty-seven players were
> implicated in a financial scandal that the feds call "perhaps the largest centralized
> fraud upon the federal Pell Grant program ever committed." And among numer-
> ous cases of improper payments to players from agents was one in which the non-
> delivery of a promised installment led a Hurricane player to barge into the agent's
> office and put a gun to his head. The illegal acts with which your Hurricanes have
> been charged run the gamut from disorderly conduct and shoplifting to drunken
> driving, burglary, arson, assault and sexual battery.... *No fewer than one of every
> seven scholarship players on last season's team has been arrested while enrolled
> at your university.*[54]

The list of crimes goes on and on. Criminal assaults by athletes have occurred
at the University of Oklahoma, the University of Wisconsin, the University of
Minnesota, Virginia Tech, and Iowa State University, to name a few.

Two large studies reveal that these examples are not anomalies. A study of
reported violence against women (battering and sexual assaults) at ten Division I schools over a three-year period found that male student-athletes, who

composed 3 percent of the total male population, nevertheless represented 35 percent of the reported perpetrators.[55] A 1990 national survey of 13,000 students found that male athletes were three and a half times more likely than nonathlete males to admit to having committed date rape.[56]

Although an extremely small percentage of student-athletes actually engage in criminal acts, college athletes are, nevertheless, disproportionately involved in deviance. There are a number of reasons for this, but I shall focus on two that have special relevance. First, many big-time programs recruit players who were in trouble before college. For example, five big-time college programs tried to recruit New York City high school star Richie Parker despite his felony conviction for sexual abuse. Cleveland State gave a scholarship to basketball player Roy Williams even though he had been convicted of murder as a teenager in California. While he was at Cleveland State, he was arrested for rape. The University of Cincinnati basketball program offered scholarships to three athletes who had criminal problems before college. Clearly, some coaches are willing to add a criminal element to their player mix if they believe that it will increase their chances of success on the field. Second chances and redemption have their place, but should a university's scarce scholarship dollars go to convicted felons just because they are big, strong, and fast?

Second, many athletes come from deprived economic backgrounds. They are on scholarship but nevertheless lack money for clothes, food, and entertainment. These athletes are well aware that the school, the administrators, the coaches, and seemingly everyone else connected to the athletic program make money from their athletic performance. Logically, it seems to many of them, they deserve a piece of the action. So they may take money from an agent, use the athletic department's long-distance telephone credit card, accept money under the table from a booster or assistant coach, shoplift, or steal a stereo from a dorm room.

Whatever the reason for the disproportionate criminality among college athletes, universities ought to do some soul searching regarding their possible complicity in such deviance. The evidence is that the problem athletes are male and are involved with the revenue-producing sports of football and basketball. This clearly raises serious questions about the extra subsidies that are given these programs, the evaluation of athletes to be given scholarships, and the monitoring of athletes when they are on campus.

Contradictions

Big-time college sport confronts us with a fundamental dilemma. Positively, college football and basketball offer entertainment, spectacle, excitement, festival, and excellence. Negatively, the commercial entertainment function of big-time college sport has severely compromised academia. Educational goals have been superseded by the quest for big money. Because winning programs receive huge revenues from television, gate receipts, bowl and tournament appearances, boosters, and even legislatures, many sports programs are guided by a win-at-any-costs philosophy.

The enormous pressures to win result sometimes in scandalous behaviors. Sometimes there are illegal payments to athletes. Education is mocked by recruiting athletes unprepared for college studies, by altering transcripts, by having surrogate test-takers, by providing phantom courses, and by not moving the athletes toward graduation. William Reed of *Sports Illustrated* made the following comment about college basketball, but it is relevant to college football as well:

> Every fan knows that underneath its shiny veneer of color, fun and excitement, college basketball is a sewer full of rats. Lift the manhole cover on the street of gold, and the odor will knock you down. . . . The misdeeds allegedly committed by college basketball programs today are the same stuff that has plagued the game for decades—buying players, cheating in academics, shaving points, etc. And the NCAA is powerless to stop it. Make a statement by coming down hard on a Kentucky or a Maryland, and what happens? Nothing, really. The filth merely oozes from another crack.[57]

To this ugly mix can be added problems associated with the exploitation of athletes, gender inequality, and the maintenance of a male-segregated athletic subculture that, when compared to its nonathletic counterpart, tends to be more anti-intellectual, sexist, aggressive, and criminal. How can any university defend and promote this hypocritical, scandal-laden activity?

Several contradictions further delineate the dilemma that big-time college sport presents. The overarching contradiction is that we have organized a commercial entertainment activity within an educational environment, and in the process we have compromised educational goals. Ernest L. Boyer, former president of the Carnegie Foundation for the Advancement for Teaching, put it this way: "I believe that the college sports system is one of the most corrupting and destructive influences on higher education. It is obscene, and there is no way to put an educational gloss on this enterprise."[58] In short, as currently structured, big-time sport is not compatible with education.

A fundamental problem is that athletes are recruited as students. Yet demanding coaches, as well as the athletic subculture, work against the student role. At the heart of this contradiction is the fact that institutions of higher learning allow the enrollment and subsidization of ill-prepared and uninterested students solely for the purpose of winning games, enhancing the visibility of the university, and producing revenue. Sometimes these universities recruit known thugs for the same purposes.

The third contradiction is that although big-time sports are revenue producing, for most schools they actually drain money away from academics. As I have demonstrated, athletic budgets are supplemented with generous sums from student fees and subsidies from the academic budgets.

The fourth contradiction is that although the marketing/sales side of big-time sport is big business, the production side is an amateur extracurricular activity in which athletes are "paid" only with an "education."[59] Meanwhile, individuals and organizations make huge amounts of money.

A final contradiction involves the issue of whether or not participation in sport is educational. University administrators often advance this as a rationale for college sport. But such administrators are caught in a contradiction because most of them willingly accept the present maldistribution of resources, scholarships, and opportunities for women's sport. Sociologist Allen Sack argues:

> If one accepts the notion that student athletes are the prime beneficiaries of college sport, how in the world can women's programs receive less financial support than men's? If sport is educational, what possible academic justification can there be for denying this aspect of education for women? Wouldn't the denial of equal athletic opportunities be tantamount to saying that men should have more microscopes, laboratory facilities and library privileges than women?[60]

And, I would add, if sport is a useful, educational activity, why limit these benefits to the athletic elite? Why should the best athletic facilities be reserved for their exclusive use? Why are we limited to one team in each sport, rather than several teams based on differences in size and skill? If sport is justifiable as an educational experience, why limit the number of men's so-called minor sports? Should they not be expanded to meet the wishes of the student body? In my view, participation in sport is good and we should maximize it instead of limiting its benefits to the few.

Alternatives

How are we to respond these dilemmas? Do we ignore them and maintain the shame and the sham of the status quo? Or do we seek true reform? Can the corporate and corrupted sports programs at our major universities be changed to redress the wrongs that make a mockery of academe's educational goals? Can these wrongs be eliminated while the high level of achievement by the athletes and the excitement generated by college sports spectacles are maintained?

I offer two scenarios, one based on what I wish would happen and one based on what is more likely to happen. Let me begin by outlining what I wish would happen. I would like to see a significant reform effort led by college presidents that would clean up college sports programs so that they are consonant with the educational objectives of the institutions they represent. In that spirit, I propose a three-pronged attack, beginning with changes in the administration of sport.

Athletic departments must *not* be self-contained corporate entities that are separate from the university, as is so often the case. They must be under the direct control of university presidents. Presidents must set up independent impartial review boards or other mechanisms to monitor athletic programs for illegalities such as the use of illicit drugs, dehumanizing behaviors by coaches, recruiting violations, and other unethical acts. Most crucially, college sports programs must be monitored and when warranted sanctioned externally. The NCAA is not the proper external agent, since it has a fundamental conflict of interest. That organization is too dependent on sport-generated television moneys and tournament revenues to be an impartial investigator and jury. An independent educational body such as the North Central Accrediting Association (ironically, also with the acronym NCAA) must oversee all aspects of universities, including the sports sphere, to assess whether educational goals are being met. Any school not meeting such goals in regard to athletics would lose accreditation, just as it would if the library was inadequate or too few professors held doctorates. Also, federal district attorneys and the courts should become involved in the investigation and prosecution of crimes by schools because big-time sports are involved in interstate commerce.

Coaches must be part of the academic community, thus gaining reasonable job security and being recognized as teachers. This means that coaches must be part of the tenure system as are other educators. As educators with special responsibilities, their salaries would be similar to academic administrators. Their outside income must be sharply curtailed. In particular, they should not be allowed to participate in commercial ventures as coaches (e.g., advertising, shoe contracts) or to receive the free use of automobiles. And they should not be permitted to participate in "sweetheart" business deals with boosters.

The performance of coaches should be evaluated on a number of criteria. It would be naive to suggest that winning is unimportant. Winning is important, but it is just one criterion for being a successful coach. Other factors should include teaching skills, the humane treatment of players, and, most critically, the proportion of athletes who graduate in six years. The number of scholarships available for the new recruits should be contingent on the graduation rate of previous athletes in the program.

The second point of attack involves the education of athletes. Academic institutions worthy of that label must make a commitment to their athletes as students. This requires, first, that only those students who have the potential to compete as students be admitted. Athletes must meet the minimum requirements demanded all students for admission: no special admissions and no special curricula for athletes. Academically marginal student-athletes must be the recipients of an extraordinary effort by the university to raise their skills through remedial classes and tutorials so that they can achieve academic success. Second, no freshman eligibility; freshmen may practice but are prohibited from playing in intercollegiate contests. This requirement has symbolic value because it shows athletes and the academic community that school performance is the ultimate priority of the institution. Most important, this requirement allows incoming athletes time to adjust to the demanding and competitive academic environment before taking on the pressures of big-time sports participation. Third, the schools must insist that student-athletes make satisfactory progress toward a degree. Fourth, the time demands on athletes must be reduced: No spring practice and no fall practice before classes start. Abolish mandatory off-season workouts. Reduce the number of football and basketball games. Start basketball games after the second semester begins. Lower the in-season demands on athletes (practice, weight training, film sessions, meetings, and travel) to manageable limits. Finally, give athletes a four-year scholarship, no strings attached. Those athletes who compete for three years should be given an open-ended scholarship guaranteeing that they will receive aid as long as it takes to graduate.

The final plank of my reform package has to do with finances. Moneys from student fees should be funneled exclusively to women's sports and to minor men's sports to achieve greater equity. Reduce the expenditures for football by limiting scholarships and squads to sixty, reducing the number of coaches, and eliminating hotel stays by the squad and coaches the night before home games. In addition, stop the athletic arms race by placing limits on the amount that can be spent on weight rooms, locker rooms, and the like. Finally, pay athletes in the revenue-producing sports fair compensation for the revenues they generate. Clearly, college athletes are not amateurs, but just as clearly, they are not well-paid professionals either. Athletes should receive a monthly stipend for living expenses, paid insurance, and paid trips home during holidays and for family emergencies. Their parents should be given two paid trips to see their sons play annually.

The problem with the plan that I just outlined is that it will never be implemented. The presidents of the universities involved in big-time college sport are too weak or too meek or too unwilling to change. If history is a guide, they will push the NCAA to make cosmetic changes, but they will balk at meaningful structural changes and will continue to look the other way while athletic programs do what they have to do to win. Moreover, the NCAA will not promote changing the present system because it is compromised by a massive conflict of interest.

Another alternative, some version of which will eventually emerge, will take the hypocrisy out of big-time college sports by decriminalizing them. The public wants big-time college sport. Corporations want big-time college sport. Television and cable networks want big-time college sport. These demands will result, I suspect, in the money from television and bowl/tournament appearances going to fewer and fewer teams. The best athletes will gravitate to those relatively few teams because of the media exposure, which they believe will translate into greater opportunities for a professional career. This will lead to a bifurcation of the schools into a two-tiered system. At the big-time level, there will be an elite composed of, say, sixty-four premier schools, divided into eight conferences and an overarching administrative organization. These schools will have sports programs explicitly designed and packaged commercially as part of a mega-entertainment industry. They will have a monopoly of the national television revenue. They will be partially subsidized by the professional leagues because they provide a developmental program for future professional players. Players will be professionals, recruited as entertainers with contracts, salaries, bonuses, and insurance. They will not be required to register as students, although this would be an option and, if chosen, funded. No more rules concerning academic eligibility. No more empty rhetoric about the ideals of amateurism. No more talk of making big-time sport compatible with the educational mission of universities. This plan removes the hypocrisy present in current programs but, of course, if implemented it mocks the purpose of the university.

The dilemma is this: We like (I like) big-time college sport—the festival, the pageanty, the exuberance, the excitement, and the excellence. But are we then willing to accept the hypocrisy that goes with it. I long for a more pristine sports system for our schools such as the one that exists at the NCAA Division III level or among the NAIA level schools. Here the athletic programs are in harmony with what college sport, in my view, should be. That is, athletic scholarships would be partial and based on academic potential. Schedules and recruiting would be regional in scope. There would be a full complement of minor sports for men and the absolute implementation of Title IX, financed by student fees and discretionary funds from the administration, as well as from legislatures. I like this part of the scenario. Here college sport is in balance with other activities and academics; participation opportunities are maximized. This would truly eliminate the sham and the shame from college sports. If academic institutions really stand for educational values, they would move to this lower level of sports programming. In doing so, they would leave the professional level to the professional leagues, which would fund minor league systems that are outside the school system.

Notes

1. Mike Krzyzewski, "Despite Loss, Kryzewski Lauds His Team," *New York Times,* March 28, 1993, sec. 8, p. 9.
2. Mike Littwin, "The Dean Comes Clean in Dirty Business," *Rocky Mountain News,* October 12, 1997, p. 2C.
3. John Feinstein, "Why the Ryder Cup Makes Legs Shake," *USA Today,* September 25, 1997, p. 15A.
4. Ibid.
5. Big-time college sport refers exclusively to men's football in the 106 Division I-A schools and the 305 men's basketball programs in NCAA Division I.

6. Douglas Lederman, "Athletic Merit vs. Academic Merit," *Chronicle of Higher Education,* March 30, 1994, pp. 37A–38A.

7. The following is taken from Sam Fulwood III, "Blacks Find Support in Sports But Not as Scholars," *Los Angeles Times,* July 25, 1995, pp. 1A, 10A.

8. Ibid., p. 10A.

9. Quoted in Richard G. Sheehan, *Keeping Score: The Economics of Big-Time Sports* (South Bend, Ind.: Diamond Communications, 1996), p. 261.

10. Murray Sperber, *College Sports Inc.: The Athletic Department vs. the University* (New York: Holt, 1990), pp. 1–2.

11. Gary Mihoces, "Football Programs Try Settling Score," *USA Today,* December 22, 1993, pp. 1C–2C; 6C.

12. Paul W. Bryant and John Underwood, *Bear: The Hard Life and Good Times of Alabama's Coach Bryant* (Boston: Little, Brown, 1974), p. 325.

13. See, for example, Allen L. Sack and Robert Thiel, "College Basketball and Role Conflict: A National Survey," *Sociology of Sport Journal* 2, no. 3 (1985): 195–209.

14. Patricia A. Adler and Peter Adler, *Backboards and Blackboards: College Athletics and Role Engulfment* (New York: Columbia University Press, 1991).

15. Ibid., p. 247.

16. Steve Wieberg, "Grad Rates for Scholarship Athletes Hold Steady," *USA Today,* June 27, 1997, p. 10C; Marc Ethier, "Male Basketball Players Continue to Lag in Graduation Rates," *Chronicle of Higher Education,* July 3, 1997, 39A.

17. Harry Edwards, "The Black 'Dumb Jock': An American Sports Tragedy," *College Board Review,* Spring 1984, p. 8.

18. Ibid., p. 9.

19. Goldie Blumenstyk, "Money-Making Champs," *Chronicle of Higher Education,* April 19, 1996, p. 49A.

20. Jim Armstrong, "Just Don't Over Do It: Money Talks, Nike Walks Fine Line with Tradition," *Denver Post,* July 6, 1997, pp. 1C, 10C.

21. Jim Naughton, "Exclusive Deal with Reebok Brings U. of Wisconsin Millions of Dollars and Unexpected Criticism," *Chronicle of Higher Education,* September 6, 1996, p. 65A.

22. Gary R. Roberts, "Financial Incentives Wrong for College Athletics," *NCAA News,* November 4, 1991, p. 4.

23. Sperber, *College Sport Inc.;* Ben Brown, "Most Schools Losing Money on Athletics," *USA Today,* November 9, 1993, pp. 1C–2C.

24. Robert Brustad, "Title IX Unfairly Blamed for Sports Cuts," *Fort Collins Coloradoan,* September 14, 1997, p. 2C.

25. John Silber, quoted in Sperber, *College Sports Inc.,* p. 65.

26. B. G. Brooks, "CU, Boosters Help Neuheisel Purchase $1.5 Million Home," *Rocky Mountain News,* July 10, 1997, p. 3C.

27. Tony Phifer, "More Than They Bargained For," *Fort Collins Coloradoan,* July 26, 1998, p. 4D.

28. Debra E. Blum, "Faculty Is Furious over Six-Fold Budget Increase for Athletics," *Chronicle of Higher Education,* February 16, 1996, p. 40A.

29. Douglas Lederman, "Do Winning Teams Spur Contributions? Scholars and Fund Raisers Are Skeptical," *Chronicle of Higher Education,* January 13, 1988, pp. 1A,

32A–33A; Barabara R. Bergmann, "Do Sports Really Make Money for the University?" *Academe* 77 (January–February, 1991): 28–30.

30. Curtis Eichelberger, "The Party May Be Over at CU," *Rocky Mountain News,* April 9, 1995, p. 28B.

31. Jim Naughton, "Who Runs College Sports? A Million-Dollar Contract for a Football Coach in Florida Raises That Question," *Chronicle of Higher Education,* November 22, 1996, pp. 37A–38A.

32. Sperber, *College Sports Inc.,* p. 65.

33. Don Yaeger and Alexander Wolff, "Troubling Questions," *Sports Illustrated,* July 7, 1997, pp. 70–79.

34. For an expose on how a Bible college, Southeastern College, was used by various colleges and junior colleges for bogus academic credits, see Alexander Wolff and Don Yaeger, "Credit Risk," *Sports Illustrated,* August 7, 1995, pp. 47–55.

35. Jack McCallum, "Paper Trail," *Sports Illustrated,* November 28, 1994, pp. 45–48. See also Wolff and Yaeger, "Credit Risk," pp. 46–55.

36. John Underwood, "A Game Plan for America," *Sports Illustrated,* February 23, 1981, p. 81.

37. Philip Taubman, "Oklahoma Football: A Powerhouse That Barry Built," *Esquire* 90 (December 1978): 91.

38. *Sports Illustrated,* December 12, 1994, p. 18.

39. *USA Today,* "Women's Group Grades Colleges," June 19, 1997, p. 3C; R. Vivian Acosta and Linda Jean Carpenter, "Women in Intercollegiate Sport: 1977–1996" (manuscript, Department of Physical Education, Brooklyn College, 1996).

40. Carol Slezak, "Colleges Still Lag on Title IX," *Chicago Sun-Times,* March 2, 1997, p. 3A.

41. Steve Wieberg, "NCAA Finds Too Little Progress," *USA Today,* June 20, 1997, p. 11C.

42. John C. Weistart, "Can Gender Equity Find a Place in Commercialized College Sports?" *Duke Journal of Gender Law and Policy* 3 (Spring 1996): 193.

43. Alexander Wolff and Richard O'Brien, "The Third Sex," *Sports Illustrated,* February 6, 1995, p. 15.

44. Ibid.

45. Ibid.

46. Tanya Albert, "Women's Programs Show Revenue Gains," *USA Today,* March 4, 1997, p. 6C.

47. D. Stanley Eitzen and Maxine Baca Zinn, "The De-athleticization of Women: The Naming and Gender Marking of Collegiate Sport Teams," *Sociology of Sport Journal* 6 (1989): 362–370.

48. Weistart, "Gender Equity," p. 264.

49. Donna Lopiano, "Stop the Rhetoric: Daughters Deserve What Law Requires," *USA Today,* July 2, 1993, p. 12C.

50. Allen L. Sack, "Amateurism as an Exploitative Ideology" (paper presented at the annual meeting of the American Alliance for Health, Physical Education, Recreation, and Dance, Detroit, 1980).

51. D. Stanley Eitzen, "The Sociology of Amateur Sport: An Overview," *International Review for the Sociology of Sport* 24, no. 2 (1989): 95–105.

52. Mike Littwin, personal correspondence with the author, July 1998.

53. Reported in Jeffrey R. Benedict, "Colleges Must Act Decisively When Scholarship Athletes Run Afoul of the Law," *Chronicle of Higher Education,* May 6, 1997, pp. 6B–7B.

54. Alexander Wolff, "Broken Beyond Repair: An Open Letter to the President of Miami Urges Him to Dismantle His Vaunted Football Program to Salvage His School's Reputation," *Sports Illustrated,* June 12, 1995, p. 22.

55. Todd W. Crosset et al., "Male Student-Athletes and Violence against Women," *Violence against Women* 2 (June 1996): 163–179.

56. Reported in Tim Larimer, "Asking for Trouble: Under Pressure to Produce Winners, Some Coaches Turn to Risky Recruits," *Sporting News,* December 16, 1991, pp. 9–12.

57. William F. Reed, "Absolutely Incredible!" *Sports Illustrated,* March 26, 1990, p. 66.

58. Quoted in Michael Goodwin, "When the Cash Register Is the Scoreboard," *New York Times,* June 8, 1986, pp. 27–28.

59. Gary Roberts, "Should College Athletes Be Paid? Yes: Trends Make Changes Inevitable," *USA Today,* June 8, 1994, p. 2C.

60. Allen L. Sack, "College Sports Must Choose: Amateur or Pro?" *New York Times,* May 3, 1981, p. 2S.

Chapter 9

The Path to Success? Myth and Reality

Lee Trevino was born to an impoverished, illiterate single mother. He was raised in a shack (next to a golf course) with no electricity or running water in North Dallas by his mother, who cleaned houses, and his grandfather, who worked as a gravedigger. As a youngster he caddied and taught himself how to play golf. He quit school after the seventh grade and took a job on the grounds crew for a country club. He played as often as he could, honing his self-taught skills and hustling bets. Against all odds—a poor, uneducated Mexican playing a sport dominated by affluent, influential whites and often played at racially segregated country clubs—Lee Trevino became one of the top three golfers of his generation. He won twenty-seven PGA tournaments, including six majors. At age fifty he joined the Senior Tour and won twenty-eight tournaments, including four major senior championships. As of 1998 he is the all-time career leading money winner on the Senior Tour. Lee Trevino is clearly an example of "rags-to-riches" through sports. Is he the rule or the exception?

Compared to much of the world, the United States is a society that allows social mobility. It is possible for poor children and penniless immigrants to become prosperous or even wealthy adults, based on some combination of hard work, educational attainment, skills/talents, and luck. Upward mobility within the system of social stratification is not only permitted but is part of the American creed that everyone should aspire to a higher social position. Americans, moreover, firmly believe that the United States is a "meritocratic" society in which social status is determined by achievement.

The primary source for this chapter is D. Stanley Eitzen and George H. Sage, *Sociology of North American Sport,* 6th ed. (Madison, Wis.: Brown and Benchmark, 1997), pp. 251–258, 264–276. Also D. Stanley Eitzen and Maxine Baca Zinn, *In Conflict and Order: Understanding Society,* 8th ed. (Boston: Allyn and Bacon, 1998), chaps. 9–10.

This belief, however, is largely a myth. Income statistics show that by far most children in this country remain in the social class of their parents. If there is movement, it tends to be slight. Traditionally, this mobility was more likely to be up than down, but Greg Duncan's research has found that the degree of social mobility has slowed in recent decades. This he attributes to the shrinkage of the middle class and to the fact that the extremes of wealth and poverty have become more intransigent.[1] Race and gender issues continue to hinder racial minorities and women. White males have higher pay and higher-status jobs than women and racial minorities even when their parents have similar status.[2]

Sport as an Avenue of Social Mobility

Typically, Americans believe that sport is a path to upward social mobility. Poor boys (rarely girls) from rural and urban areas, whether white or black, sometimes skyrocket to fame and fortune through success in sports. The financial rewards can be astounding, such as the high pay that some African-American athletes have received in recent years.[3] In 1997 Tracy McGrady, an NBA-bound high school star, bypassed college, and signed a $12 million deal over six years with Adidas. Golfer Tiger Woods in his first year as a professional made $6.82 million in winnings (United States and worldwide) and appearance fees. He signed a series of five-year deals with Nike, Titleist, American Express, and Rolex worth $95.2 million. In 1998 Woods's earnings from endorsements totaled $28 million. Boxer Mike Tyson made $75 million in 1996. It is estimated that basketball phenomenon Michael Jordan made over $100 million in 1997, including salary and endorsements, as well as box office, merchandise, and video income from his movie *Space Jam.* Jordan's salary and endorsement money alone add up to an average of $123.60 for every minute, twenty-four hours a day.[4] Baseball stars Barry Bonds and Albert Belle made $11.45 million and $11 million, respectively, in 1997 in salaries alone. Two-thirds of the players in the NBA (80 percent of the players in the leagues are African Americans) earn at least $1 million in annual salary.

High salaries and endorsement contracts are not the only financial opportunities provided by sport. The road to success in football, basketball, and some other sports virtually requires the athletes to attend college. Thus sports participation has the effect of encouraging athletes to attain more education and increasing the opportunities for success outside the sports world for those who do not find positions as players. Higher education also widens athletes' opportunities after a professional career.

Several studies indicate that after graduation male college athletes are more upwardly mobile than their nonathletic peers.[5] There are at least three possible reasons for this. First, athletic participation may lead to various forms of "occupational sponsorship." The male college athlete, especially in big-time sport, is a popular hero and therefore is more likely to date and marry a woman of higher socioeconomic status and may acquire a father-in-law who can provide him with benefits in the business world much greater than those available to the average nonathlete male. Another form of sponsorship may come from well-placed alumni who offer former athletes positions in their businesses after graduation. This may be done to help the firm's public relations, or it may be part of a payoff in the recruiting wars that some alumni are willing to underwrite.

A second reason for athletes' better outcomes is that the selection process for many jobs requires the applicant to be "well-rounded," meaning that a premium is placed on participation in extracurricular activities in addition to classes taken and grade point averages.

Finally, participation in highly competitive sports situations may lead to the development of attitudes and behavior patterns highly valued in the larger occupational world. If attributes such as leadership, human relations skills, teamwork, good work habits, and a well-developed competitive drive are acquired in sports, they may ensure that athletes will succeed in other endeavors. Considerable debate surrounds the question, Does sports participation build character? Or is it that only certain kinds of personalities survive the sports experience (see chapter 4)? There may be a self-fulfilling prophecy at work here, however. Employers who assume that athletes possess these valued character traits will make hiring and advancement decisions accordingly, giving former athletes the advantage. Yet a closer look at the situations that actually exist shows that for the vast majority, these benefits are fleeting at best.

Myths about Social Mobility through Sport

The belief that sport is a social mobility escalator is built on a succession of myths, including (1) sport provides a free college education; (2) sport leads to a college degree; (3) a professional sports career is possible; (4) sport is a way out of poverty, especially for racial minorities; (5) Title IX has created many opportunities for upward mobility through sport for women; and (6) a professional sports career provides security for life.

Myth 1: Sport Provides a Free College Education

Good high school athletes get college scholarships. These athletic scholarships are especially helpful to poor youth who otherwise would not be able to attend college because of the high costs. But, in reality, very few high school athletes actually receive full-ride scholarships. Football provides the easiest route to a college scholarship because Division I-A colleges each have eighty-five football scholarships, but even this avenue is exceedingly narrow. In Colorado 3,481 high school seniors played football during the 1994 season, thirty-one of whom received full-ride scholarships at Division I-A schools (0.0089 percent).[6] Of all the varsity athletes at all college levels in 1993, only about 15 percent to 20 percent had full scholarships. Another 15 percent to 25 percent had partial scholarships, leaving 55 percent to 70 percent of all intercollegiate athletes without any sport-related financial assistance.[7] As low as the chances are for men, women athletes have even less chance to receive an athletic scholarship. Although women make up about 52 percent of all college students, they make up only 35 percent of intercollegiate athletes, with a similar disproportionate distribution of scholarships (see chapter 8). Another reality debunking the notion that sport is an easy avenue to free access to a college education is that the chances of a full-ride scholarship for a male athlete in a so-called minor sport (swimming, tennis, golf, gymnastics, cross-country, wrestling) are virtually nil. At most, such an athlete can hope for a partial scholarship, since these sports are underfunded and stand to be eliminated at many schools.

Myth 2: Sport Leads to a College Degree

College graduates exceed high school graduates by hundreds of thousands of dollars in lifetime earnings. Since most high school and college athletes never play at the professional level, the attainment of a college degree is a crucial determinant of upward mobility through sport. The problem is that relatively few athletes in the big-time revenue-producing sports, compared to their nonathlete peers, actually receive college degrees (see chapter 8). This is especially the case for African Americans, who are overrepresented in the revenue-producing sports. In 1996, for example, of the athletes who entered Division I schools in 1990, only 45 percent of African-American football players and 39 percent of African-American basketball players had graduated (compared to 56 percent of the general student body).[8]

There are a number of barriers to graduation for athletes. The demands on their time and energy are enormous, even in the off-season. To cope with these pressures, many athletes take easy courses, to maintain eligibility, that do not lead to graduation. This strategy either delays graduation or makes it an unrealistic goal.

Another barrier to graduation for many college athletes is that they are recruited for athletic prowess rather than academic ability in the first place. Recent data show that football players in big-time programs are, on average, more than two hundred points behind their nonathlete classmates.[9] Poorly prepared students are the most likely to take easy courses, cheat on exams, hire surrogate test takers, and otherwise do the minimum. In other words, although they are in school, they are not receiving an education that will be an asset when they leave school.

A third barrier to graduation for college athletes is their attitude, as they may not take advantage of their scholarships to obtain a quality education and graduate. This is especially the case for those who perceive their college experience only as preparation for a professional career in sport. Study for them is important only to maintain their eligibility. The goal of a professional career is unrealistic for all but the superstars. And the superstars who do make it at the professional level probably do not graduate from college; nor do they go back to finish their degrees when their professional careers are over. Even a successful professional athletic career is limited to a few years, and not many professional athletes are able to translate their success in the pros to success in postathletic careers. Such a problem is especially true for African Americans, who often face employment discrimination in the wider society.

The Center for the Study of Sport and Society (CSSS) of Northeastern University in Boston has several programs that are aimed at keeping the "student" in the student-athlete. Richard Lapchick, director of CSSS, has brought together a consortium of 140 colleges and universities, the National Collegiate Athletic Association, and several professional leagues to entice former athletes back to school to get their degrees. In particular, when a university joins the National Consortium for Academics and Sports, it agrees to bring back, tuition-free, its former student-athletes who competed in revenue sports and were unable to complete their degree requirements. In return, the student-athletes agree to participate in the school's outreach and community service programs. This program has achieved very positive results. From 1984 to 1996, some 13,122 students have gone back to school to complete their degrees (8,594 athletes who did not make it to the professional level, 171 Olympians, and 4,528 professional athletes).[10] These results are terrific, but I have two concerns. First, many schools, including my own, have chosen not to belong to the consortium. My second concern is that this approach addresses the consequences of the problem rather than attacking the essence of the problem—schools that exploit athletes instead of educating them in the first place.

Myth 3: A Professional Sports Career Is Possible

A recent survey by the Center for the Study of Sport in Society found that two-thirds of African-American males between the ages of thirteen and eighteen believe that they can earn a living playing professional sports (more than double the proportion of young white males who hold such beliefs). Moreover, African-American parents were four times more likely than white parents to believe that their children are destined for careers as professional athletes.[11]

If these young athletes do play as professionals, the economic rewards are excellent, especially in basketball and baseball. In 1998 the average annual salary for professional basketball was $2.24 million. In baseball the average salary was $1.37 million; 280 of the 774 players on opening day rosters made $1 million or more (197 exceeding $2 million or more and 32 making $6 million or more). The average salaries for the National Hockey League and

National Football League were $892,000 and $795,000, respectively. In foot-ball, for example, 19 percent of the players (333 of 1,765) exceeded $1 million in salary. These numbers are inflated by the use of averages, which are skewed by the salaries of the superstars. Use of the median (in which half the players make more and half make less) reveals that the median salary in basketball was $1.4 million; baseball, $500,000; football, $400,000, and hockey, $400,000.[12] Regardless of the measure, the financial allure of a professional sports career is great.

The dream of financial success through a professional sports career is just that, however, a dream for all but an infinitesimal number. A career in profes-sional sport is nearly impossible to attain because of the fierce competition for so few openings. For example, in 1992 there were approximately 1.9 million American boys playing high school football, basketball, and baseball. That same year about 68,000 men were playing those sports in college, and 2,490 participated at the major professional level. In short, one in twenty-seven high school players in these sports will play at the college level, and *only one in 736 high school players will play at the major professional level (0.14 percent)*. In baseball about 120,000 players are eligible each year for the free-agent draft (high school seniors, college seniors, collegians over twenty-one, junior col-lege players, and foreign players). Only about 1,200 (1 percent) are actually drafted, and most of them will never make it to the major leagues. Indeed, only 10 percent of the players who sign a professional baseball contract ever play in the major leagues for at least one day.[13]

The same rigorous winnowing process occurs in football. About 15,000 players are eligible for the NFL draft each year. Of them, 336 are drafted and about 160 actually make the final roster. About forty new players are added to the rosters in the NBA, and sixty rookies make it into the NHL each year. In tennis about a hundred men and an equal number of women make enough money to cover expenses. Of the 165 men eligible for the PGA tour in 1997, their official winnings ranged from $2,066,833 (Tiger Woods) to $10,653 (Chip Beck).[14] The competition among these golfers is fierce. On average, the top hundred golfers on the tour play within two strokes of each other for every eighteen holes, yet Tiger Woods, the tops in winnings, won over $2 million, and the hundredth finisher won only $250,000.[15] Below the PGA tour is the Nike Tour, in which the next best 125 golfers compete. Their win-nings ranged from a top of $225,201 (Chris Smith) to a low of $9,944 (Dick Mast).[16]

Myth 4: Sport is a Way Out of Poverty, Especially for Racial Minorities

Sport appears to be an important avenue out of the ghetto for African Ameri-cans. The major professional sports are dominated numerically by African Americans. Although they constitute only 12 percent of the population, African

Americans make up about 80 percent of the players in professional basketball, about 67 percent in professional football, and 18 percent in professional baseball (Latinos account for about 18 percent of professional baseball players). Moreover, as noted earlier in this essay, African Americans dominate the list of the highest moneymakers in sport (salaries, commercial sponsorships). These facts are nevertheless illusory.

Although African Americans dominate professional basketball, football, and, to a lesser extent, baseball, they are rarely found in other sports, such as hockey, automobile racing, tennis, golf, bowling, and skiing. Moreover, African Americans are severely underrepresented in positions of authority in sport—head coaches, referees, athletic directors, scouts, general managers, and owners. In the NFL in 1997, for example, where more than two-thirds of the players were African Americans, only three head coaches and five offensive or defensive coordinators were African Americans. In that year eleven head coaching vacancies were filled, none by African Americans. Writing about the reason for this racial imbalance in hiring, white sports columnist Bob Kravitz remarks that "something here stinks, and it stinks a lot like racism."[17]

Although African-American males have better odds of making it as professional athletes than whites (about 1 in 3,500 African-American male high school athletes, compared to 1 in 10,000 white male high school athletes),[18] their odds remain exceedingly slim. Of the 40,000 or so African-American boys who play high school basketball, only thirty-five will make the NBA and only seven will be starters. Referring to the low odds for young African Americans, Harry Edwards, an African-American sociologist specializing in the sociology of sport, said with a bit of hyperbole: "Statistically, you have a better chance of getting hit by a meteorite in the next 10 years than getting work as an athlete."[19] These low odds are for African-American males. The chances for African-American females are virtually nonexistent (except for the one fledgling women's professional basketball league).

Despite these discouraging facts, the myth is alive for poor youth: Two-thirds of young African-American boys believe they can be professional athletes. Their parents too accept this belief. The film *Hoop Dreams* and Darcey Frey's book *The Last Shot: City Streets, Basketball Dreams* document the emphasis that young African-American men place on sport as a way up and the disappointment that they experience.[20] For many of them, sport represents their only hope of escape from a life of crime, poverty, and despair. They latch on to the dream of athletic success partly because they have few opportunities for middle-class success. They spend many hours per day developing their speed, strength, jumping height, or "moves," to the virtual exclusion of abilities that have a greater likelihood of paying off in upward mobility, such as reading comprehension, mathematical reasoning, communication skills, and computer literacy. Sociologist Jay Coakley puts it this way:

My best guess is that less than 3,500 African Americans . . . are making their livings as professional athletes. At the same time (in 1996), there are about 30,015 black physicians and about 30,800 black lawyers currently employed in the U.S. Therefore, there are twenty times more blacks working in these two professions than playing top-level professional sports. And physicians and lawyers usually have lifetime earnings far in excess of the earnings of professional athletes, whose playing careers, on average, last less than five years.[21]

This futile pursuit of sports stardom has serious consequences for individual African Americans as well as for the African-American community. First and foremost, they spend their time learning skills that are worthless in the job market. Harry Edwards posits that by spending their energies and talents on athletic skills, young African Americans are not pursuing occupations that would help them meet their political and material needs. Thus their belief in the "sports as a way up" myth causes them to remain dependent on whites and white institutions.[22] Salim Muwakkil, an African-American political analyst, argues,

If African-Americans are to exploit the socio-economic options opened by varied civil rights struggles more fully, blacks must reduce the disproportionate allure of sports in their communities. Black leadership must contextualize athletic success by promoting other avenues to social status, intensifying the struggle for access to those avenues and better educating youth about those potholes on the road to the stadium.[23]

John Hoberman also challenges the assumption that sport has progressive consequences.[24] The success of African Americans in the highly visible sports gives white America a false sense of black progress and interracial harmony. But the social progress of African Americans in general has little relationship to the apparent integration that they have achieved on the country's playing fields:

The illusory sense of racial harmony on countless playing fields across America masks the true depth of the racial conflict that survives in one and the same society. In this sense, the material gains of a Michael Jordan or a Tiger Woods impede the process of social change. For every black Superstar, there are thousands of blacks behind bars.[25]

Hoberman also contends that the numerical superiority of African Americans in sport, coupled with their disproportionate underrepresentation in other professions, reinforces the racist ideology that African Americans are physically superior to whites but are inferior to them intellectually. In short, sport harms African Americans by serving up imagery and metaphors that reinforce racism and the racial divisions that continue to plague U.S. society.

I do not mean to say that talented African Americans should not seek a career in professional sport. Professional sport is a legitimate career with the potential for exceptional monetary rewards. What is harmful, to reiterate, is that the odds of success are so slim, rendering extraordinary, sustained effort futile and misguided for the vast majority. If this effort were directed at areas having better odds of success, then upward mobility would occur for many more. The late African-American tennis star Arthur Ashe argued that "we have been on the same roads — sports and entertainment — too long. We need to pull over, fill up at the library and speed away to Congress, and the Supreme Court, the unions, and the business world."[26]

Myth 5: Title IX Has Created Many Opportunities for Upward Mobility through Sport for Women

Since Title IX was passed in 1972, requiring schools receiving federal funds to provide equal opportunities for women and men, sports participation by women in high school and college has increased dramatically. In 1973, for example 50,000 men received some form of college scholarship for their athletic abilities; only fifty scholarships went to women. Now women receive about 35 percent of the money allotted for college athletic scholarships (this is a dramatic improvement but should not be equated with gender equality; see chapter 8). Scholarships allow many women to attend college who otherwise could not afford it, and college attendance is directly related to upward social mobility.

Upward mobility from sport is another matter for women. Women have fewer opportunities than men in professional team sports. Beach volleyball is a possibility for a very few, but again the rewards are minimal. Two professional women's basketball leagues began in 1997, but the pay is very low compared to what men make, and the leagues are on shaky financial ground; one of the leagues failed after one season. The other option for women is to play in professional leagues in Europe, Australia, and Asia, but again the pay is relatively low.

Women have more opportunities as professionals in individual sports such as tennis, golf, ice skating, skiing, bowling, cycling, and track. Ironically, the sports with the greatest monetary rewards for women are those of the middle and upper classes (tennis, golf, and ice skating). These sports are expensive, and they require considerable individual coaching as well as access to private facilities. In short, sport does not offer poor women, even in a very limited way, the potential for upward mobility. Speaking of African Americans in this regard, Harry Edwards has observed, "We must also consider that to the extent that sport provides an escape route from the ghetto at all, it does so only for black males."[27]

Opportunities in sport apart from the athlete role are more limited for women than for men. Ironically, with the passage of Title IX, which increased the participation rates of women so dramatically, there has been a decline in the number and proportion of women as coaches and athletic administrators.[28] In addition to the glaring pay gap that exists between coaches of men's teams and coaches of women's teams, men who coach women's teams tend to have higher salaries than women coaching women's teams. Women also have fewer opportunities than men as athletic trainers, officials, sports journalists, and other adjunct positions.

Myth 6: A Professional Sports Career Provides Security for Life

Even among those who attain a career in professional sport, fame and fortune are in short supply. Of course, some athletes make an income from salaries and endorsements that, if invested wisely, provides financial security for life. But many professional athletes make relatively low salaries. During the 1996 season, for example, 17 percent of major league baseball players made the minimum salary of $247,500 for veterans and $220,000 for rookies. This is a lot of money, but the careers of these marginal players may not last very long. Indeed, the average length of a professional career in a team sport is about five years. Marginal athletes in individual sports, such as golf, tennis, boxing, and bowling, struggle financially. They must cover their travel expenses, health insurance, equipment, and the like with no guaranteed paycheck. And that brief sports career diverts the young athletes from developing other career skills and experiences that would benefit them throughout life.

A career as a professional athlete is short, even for those who extend their playing days beyond the average. Athletes leave sport involuntarily when they are injured or when they are replaced by more talented athletes. They leave voluntarily when age slows them down so much that they cannot continue to compete successfully.

Ex-professional athletes leave sport, on average, when they are in their late twenties or early thirties, at a time when their nonathlete peers have begun to establish themselves in occupations leading toward retirement in forty years or so. What are the ex-professional athletes to do with their remaining productive years?

Exiting a sports career can be relatively smooth or it can be difficult. Some athletes plan ahead, preparing themselves for other careers in sport (coaching, scouting, administering) or for a nonsport occupation. Others do not prepare themselves for this abrupt change. They graduate from college but do not spend the off-seasons apprenticing nonsport jobs. Exiting the athlete role is difficult for many because they *lose* (1) what they have focused on for most of their lives; (2) the primary source of their personal identity; (3) their physical prowess; (4) adulation bordering on worship from others; (5) the money and the perquisites of fame; (6) the camaraderie with teammates; (7) the intense "highs" of competition; and (8) status (for most ex-athletes). As a result of these losses, many ex-professional athletes have trouble adjusting to life after sport.[29] A study by the NFL Players Association found that emotional difficulties, divorce, and financial strain were common problems for retired athletes.[30]

For most, the real world is a big step down. Big-time pro athletes are pampered like royalty. They fly first class while hired hands pay the bills and tote the luggage. High-powered executives and heads of state fawn over them. "You begin to feel like Louis XIV," says Wilbert McClure, a two-time Golden Gloves boxing champion who is now a psychologist and counselor to basketball players. Step off the pedestal and everything changes. McClure likens it to "being dipped into hell."[31]

Often retirement occurs because the athlete has "failed," that is, is demoted to nonstarter, is let go by management, or no longer meets the qualifications, such as not making the cut in tournament after tournament in golf. These once successful athletes now face marginality, degradation, and the stigma of failure.[32]

A survey of 645 former NFL players in 1988 found that many had problems adjusting to life after professional football. Some 42 percent had made three or more career changes, and 62 percent had "some" emotional problems during the first six months. Moreover, 62 percent said that they had "permanent injuries" from football.[33]

An athlete has some potential for a sport-related career after his or her playing days are over, such as coaching, managing, scouting, sportscasting, public relations, and administration. For all but superstars, however, the opportunities are severely limited. Racial minorities and women rarely attain such a career.

In summary, the evidence supports the contention that sports participation has limited potential as a social mobility escalator. The allure in its potential, however, remains strong, and this has at least two negative consequences. First, ghetto youngsters who devote their lives to the pursuit of athletic stardom are, except for the fortunate few, doomed to failure in sport and in the real world as well, since sports skills are essentially irrelevant to occupational placement and advancement. The second negative consequence is more subtle but is very important. Sport contributes to the ideology that legitimizes social inequalities and promotes the myth that all it takes to succeed is extraordinary effort. Sport sociologist George H. Sage makes this point forcefully:

Because sport is by nature meritocratic—that is, superior performance brings status and rewards—it provides convincing symbolic support for hegemonic [the dominant] ideology—that ambitious, dedicated, hard-working individuals, regardless of social origin, can achieve success and ascend in the social hierarchy, obtaining high status and material rewards, while those who don't move upward simply didn't work hard enough. Because the rags-to-riches athletes are so visible, the social mobility theme is maintained. This reflects the opportunity structure of society in general—the success of a few reproduces the belief in social mobility among the many.[34]

Notes

1. Greg J. Duncan, "Slow Motion: Earnings Mobility of Young Workers in the 1970s and 1980s" (paper presented at the annual meeting of the Midwest Sociological Society, Chicago, 1996).
2. John E. Farley, *Sociology*, 4th ed. (Englewood Cliffs, N.J.: Prentice-Hall, 1998), p. 199.
3. Documentation for these examples comes from Bill Meyers, "Prep Star Signs $12M Adidas Deal," *USA Today*, June 19, 1997, p. 1C; Ron Sirak, "Tiger Woods' $653 Million Financial Roar for Golf," *Rocky Mountain News*, August 27, 1997, p. 2A; "Tyson's '96 Pay Hits Record $75M," *USA Today*, December 2, 1996, p. 3A; Erik Brady, "Just How High Can Players' Salaries Go?" *USA Today*, April 3, 1997, pp. 1A–2A.
4. "Numbers Game," *Denver Post*, June 10, 1997, p. 2D.
5. John W. Loy Jr., "The Study of Sport and Social Mobility," *International Review of Sport Sociology* 7 (1972): 5–23; Allen L. Sack and Robert Thiel, "College Football and Social Mobility: A Case of Notre Dame Football Players," *Sociology of Education* 52 (January 1979): 60–66; and Douglas Lederman, "Students Who Competed in College Sports Fare Better in Job Market Than Those Who Didn't, Report Says," *Chronicle of Higher Education*, September 26, 1990, pp. 47A–48A.
6. Scott Stocker, "Don't Bank on Earning a Division I-A Football Scholarship," *Rocky Mountain News*, February 7, 1995, p. 16B.
7. Jay J. Coakley, *Sport in Society*, 5th ed. (St. Louis: Mosby, 1994), p. 296.
8. Steve Wieberg, "Grad Rates for Scholarship Athletes Hold Steady," *USA Today*, June 27, 1997, p. 10C; Marc Ethier, "Male Basketball Players Continue to Lag in Graduation Rates," *Chronicle of Higher Education*, July 3, 1997, p. 39A.
9. Gary Mihoces, "Football Programs Try Settling Score," *USA Today*, December 22, 1993, pp. 1C–2C, 6C.
10. *Academics and Sports: Annual Report of the National Consortium for Academics and Sports* (Boston: Center for the Study of Sport and Society, 1997), p. 4.
11. Cited in John Simons, "Improbable Dreams: African Americans Are a Dominant Presence in Professional Sports. Do Blacks Suffer as a Result?" *U.S. News & World Report*, March 24, 1997, pp. 46–52.
12. Erik Brady, "Just How High Can Players' Salaries Go? *USA Today*, April 3, 1997, pp. 1C–2C.
13. *NCAA News*, October 21, 1991, p. 16.
14. "1997 PGA Tour Statistics," *Golfweek's Pro Golf '98* 24, no. 1 (1998): 18–20.
15. "PGA Rests Its Cart Case," *Denver Post*, February 9, 1998, p. 5C.
16. "Nike Tour Year in Review," *Golfweek*, October 25, 1997, p. 12.
17. Bob Kravitz, "NFL Hiring Practices Look Like Racism," *Rocky Mountain News*, January 21, 1998, p. 3N; see also Alex Marvez, "System Works against Minority Coaches," *Rocky Mountain News*, January 18, 1998, p. 26N; and Paul Tagliabue, "Fair Play underneath the Headsets," *New York Times*, January 4, 1998, p. 22.
18. George H. Sage, *Power and Ideology in American Sport: A Critical Perspective* (Champaign, Ill.: Human Kinetics, 1990), p.40.
19. Harry Edwards, quoted in Bob Oates, "The Great American Tease: Sport as a Way Out of the Ghetto," *New York Times*, June 8, 1979, p. 32A.

20. *Hoop Dreams,* film documentary directed by Steve James (1994); Darcy Frey, *The Last Shot: City Streets, Basketball Dreams* (Boston: Houghton Mifflin, 1994).

21. Jay J. Coakley, *Sport in Society: Issues and Controversies,* 6th ed. (New York: McGraw-Hill, 1998), p. 313.

22. Harry Edwards, "The Black Athletes: 20th Century Gladiators for White Americans," *Psychology Today* 7 (November 1973): 43–52.

23. Salim Muwakkil, "Which Team Are You On?" *In These Times,* May 3, 1998, p. 16.

24. John Hoberman, *Darwin's Athletes: How Sport Has Damaged Black America and Preserved the Myth of Race* (Boston: Houghton Mifflin, 1997).

25. Jim Nadell, review of *Darwin's Athletes: How Sport Has Damaged Black America and Preserved the Myth of Race,* by John Hoberman, *Z Magazine* 10 (December 1997): 54.

26. Arthur Ashe, "Send Your Children to the Libraries," *New York Times,* February 6, 1977, p. 2S.

27. Harry Edwards, "Black Athletes," p. 47.

28. R. Vivian Acosta and Linda Jean Carpenter, "Women in Intercollegiate Sport: 1977–1996" (manuscript, Department of Physical Education, Brooklyn College, 1996).

29. Jo Anne Tremaine Drahota and D. Stanley Eitzen, "The Role Exit of Professional Athletes," *Sociology of Sport Journal* 15 (September 1998): 263–278; Jo Anne Tremaine Drahota, "The Role Exit of Professional Athletes" (Ph.D. diss., Colorado State University, 1996); and Michael A. Messner, *Power at Play* (Boston: Beacon, 1992).

30. Reported in a five-part series by Brian Hewitt, *Chicago Sun-Times,* September 19–22, 1993.

31. Andrea Rothman and Stephanie Anderson Forest, "The Thrill of Victory, the Agony of Retirement," *Business Week,* June 3, 1991, pp. 54–55.

32. Donald W. Ball, "Failure in Sport," *American Sociological Review* 41 (1976): 726–739. See also Donald S. Harris and D. Stanley Eitzen, "The Consequences of Failure in Sport," *Urban Life* 7 (1978): 177–188.

33. Gary Mihoces, "Less-Visible Players Find Little Glory after Football," *USA Today,* May 10, 1988, p. 12C.

34. Sage, *Power and Ideology,* p. 41.

Chapter 10

Professional Sport Franchises: Public Teams, Private Businesses

Most public address announcers at professional sports events, when introducing the teams, refer to the home team as your *team, as in* your *Denver Broncos,* your *New York Yankees, or* your *Atlanta Hawks. The home fans do identify, often passionately, with the home team, the team representing their city or region. The team* is *their team in this respect. The fans also have a financial stake in these teams by purchasing the high-priced tickets and, with the exception of a few teams, helping to subsidize the stadiums and arenas in which the professional teams play.*

But the professional team to which they give their allegiance is not really theirs. With the exception of only one major league franchise in the four major sports—the Green Bay Packers—every professional team is owned by an individual, a family, a small group of business partners, or a corporation. The owner can sell and trade players, including players who are true heroes to the fans. The owner determines ticket prices. The owner can move the team to another city. Examining professional sport as a monopoly, ownership for profit, and public subsidies to professional team franchises raises a question: Who profits and who loses in the way professional sport is organized?

Professional Sport as a Monopoly

Each major professional league is an unregulated monopoly. Each league regulates itself, unfettered by government oversight and government rules against monopolies that apply to other industries. Each league operates as a cartel—as competitors joined together for mutual benefit. This means that the teams making up each league make agreements on matters of mutual interest such as rules, schedules, promotions, expansion, and media contracts. In professional sport cartels exist to restrict competition for athletes, to limit franchises, and to divide markets among the league's teams.[1] Such arrangements are illegal in most other businesses because they lead to collusion, price-fixing, and restraint of trade.

Being a cartel gives each league enormous advantages. The cartel limits competition in several ways. Competitive bidding among teams for players is controlled through player drafts, contracts, and trades. A cartel keeps competition among the teams at a minimum by restricting the number of teams in the league and where they can locate. The owner of the Kansas City Royals, for instance, is protected from a rival team locating in his territory. There are some metropolitan areas with two major league baseball teams, but these exceptions occurred before baseball agreed to territorial exclusivity. Even for the few exceptions, the teams are in different leagues (Chicago White Sox and Chicago Cubs, and the New York Yankees and the New York Mets). This protection from competition eliminates price wars. The owners of a franchise can continue to charge the maximum without fear of price cutting by competitors.

The league cartel also controls the number of franchises allowed. Take the case of baseball. In 1901, when the population of the United States was about 76 million, there were sixteen major league teams. No new teams were added between 1901 and 1961, yet the population more than doubled to 179 million. From 1961 to 1998, twelve teams were added, for a total of thirty teams in a nation of approximately 270 million. Using 1901 as a standard, and assuming that the United States is capable of developing the same proportion of major league caliber baseball players today as was the case at the turn of the century, there should now be fifty-seven major league teams rather than the current thirty.[2] This calculation does not account for the exclusion of African Americans from major league baseball until 1947 and the influx of Latinos in the last couple of decades (African Americans and Latinos combined now make up about 36 percent of major league rosters), which means that the number of teams should be even more than the hypothetical fifty-seven.

Sport sociologist George Sage asserts that this is clearly the result of major league baseball's reluctance to expand because the owners do not want to "diminish their political and economic power by adding new franchises. It seems obvious that expansion has little to do with the availability of capable baseball players."[3] When major league baseball does expand, it does so to benefit the league. The last four additions reveal why. In 1993 the Florida Marlins and the Colorado Rockies were admitted because neither Florida nor the Rocky Mountain time zone had a major league team. These additions tapped new populations and media markets, which would benefit the other league members. So too did the $95 million each team paid to join. Neither team was allowed to share in television revenues for two seasons, which had the effect, when the initiation fee was added, of totaling $106 million. In 1998 the Arizona Diamondbacks and the Tampa Bay Devil Rays played their first seasons, having each paid $125 million to become members of the cartel. Both of these teams were added for reasons similar to the ones dictating the addition of the Marlins and Rockies—Arizona had no major league team and Tampa Bay was located in a large, heretofore untapped market that did not infringe on Miami, 275 miles away.

Each league is generally reluctant to add new teams because scarcity permits higher ticket prices, more beneficial media arrangements, and continued territorial purity. In short, the value of each franchise increases by the restriction on the number of teams.

This monopolistic situation enables a league to negotiate television contracts for the benefit of all members of the cartel. The 1961 Sports Broadcast Act allowed sports leagues to sell their television rights as a group without being subject to antitrust laws. As a result, the national networks and cable systems may bid for the right to televise the games for a particular league. The deal struck at the end of 1997 totaled $17.6 billion for the right to televise NFL games until 2005 (double the previous contract). This amounts to about $75 million a team per season, a gain of $37 million from the former contract. Similarly, the four-year deal made by the National Basketball Association was for $2.65 billion—twice the provisions of the old contract.

Another advantage of the monopoly enjoyed by the professional leagues is that the players are drastically limited in their choices and bargaining power. The sports cartel holds down wages because the athletes have few options besides playing in the league. In football, players are drafted out of college. If they want to play in the NFL, they must negotiate with the team that drafted them. Their other choices are to play in the Arena League or to play in Canada. These other options offer much less pay, and the Canadian teams limit the number of Americans allowed per team.

A final advantage of the cartel's controlling the number and location of franchises is that the owners prosper. Since the owners rarely add teams to the cartel, their teams are scarce commodities, which means that their worth appreciates much faster than other investments.[4] In 1997, for example, the 113 professional team franchises valued by *Financial World* were worth an average of $146 million, an 18 percent increase in one year.[5] A few examples can be cited that represent the growth curve in professional team franchise value:[6]

- The Dallas Cowboys were purchased in 1960 for $600,000; in 1984 they were sold for $60 million and in 1989, for $150 million. In 1997 the value of the franchise was estimated at $320 million.
- The Denver Broncos were purchased in 1981 for $30 million and sold three years later for $72 million. The 1997 value of the Broncos was estimated at $182 million. When the Denver voters decided to build a new stadium for the Denver Broncos, some observers estimated an addition of $10.3 million in profits—or more—annually from advertising, parking, concessions, as well as income from skyboxes and club seating.[7]
- The Tampa Bay Buccaneers, a perennially losing team, were bought for $16 million in 1976 and sold for $192 million in 1995.

- The sale of the Baltimore Orioles brought $12 million in 1979. In 1988 that franchise cost the new owner $70 million. The team's estimated market value in 1997 was $207 million.
- The Quebec Nordiques (now the Colorado Avalanche) franchise was purchased in 1979 for $6 million. In 1988 it sold for $14.8 million, and in 1995 it went for $75 million (and moved to Denver). The 1997 estimate of that franchise's market value was $81 million.
- The Portland Trail Blazers were purchased for $3.5 million in 1970 and sold for $70 million in 1988. In 1997 the value of the franchise was estimated to be $179 million.
- The Texas Rangers were purchased in 1989 for $86 million and sold in 1998 for $250 million. George Walker Bush, now governor of Texas, was one of the early investors, putting up $606,302. His 2 percent share of the proceeds (plus an additional 10 percent for serving as managing partner) was $14.9 million. The value of the Rangers was high because of the taxpayer-built field (a topic considered later in this chapter). A political opponent of Bush said, "I don't think that when voters approved this [building the baseball stadium] they thought Governor Bush would make $14.9 million. The citizens haven't got close to the kind of return Governor Bush has gotten."[8]

Public Subsidies to Professional Team Franchises

The scarcity of professional teams (the consequence of league monopoly) and the tremendous fan interest in having a major sports franchise in their city lead to large public subsidies for the relatively few teams. The subsidies to franchise owners take two forms—tax breaks and the availability of arenas at very low cost.

The tax code benefits team owners in two ways. First, the typically enormous profits from the sale of a team are counted as capital gains for team owners (as with the sale of other American businesses) and thus are taxed at a lower rate than other sources of income such as salaries and wages. A second tax benefit is indirect but bountiful nonetheless. This financial advantage accrues to team owners as businesses purchase tickets, food, and skyboxes. They are permitted to write off 50 percent of these costs as business expenses. This tax subsidy to businesses and corporations makes the high cost of attending sports events more palatable to them, which helps to keep the price of tickets and skyboxes inflated and profits steady. All other taxpayers, however, are left holding the bag.

Despite these advantages, team owners today paint a bleak picture of team finances. They do this to get the fans on their side in salary disputes with players, to keep the players' salary demands as low as possible, and to secure support for further subsidies, to renovate existing stadiums or build new ones. The negative financial picture painted by the owners is misleading because it refers usually to accounting losses (expenses exceeding income) that are not really losses.

Consider a hypothetical example provided by economist Richard Sheehan.[9] Let's assume someone purchases a major league baseball franchise for $100 million. For that money the new owner receives the legal right to the franchise (the franchise name), to be part of the league cartel, and to hold the player contracts. The Internal Revenue Service has ruled that the owner can claim 60 percent of the purchase price for the franchise and 40 percent for the player contracts. The tax subsidy occurs because the players under contract are assumed to lose value with age; therefore, their value can be depreciated, just as a farmer depreciates a tractor or a steel company depreciates a blast furnace for tax purposes. The right to depreciate an asset lowers taxable income. Thus, after the bills are paid in this hypothetical example, the owner has $5 million left over (profit). But since the owner can amortize that $40 million in player contracts over five years, he or she can write off 20 percent of that $40 million, or $8 million each year, and call it a cost. In effect, the owner pockets the $5 million but declares a loss of $3 million.

This legal maneuver has the effect of informing the public that the owner is losing money when that is not in fact the case. Moreover, the owner does not owe any taxes because of the "loss." If the owner were not allowed to depreciate the players, then he or she would owe taxes on the $5 million. This tax subsidy for the owners is not allowed to others, since no other business in the United States depreciates the value of human beings as part of the cost of its operation. In a curious twist of logic, but revealing of the bias of capital over human rights, the players whose skills diminish with age do not receive a tax write-off; only their owners do. This tax subsidy is a gift to team owners paid for by the rest of us.

Sheehan provides another example of creative accounting that is used to misrepresent the fiscal health of professional teams, although it is not a tax subsidy to owners. In this instance, the owner pays himself or herself a significant salary, which is counted as a business expense that lowers profits. Some NFL owners have paid themselves "salaries" as high as $7.5 million. The bottom line, the line that the public hears, is that the team is losing money, when the owner is simply taking the profit as salary.

Another manipulation of the financial balance sheet intended to project financial weakness occurs when the prospective owner loans the money to the newly created team ownership corporation for the down payment to purchase the team. This loan and the accrued interest have to be repaid from the subsequent income of the team, thus lowering, for accounting purposes, the team's stated profit. Thus the owner pockets the money, which the accounting department registers as an expense.[10]

The second type of public subsidy of professional sport is the provision of sports facilities to most franchises at very low cost. These arenas and stadiums are essential to the financial success and spectator appeal of professional sports. Team owners seek new and improved sports facilities, usually at taxpayer expense, and typically they get them. If not, they move. This threat to move (some would call it blackmail), real or implied, has resulted in a construction boom. In the decade of the 1990s some $9 billion in stadium construction occurred in the United States ("stadia mania"), most of which was subsidized by the taxpayers.

Community subsidies take several forms. Stadiums are built by the taxpayers. So too are new roads and overpasses, access to freeways, and the like. Owners may be given other economic considerations as well. Consider, as an extreme example, the lucrative deal given the owners of the Colorado Rockies by local taxpayers.[11]

Case Study: The Rockies Stadium Deal

Citizens of the six counties surrounding and including Denver passed a 0.1 percent sales tax proposal to fund a new stadium for the Colorado Rockies baseball team. The stadium was projected to cost $139 million, with $97 million to come from taxpayers and $42 million from private sources. Eventually, as is common, the original cost estimate turned out to be too low. The stadium actually cost $180 million, the taxpayers' obligation rising to $156 million rather than the $96 million they voted on. The stadium district board gave its chairperson, John McHale Jr., the power to negotiate the terms of the stadium lease with the Rockies. The deal struck between these two parties included the following generous provisions:

1. The owners of the Rockies were given the right to name the stadium, which they sold to Coors Brewing Company for $15 million.
2. The team owners will not pay rent or maintenance until the year 2000. After that they will pay the stadium district less than 2.5 percent of the team's net profits and $150,000 a year to cover the stadium's operating costs.
3. The team owners received seat rights, luxury suites, advertising, parking, and concession rights for seventeen years *at no cost*. They keep 40 percent of all concession sales (at least $10 million annually). All the revenue from sixty-four private suites (ranging in price from $60,000 to $90,000 annually) goes to the Rockies.
4. The owners receive all revenues from nonbaseball events for parking, concessions, and rent. For a sold-out rock concert, for example, the owners would receive about $500,000.
5. As stadium managers, the owners of the Rockies receive an annual fee of $2.65 million.

As sport sociologist George Sage observed, "Incredible as it may seem, the lease gave the Rockies every source of revenue generated by the stadium including concessions, parking, advertising, and non-baseball events there. The agreement sent no revenue streams back to taxpayers who were footing the construction bill through the sales tax hike."[12]

The Rockies have done extremely well financially, given this cozy arrangement. Since the team moved into Coors Field, it has led the major leagues in attendance, averaging almost 4 million a year. These 4 million at an average of $15, spending, typically, $5 in concessions and arriving in one million cars parked at $5 a car, mean something in the neighborhood of $85 million annually from fans—the same fans whose taxes helped to pay for the stadium construction and maintenance. In 1997, the market value of the Rockies was estimated to be $184 million, which is probably a conservative figure.

As a postscript, there are three items of note. First, the election was passed by a 54 percent to 46 percent majority after a vigorous campaign by local politicians, business interests, and the local media. Among the media, Denver's largest newspaper, the *Rocky Mountain News,* was an unabashed cheerleader, urging a yes vote in editorials and in the slant of its coverage. Editorials referred to opponents of the subsidy as "forces of caution and stagnation," "skeptics," "wearing dust-covered glasses," "shortsighted," and "envy-wracked."[13] After the vote, it was revealed that the *Rocky Mountain News* was involved in negotiations to become a part owner of the franchise (these negotiations were successful). A second interesting bit of information concerning this one-sided arrangement for the Rockies is that the taxpayers were represented in the negotiations, as noted earlier, by John McHale Jr. Four months after the lease was signed, McHale joined the Rockies as the team's executive vice president for baseball operations.

Finally, the Colorado Rockies made a profit of $23 million in 1996, according to *Financial World,*[14] none of which was returned to the taxpayers who paid for the stadium. Rather, ticket prices were raised for the 1997 season and again for the 1998 season.

Other Egregious Examples of Subsidies to Team Owners

In the 1990s states and localities built six baseball parks, with team owners putting up only 6 percent of the $1.07 billion. The public funding came from a variety of sources, for example, a 2 percent hotel room tax pays for the new park for the White Sox; the sports lottery pays for Oriole Park; a 1.9 cent tax on every twelve-ounce beer is the primary source for the Cleveland Indians field; the Texas Rangers have a stadium in Arlington, paid for through $135 million in thirty-year bonds; and Coors Field of the Rockies is financed with a 0.1 percent sales tax in a six-county metropolitan area.[15]

St. Louis enticed the Rams to leave Los Angeles with a package that included a new $300 million stadium, all proceeds from concessions, parking, club seats and luxury suites, and a $15 million practice facility. To pay for the stadium Missouri taxpayers pay $24 million a year, St. Louis taxpayers pay another $12.5 million, and visitors to the county pay a 7.25 percent room tax to raise another $6 million. Federal taxpayers (i.e., all of us) also help out— $2 million not received in federal taxes because of the use of tax-exempt bonds; $2 million because businesses deduct half the cost of club seats and luxury suites; and the deductions allowed owners through the depreciation of players.[16]

Art Modell, owner of the Cleveland Browns (which averaged 70,000 fans per game), decided to move his team to Baltimore because he was given a $200 million stadium with 108 luxury boxes and 7,500 club seats, $75 million for moving expenses, $50 million for doing the deal, all revenues from ticket sales, concessions, parking, and stadium advertising. Finally, taxpayers will guarantee ten years of sellout crowds for the new stadium. When the stadium is used for other events, Modell will collect a 10 percent management fee plus half the profits. Use of the stadium is rent-free for thirty years, although Modell will pay back $24 million in construction costs.[17]

The Rationale for Public Subsidization
of Professional Sports Teams

Citizens have, for the most part, been willing to underwrite these subsidies to teams for four reasons. First, conventional wisdom holds that the presence of major league sports teams enhances a city's prestige. Image is important, at least to civic boosters, and having a major league team gives the impression of being a first-class city. Civic boosters believe above all that a world-class city has world-class sports teams engaged in contests with other teams representing world-class cities. A professional team housed in a stadium downtown restores the image and prosperity of the downtown area with the gentrification of stadium environs (e.g., warehouses are converted into upscale lofts; trendy restaurants, nightclubs, and boutiques locate nearby).[18] Tourists and television viewers now see the city in a new, more positive light.

Second, the presence of a major league team representing a city means a lot to the sports fans in that city and nearby environs. These fans can now identify with that team instead of watching a televised game between opponents from other places. This collective rooting for a major league team is believed to provide some social glue holding together a sprawling metropolitan area by bringing people together with a common identity. As Marilyn Geewax, a reporter for the *Atlanta Constitution* puts it, "When I see 50,000 people in Turner Field, cheering and chopping [doing the Tomahawk chop for the Atlanta Braves, see chapter 3] together, I feel as though I live in a richer, more cohesive community. I can't name the price, but I know that feeling has value."[19]

Third, fans want to see games in person, not only the heroics of the home team but also sports stars from the visiting team as well. Attending a major league game is a noteworthy event for many.

Fourth, it is commonly asserted that a major league team creates substantial economic growth. This is an important issue: Does a major league sports franchise generate a significant investment return for the community? And if there are economic benefits, who benefits and who does not?

Let's consider the claim that having a major league team and building a bigger and better stadium benefits the community economically. The following eight points represent a summary of scholars' conclusions refuting the myth of professional sport as an economic force in the community.[20]

1. Professional sports teams are relatively small firms, when compared with the corporations and universities in a locality. Urban scholar Mark Rosentraub concludes that "sports is just too small a component of any community's economy to be the engine that propels jobs and growth."[21] "Professional sports may be the 'icing on a region's or city's economic cake,' but it is not an 'engine' that drives any economy."[22]

2. A common belief is that the presence of a professional sports team increases expenditures in restaurants and hotels, thereby stimulating growth and creating jobs. To a degree this is true—restaurants and hotels do locate near the stadium, revitalizing the area and bringing jobs. But most of this activity, about 80 percent of it, is just a transfer of spending from some parts of the metropolitan area to a more focused location. There is also less spending on other forms of recreation as attention is directed at the professional team. For example, on game days there is a decline in movie attendance, skiing on the nearby ski slopes, and even shopping in the malls.

3. Corporations do not move to an area because of a sport team or teams but primarily because of such factors as a suitable workforce, a positive (for management) labor climate, good schools, and relatively low taxes.

4. Economists have a concept called the "multiplier effect," which refers to money paid in profits or wages that is then spent (recirculated) in the community. The common argument by the proponents of civic growth is that the regional multiplier for any tourist industry is three. Rosentraub, however, makes the case for a multiplier effect of two when it comes to professional sports teams. Consider, for example, the money paid to players. About half of the money earned by sports teams is paid to players, with most making hundreds of thousands (if not millions) of

dollars each season. At least half of this money, however, is spent else-where (e.g., agent fees, investments, permanent home, vacation home, purchase of luxury items not produced in the local economy).

5. When teams relocate, there is some economic gain to the community (no more than $10 to $15 million in new economic activity) but that gain is another community's loss, again, a transfer of economic activ-ity rather than the creation of new economic activity.

6. Despite claims by public relations firms and civic boosters to the con-trary, scholarly analyses of the economic impact of a stadium and a pro-fessional team show consistently that sport has a negligible impact on metropolitan economies.[23] In short, "professional sports have been oversold by professional sports boosters as a catalyst for economic de-velopment."[24] Economist Robert Baade concludes, "Using economics as a justification for the subsidy is a political expedient, perhaps neces-sity, but it is inconsonant with the statistical evidence."[25]

7. Although sports teams may not have a tangible economic impact on a metropolitan community, they do have intangible benefits. Rosentraub says that "it may be important to attract millions of visitors to a down-town if only to remind them of the vitality and creativity contained in America's cities. If sports teams and their facilities accomplish that goal and establish pride in central cities, they may well be . . . 'major league.' . . . Further, if cities are to remain integral components of American life, then keeping sports in cities is important. Sport is too important a part of Western society for us to think that cities can exist without the teams and the events which define essential dimensions of our society and life."[26]

8. Although sports are an important part of a community's quality of life, the citizens of every community have to decide whether the public sub-sidization of professional sports enhances the quality of life enough to warrant the investment and, more important, whether there are other ar-eas that are better community investments. As Rosentraub wonders, "What are we to say to the residents of Cleveland, Indianapolis, and St. Louis who need better schools, health care, and neighborhoods when we refuse to raise some taxes but consent to give sports owners and ath-letes hundreds of millions of dollars in support?"[27]

I want to elaborate on this last point because it presents an interesting but dis-turbing inconsistency—U.S. society approves a welfare system to wealthy team owners and affluent athletes while condemning the social welfare system for the poor.[28]

From 1935 to 1996 the United States had a minimal welfare safety net for those in need (minimal when compared to the more generous welfare states of Western Europe and Scandinavia). Beginning with the Reagan administration, this welfare program has gradually been dismantled. This dismemberment accelerated in 1996 when the federal government made welfare assistance to families temporary and withdrew $55 billion in federal aid to the poor. At the federal and state levels politicians from both major political parties favored doing away with welfare and substituting programs that would provide market-based solutions. The leaders of both political parties sought to reduce taxes or at least resist tax increases. This significant reduction of welfare for the poor occurred at a time when 14 percent of the population, including 20 percent of all American children, were living in poverty, 41 million Americans did not have health insurance, urban schools were desperately behind suburban schools in resources, and only one-third of those children who qualified for Head Start received it. In short, the politicians, with the apparent support of the populace, embarked on a social experiment that, at least in the short run, would make life much more difficult for the economically disadvantaged. This inhumane approach was rationalized as necessary to rid the nation of a welfare system that was contrary to the American values of individualism, competition, and self-reliance.

At the same time, however, these same politicians, with the consent of the citizens (except for the voters in Minneapolis and Pittsburgh; in 1997 they rejected tax increases to build new stadiums), have encouraged a welfare system for wealthy team owners and their high-paid athletes. The system of subsidies to emerge has, as economist Robert A. Baade described it, created a *reverse* "Robin Hood" effect—taking from the poor, the near poor, the working class, and the middle classes and giving to the rich.[29] This welfare to owners takes several forms, some of which I have already discussed. Federal law allows cities to issue tax exempt bonds to finance the building of stadiums and arenas. The Congressional Research Service estimates that the cost to the federal treasury of such exemptions is $100 million in lost tax revenue. The 50 percent deductions of the cost of luxury suites and the like for businesses amount to a 17 percent federal subsidy for wealthy people to watch games.[30] The resulting lost tax revenues to the federal treasury come from other sources, which we all pay.

When the stadiums are built and paid for by taxpayers, there is a clear transfer of wealth from the taxpayers to the owners and the players. Urban scholar Mark Rosentraub says:

> Sales taxes paid by lower-income people produce excess profits that are divided between players and owners, all of whom enjoy salaries about which the taxpayers can only dream. A subsidy spread across hundreds of thousands of people amounts to a small charge each year. It is still, however, a transfer of wealth from the lower and middle classes to the upper class.[31]

This transfer occurs as the new stadium increases the value of the team. When it is sold, the owner reaps greater capital gains. For example, in 1993 the

Cleveland Indians had a market value of $81 million. The next year, with the opening of Jacobs Field, the value of the team jumped immediately to an estimated $100 million, and by 1996 to $125 million (a return of 54.3 percent in the three years following the opening of a new stadium).[32] The transfer of wealth also occurs when luxury suites and club-level seats are built and the additional revenues generated go to the owners. So too with revenues from parking and concessions. Sometimes cities provide owners with moving expenses, practice facilities, office space, land, and special investment opportunities to entice them to stay or to move to their team to the city.

Even though the public votes on raising taxes for a stadium, the obligation is not finite. The public sector ends up with the responsibility for any cost overruns, which are common. Most telling, stadiums are generally built with the owner investing some money but the public raising usually at least 80 percent of the funds, amounting to hundreds of millions of dollars. The asymmetrical nature of this relationship is revealed in the division of the revenues generated from the operation of the stadium—the owner who put up about 20 percent (on average) receives 100 percent of the proceeds! The public, which invested most of the money for construction and maintenance of the facility, receives none of the proceeds!

To summarize, the professional team owner–city relationship entails several related contradictions. First, the mayors, governors, and legislators who work against welfare for the poor are more than generous with their subsidies to the rich. Second, the wealthy owners who favor private enterprise and marketplace solutions in their other business activities insist on subsidies to maintain their lucrative professional teams. Paul Allen, for example, the third richest individual in the United States (today worth some $20 billion) insisted that he would move the Seattle Seahawks unless the residents of Seattle voted to build a stadium for his team (which they did). Third, team owners faced with what they consider inadequate subsidies will move their franchise to a locality that provides more generous subsidies. Fourth, the citizens of cities put up with this hypocrisy. Fifth, the public, which underwrites the largesse to the wealthy, ends up being *less likely to be able to afford to see the games in person*. The cost of tickets, tending to go up anyway, escalates with a new stadium. Some stadium commissions require the purchase of a "personal seat license" (at a cost of $2,500, for example, in Charlotte for the right to purchase a season ticket). As a result of these practices, the crowds in these new arenas are becoming more and more elite.

This trend takes two other forms as well. Publicly financed arenas are for sports that appeal especially to the affluent. Sports for the working classes, such as automobile racing, usually take place in privately owned arenas. Also, publicly funded arenas are for men. In this regard, Mariah Burton Nelson asks, "Who loses when a community spends millions of dollars in tax revenue to construct a new stadium and only men get to play in it, and only men get to work there?"[33] Sport sociologist Bruce Kidd makes the same point in his essay on the building of a domed stadium in Toronto: "It constitutes a massive subsidization and celebration of the interests of men. . . . If a city gave pride of place to a stadium where only Anglo-Saxons could play, there would be howls of protest, but in the matter of gender and sports, such favouritism is usually taken for granted."[34]

Finally, as Mark Rosentraub observes, "If It Quacks, It Is Still a Duck," meaning that no matter what the spin, the subsidies that owners receive constitute welfare.[35] Ironically, it is a reverse type of socialism that redistributes wealth upward. Yet owners, civic boosters, editorial writers, and politicians who spend much of their time defending capitalism and the free market support it unabashedly and uncritically.

An Alternative Structure

There is another way—a fairer way—to structure professional sport. Teams could be owned by local governments (cities, counties, or region) or by community stockholders rather than individuals or corporations, as is now the case. Localities already subsidize the teams but do not own them, which allows the owner to insist on more and better subsidies with the threat of moving the team to a more lucrative situation. The Green Bay Packers football team is the only major professional team that is owned by the people.

Some 1,900 of the locals, including truckers, barkeeps, merchants, and bus drivers, own a piece of the Pack, organized back in 1923 as a community-owned, nonprofit company. The stockholders draw no profit, and the locally elected board of directors that operates the team is unpaid, but all concerned draw great pleasure from knowing that the Packers are *theirs*.

What a difference ownership makes. Not a dime needs to be spent to hype up fan support, since the team literally belongs to them. The town of 96,000 built Lambeau Stadium, owns it, operates it, and fills each of the 60,790 seats in it for every home game—forty straight years of sellouts, whether the team is winning or not, and the season ticket waiting list has 20,000 names on it.

Get this: No ticket costs more than $28, no parking space is more than $7, there is free parking within four blocks of the stadium. . . . Charities run the stadium's concessions. . . . Off-duty police provide stadium security, and are paid overtime by the team.

Green Bay fans and citizens never have to worry that some pirate of an owner is going to hijack the Pack and haul their team to Los Angeles or any other big-city market, because Green Bay *is* their team. It stands as a shining model of how fans in other cities could get control of their teams and stop corporate rip-offs.[36]

Shifting team ownership to community ownership is relatively easy. Each locality could buy the local team at its market value, which would amount to something less than what they now pay to build the owner a new stadium. There is only one catch: The owners in each league have passed a rule specifically banning any future team from being community owned! In other words, the teams will continue to be owned by individuals and corporations but financed by the public. This maintains the situation where each team may claim that it is *yours* but it is really *theirs*.

Notes

1. Roger G. Noll, "The U.S. Team Sports Industry," in *Government and the Sports Business,* ed. Roger G. Noll (Washington, D.C.: Brookings Institution, 1974), p. 2.

2. George H. Sage, "Stealing Home: Political, Economic, and Media Power and a Publicly-Funded Stadium in Denver," *Journal of Sport and Social Issues* 17 (August 1993): 112. I have updated Sage's calculation of the number of teams by population, using current population data and the addition of two franchises.

3. Ibid. See also Andrew Zimbalist, *Baseball and Billions* (New York: Basic Books, 1992).

4. George H. Sage, *Power and Ideology in American Sport* (Champaign, Ill.: Human Kinetics, 1990), p. 145.

5. Kurt Badenhausen and Christopher Nikolov, "More Than a Game: An In-depth Look at the Raging Bull Market in Sports Franchises," *Financial World,* June 17, 1997, pp. 40–59.

6. These examples are taken from Richard G. Sheehan, *Keeping Score: The Economics of Big-Time Sports* (South Bend, Ind.: Diamond Communications, 1996), pp. 96–97, 120–121; Sage, *Power and Ideology,* p. 145; and Badenhausen and Nikolov, "More Than a Game."

7. Steven K. Paulson, "New Stadium Would Double Broncos' Profits," reprinted in *Fort Collins Coloradoan,* September 15, 1996, pp. 1E, 4E.

8. Quoted in Juan B. Elizondo Jr., "Governor Pockets 14.9 Million from Rangers Sale," *Mexico City Times,* June 19, 1998, p. 8.

9. Sheehan, *Keeping Score,* pp. 23–25.

10. Mark S. Rosentraub, *Major League Lo$ers: The Real Cost of Sports and Who's Paying for It* (New York: Basic Books, 1997), pp. 119–120.

11. The following is from Sage, "Stealing Home," pp. 110–124; Fawn Germer, "Rockies Strike Richest Deal," *Rocky Mountain News,* November 28, 1991, p. 8; Richard Corliss, "High on the Rockies," *Time,* July 19, 1993, p. 55; and Paul Hutchinson, "Coors Field Tab Up to $215.5 million," *Denver Post,* December 3, 1994, p. 1.

12. Sage, "Stealing Home," p. 118.

13. Ibid., p. 116.

14. Reported in Steve Raabe, "The Big Business of Rockies Baseball," *Denver Post,* September 7, 1997, p. 11.

15. Tracy Ringolsby, "Privately Financed Ballparks Rare," *Rocky Mountain News,* May 8, 1997, p. 8C.

16. "Sports Welfare," *USA Today,* August 19, 1997, p. 12A.

17. Jon Morgan, *Glory for Sale: Fans, Dollars and the New NFL* (Baltimore, Md.:

Bancroft, 1997); George F. Will, "Modell Sacks Maryland," *Newsweek,* January 22, 1996, p. 70; and Jim Hightower, *There's Nothing in the Middle of the Road but Yellow Stripes and Dead Armadillos* (New York: HarperCollins, 1997), pp. 20–21.

18. See David Whitson and Donald Macintosh, "Becoming a World-Class City," *Sociology of Sport Journal* 10 (September 1993): 221–240.

19. Marilyn Geewax, "Stadiums Can't Be Judged by Their Tax Costs Alone," *Rocky Mountain News,* October 22, 1997, p. 48A.

20. Rosentraub, *Major League Lo$ers,* pp.129–178.

21. Mark S. Rosentraub, "Does the Emperor Have New Clothes? A Reply to Robert J. Baade," *Journal of Urban Affairs* 18, no. 1 (1996): 23.

22. Rosentraub, *Major League Lo$ers,* p. 140.

23. Robert A. Baade, "Professional Sports as Catalysts for Metropolitan Economic Development," *Journal of Economic Affairs* 18, no. 1 (1996): 1–17; Roger G. Noll and Andrew Zimbalist, eds., *Sports, Jobs, and Taxes: The Economic Impact of Sports Teams and Stadiums* (Washington, D.C.: Brookings Institution, 1997); C. C. Euchner, *Playing the Field: Why Sports Teams Move and Cities Fight to Keep Them* (Baltimore: Johns Hopkins University Press, 1993); Dean Baim, *The Sports Stadium as a Municipal Investment* (Westport, Conn.: Greenwood, 1992); and Mark S. Rosentraub, "Sport and Downtown Development Strategy: If You Build It, Will Jobs Come?" *Journal of Urban Affairs* 16 (1994): 221–239; and Rosentraub, *Major League Lo$ers.*

24. Baade, "Professional Sports as Catalysts," p. 16.

25. Robert A. Baade, "Stadium Subsidies Make Little Economic Sense for Cities," *Journal of Urban Affairs* 18, no. 1 (1996): 37.

26. Rosentraub, "Does the Emperor Have New Clothes?" p. 29.

27. Ibid., p. 30.

28. The following is taken primarily from Rosentraub, *Major League Lo$ers,* pp. 3–17; D. Stanley Eitzen, "Dismantling the Welfare State," *Vital Speeches of the Day* 62 (June 1996): 532–536; and D. Stanley Eitzen and Maxine Baca Zinn, "New Welfare Legislation and Families" (paper presented to the American Sociological Association, San Francisco, August 1998).

29. Robert A. Baade and Alan Sanderson, "Field of Fantasies," Heartland Institute, Intellectual Ammunition web site , quoted in Morgan, *Glory for Sale,* p. 315.

30. "How You Pay $$$ for Stadiums Far, Far Away," *USA Today,* June 5, 1997, p. 14A.

31. Rosentraub, *Major League Lo$ers,* p. 447.

32. Ibid., p. 110.

33. Mariah Burton Nelson, *The Stronger Women Get, the More Men Love Football: Sexism and the American Culture of Sports* (New York: Harcourt Brace, 1994), p. 8.

34. Bruce Kidd, "The Men's Cultural Centre: Sports and the Dynamic of Women's Oppression/Men's Repression," in *Sport, Men, and the Gender Order: Critical Feminist Perspectives,* ed. Michael A. Messner and Donald F. Sabo (Champaign, Ill.: Human Kinetics, 1990), p. 32.

35. Rosentraub, *Major League Lo$ers,* p. 447.

36. Hightower, *There's Nothing in the Middle of the Road,* pp. 22–23.

Chapter 11

The Challenge: Changing Sport

Probably only death will cure my love affair with North Carolina basketball, and no doubt there are millions of people who feel the same way about their own teams. But loving the game need not mean having a romantic view of how college sports are organized. College sports are far too visible an arena in American society to be simply thrown to the wolves. Ultimately, the only productive route forward is to insist that those who love the game also fight to change it.

—Thad Williamson

This book is titled *Fair* and *Foul: Beyond the Myths and Paradoxes of Sport* because sport is both elevating and deflating, appealing and appalling, inspiring and disillusioning. Although I have tried to present the positive side of sport, my emphasis has leaned strongly toward criticism—and an examination of the "dark side" of sport. My analysis shares something with the experience of Mike Lupica, sportswriter for the *New York Daily News,* who says that he wants to celebrate sport in his column but "sports keeps making it so goddamned hard [to do so]."[1]

My bias toward the "dark side" is deliberate. My goal is to engage readers in an analysis of sport that leads them to reflect on how sport really works and how it might be improved.

Is Change Possible?

First, sport, as it is practiced in the United States, is not fated by nature or even by the "invisible hand" of the market; *it is a social construction,* the result of historical actions and choices. Americans have created the organization of sport that now exists, and Americans maintain it.[2] This means, then, that because sport is created by people, it can be changed by them as well.

Second, historically, sport has occasionally changed for the better because of the deliberate acts of individuals and the collective, organized efforts of social

161

movements and organizations. Three well-known examples illustrate this point. In these and other significant challenges to the status quo, change did not occur without a fight. Individuals and groups confronted the powerful and succeeded.

The Racial Integration of Baseball

Baseball was rigidly segregated before World War II. But in 1947 Branch Rickey, the owner of the Brooklyn Dodgers, brought talented Jackie Robinson, an African American, into the major leagues against the vehement opposition of his fellow owners (the owners voted 15 to 1 in 1946 to maintain segregation) and most major league players.[3] Rickey's bold move was not entirely altruistic, since he saw blacks as a reservoir of untapped talent and believed that racial integration would increase attendance by tapping the black fans.

Blacks soon achieved prominence in baseball and ultimately were accepted by white players and fans. Many were involved behind the scenes in effecting this extraordinary transformation. In 1944 Albert "Happy" Chandler, who was sympathetic toward the goal of racial integration, became commissioner of major league baseball, replacing a strict segregationist, Kenesaw Mountain Landis. During the war and after it, black newspapers, most prominently in New York and Pittsburgh, argued for racial integration in baseball. Their argument (used also by a few white sportswriters) was that blacks fought in World War II to protect freedom, yet American society denied blacks the freedom to compete on a level playing field with whites.

Free Agency for Athletes

Before the landmark court cases of the mid-1970s, professional athletes in team sports were trapped by the reserve clause in their contracts. Once a player signed a contract with a club, that team had exclusive rights, and the player was no longer free to negotiate with any other team. In succeeding years, the player had to sell his services solely to the club that owned his contract unless it released, sold, or traded him, or he chose to retire. The reserve clause specified that the owner had the exclusive right to renew a player's contract annually. Thus a player was bound perpetually to negotiate with only one club. The player was the club's property and could be sold to another club without the player's consent. In effect, this clause kept the salaries of players artificially low and restricted the players' freedom. As one observer put it, "After the Civil War settled the slavery issue, owning a ball club was the closest one could come to owning a plantation."[4]

The late 1960s was a period in American history when various downtrodden groups (racial minorities, women, gays) became militant in attempts to change existing power relationships. Within this society-wide framework, athletes too began to recognize their common plight and organized to change it. Most fundamentally, they felt that because the owners had all the power, the players did not receive their true value in the marketplace. The result was that athletes, as individuals and as player associations, began to assert themselves against what they considered an unfair system.

Several cases were instrumental in modifying the reserve clause in baseball. First and foremost was Curt Flood, who was traded by the baseball Cardinals in 1969 to the Philadelphia Phillies but refused to play for them, sitting out the 1970 season. He brought suit against organized baseball, alleging that the reserve system constituted a system of peonage. The U.S. Supreme Court ruled 5 to 3 against Flood but recognized that the system should be changed by congressional action.

Flood's heroic act, coupled with the decisions of arbitrators releasing three major league baseball players from their contracts (teams then bid for their services offering many times what they had been paid by their owners under the reserve clause, indicating their "true" worth), led to an agreement between the owners of professional baseball and the Players Association in 1976. This agreement killed the reserve clause by permitting free agency (after a specified time a player was free to negotiate with all teams, not just his original team).

Gender Equity

In the spirit of the 1960s the National Organization of Women (NOW) gathered data at the national and local levels on discrimination against girls and women in community and school sports. Armed with this information, the organization lobbied Congress, which ultimately passed Title IX, the act that requires schools receiving federal funds to provide equal opportunities for males and females. This landmark decision caused a huge explosion in female sports participation. Similarly, individuals have brought court cases that successfully challenged the male sports structure in various children's sports programs, school districts, and state associations. As a result, Little League baseball is no longer exclusively male, over a million girls are playing youth soccer, and girls can participate on coeducational high school wrestling teams.

Should We Change Sport?

Sport is important because if reflects society, reinforces its class, race, and gender inequities, and provides opportunities. Sport matters because it affects each of us, sometimes profoundly. It clearly has an impact on the interests and values of our children. Family life is disrupted by practice and game schedules as well as the cost of coaching, equipment, travel, and camps. Our taxes and the tax code subsidize professional teams, owners, and players. The tuition and fees of college students subsidize athletic programs. Many of the products we purchase cost more because their producers have invested heavily in sports-related advertising. Corporations intrude in high school and college sports. Money drives big-time college sport, sometimes making a mockery of athletes as students. Money, sometimes very big money, distorts the original intent of sport—the participants' pleasure in the activity. Thus play becomes work and the outcome supersedes the process.

My understanding of sport leads me to seek change in eight problem areas. First, striving to win, which is the essence of sport, sometimes leads to unethical behaviors by players, coaches, fans, and others associated with sport. Clearly, codes of conduct are required that are strictly monitored and administered at all levels of sport to keep the actions of those involved as close to the ethical high road as possible.

Second, children's sports have moved from peer control to adult control. With this change, play has become work. Participation for its own sake has become a public activity, with winning often becoming all-consuming for the children, their parents, and their coaches. The games that children play have lost their innocence. Although adult-structured activities make sense at some age, say, age twelve and above, they make absolutely no sense for four- and five-year-olds, and perhaps nine-, ten-, and eleven-year-olds as well.

Third, our youth and school programs are elitist. They provide too few resources for the majority of young people and too many for gifted (usually male) athletes. If sports participation is good (and I believe that it is), then it should be provided for everyone—skilled and unskilled, able and disabled, affluent and poor. Maximum participation should be a major goal of youth and school programs.

Fourth, college sport at the big-time level has become too big, too dominated by money concerns, too controlled by those outside the university (television networks, bowl and tournament administrators, and large contributors—individual and corporate) to make sense educationally. Big-time college sport, if anything, undermines educational goals by admitting students unprepared for college and demanding too much from the athletes in time and commitment. Organized sport at the small school level (Division III) is much more in tune with the educational mission of schools. If the current big-time programs want to maintain a high-level entertainment/commercial enterprise, then let them organize a league that is professional (the players are paid), with the athletes having the option of being students or not.[5] This plan would eliminate the hypocrisy and unethical practices in recruiting and keeping players eligible as well as removing the exploitation of athletes.

Fifth, girls and women have not received equality in school sport, although considerable progress has been made since the 1970s. Enforcement of Title IX needs to be more rigorous. Fundamentally, the interpretation of Title IX needs to be unequivocal in its insistence on gender equity. This means, of course, that football must be part of the equality equation.

Sixth, racial minorities, once denied participation, now dominate the major team sports in the United States. They dominate numerically as players but rarely as head coaches, general managers, owners, athletic directors, trainers, and sports publicists. Racial minorities must receive the experience necessary for consideration for these positions, and those who have the requisite experience and skills must be considered seriously. Public acceptance of racial minorities in positions of power is crucial.

Seventh, I believe that it is improper for cities and regions to use public money to build and maintain stadiums and provide other subsidies for the profit of privately owned professional teams. Cities should own these teams. Although the leagues have rules against city ownership, these rules can be superseded by Congress, since professional sport involves interstate commerce. If Congress does not so act, there are other options, for example, voters may refuse to subsidize owners (as has happened in a quarter of recent elections).

Eighth, attending big-time college and professional sports events, even when these enterprises are subsidized by the public, has become too costly. Average people, for the most part, are shut out, and only the well-to-do experience the thrill of watching sports in person. This is unacceptable. As sportswriter Mike Lupica puts it, "The song says, 'Take me out to the ballgame.' Not out to the cleaners."[6] Lupica says:

> We have to stop the insanity somewhere. Even if it costs the owners some money. Just because they can get top dollar, for every seat in the house, doesn't mean they have to get top dollar. Or are even entitled to get top dollar. If the owners themselves can't see this, it is the job of a good commissioner to make them see it.
>
> My idea?
>
> That there be a cheap-seat section of every major arena, every ballpark, every football stadium operating in professional sports. Not bad seats. Not nosebleed seats. Cheap seats. That means reasonably priced. Geared toward attracting minorities, geared toward attracting kids. . . . We have to get kids, and especially kids of color, watching ballplayers of color, heroes of color, on the inside.[7]

How Do We Go About Making Changes?

We can make changes in sport by making changes in social arrangements. We are not passive actors who accept society's arrangements as inevitable. To the contrary, we can be actively engaged in social life, working for the improvement or even the radical change of faulty social structures. This notion that human beings construct and reconstruct society implies another notion—that the personal is political. As individuals, we make choices—to participate or not, to accept a coach's dehumanizing behavior or not, to pay outrageously expensive prices or not, to support or undermine an African American as head coach, to encourage or discourage ethical behaviors, to place winning above all other considerations or not, to choose or reject the dominant sports—choices that promote the status quo or something else.

What is most significant at the individual level is that individuals as fans pay the cost of big-time college and professional sports. We are the ones who spend $100 billion a year on sports (equipment, memorabilia, tickets, and the like). We are the ones who have approved spending $24 billion to build sports facilities by 2005, 75 percent of it public money. We are the ones who continue to forgive and forget irresponsible behavior by players, coaches, and owners. If enough fans withdrew their financial support of professional sports in protest of the way things are, meaningful changes might occur. Dean Bonham, chief executive officer of a Denver-based sports and entertainment marketing firm, says:

> Rather than shake our fists at the antics of owners and players, I think we should simply look in the mirror. That's right: The real fault lies with you and me—"the fans." . . . If it's you and me who are at fault here, what's the solution? I believe the only way to correct our mistakes is to stop buying tickets, merchandise, concessions, and such, and to stop watching these teams on TV as long as the profligate owners and arrogant players ignore us and take us for granted. Maybe then they'll get the message that the game belongs to you and me—the fans.[8]

There is some evidence that the cumulative effects of individual acts by fans are making a difference. In a cover story entitled "Big League Troubles," *U.S. News & World Report* cited a number of problems in sport, such as gentrification (working families can't afford to go to a game), $200 basketball shoes, rich owners who blackmail cities for larger subsidies, athletes who turn down $100 million multiyear contracts because such a low-ball bid disrespects them, strikes and player lockouts, members of the U.S. Olympic hockey team who trash their rooms, and players in and out of the courts for sexual aggression, spouse abuse, assault, and drug/alcohol abuse. In the face of these and other factors, there are indicators that fans are losing interest in sports. Consider the following:[9]

- Sales of sports-related merchandise are declining (Nike, Reebok, licensed products tied to professional sports).
- Voters have rejected public funding for sports arenas in places like Minneapolis-St. Paul, Pittsburgh, South Florida, and North Carolina, where a subsidized stadium would have brought in the Minnesota Twins.
- A *Los Angeles Times* poll in 1998 found that 59 percent of those surveyed did not consider having an NFL team in the Los Angeles area important.
- The ratings for the professional sports leagues on the four major networks have fallen for the past ten years. Baseball is down 30 percent since 1987, the NBA is down 14 percent, and NFL viewership is down 22 percent. Even playoff ratings in the NFL have fallen off by 22 percent in the past decade.

These trends indicate that fans can make a difference, and some may opt out of sport because of its negatives. Nevertheless, the vast majority continue to support the sports establishment uncritically. Sports junkies mindlessly watch twenty-four-hour sports channels. Many sports fans are critical of the behavior of athletes and the high cost of sport across the country, but they still root wholeheartedly for their home teams. The 1960s liberation efforts by racial minorities, women, gays, and other downtrodden groups required not only mobilization and action but also a "raising of consciousness" to bring the formerly unconvinced into the cause. This needs to happen in the sports sphere as well. The masses need to become aware of the problems, with a keen understanding of who benefits and who does not under the current system and how their actions maintain the status quo.

There are three additional ways to initiate change.[10] First, people can work within the system, volunteering to coach youth sports teams or serve on the board of directors of a sports league. Teachers can become coaches or move into athletic administration. College professors can serve on athletic committees or serve as their institution's athletic representative to a league and the NCAA. But as people become insiders and move into positions of increasing power, there is an ever greater likelihood of acquiring a vested interest in the status quo.

A second way to affect change is to become involved in opposition groups. Only rarely can an individual make much of a difference. A better strategy is to become involved in collective action—joining with others in an effort to seek a solution to some problem by putting pressure on power wielders. This may be a group opposed to tax-subsidized construction of a stadium or a group promoting the construction of a community playing facility such as a new ice arena, baseball field, or soccer field to accommodate growing demand. Students at Duke University and others have organized and have successfully pushed administrators to adopt rules requiring that all campus athletic gear be produced in compliance with labor and human rights standards.

> These same activists should insist that corporate advertising be banned from all arenas; that universities cap athletic budgets for football and basketball and put an end to the "arms race" for bigger facilities and more amenities; and that the influence of big-money donors be limited so that students and fans can continue to attend athletic events at reasonable prices. Activists might also find unexpected common ground with coaches and fans concerned about how the integrity of the game has been subordinated to television, or how corporations are colonizing and poisoning the high school recruiting scene.[11]

Consumer advocate Ralph Nader calls for an organization that he calls FANS—Fight to Advance Nation's Sports (Nader tried to get this organization started in 1977 but it never got off the ground). Nader wishes for at least 10,000 fans who would be willing to pay dues of twenty-five dollars a year. This money would be used to get information to the public and to initiate lawsuits as necessary. Nader's concerns include the right of fans to reasonably priced tickets; the unfair tax and other subsidies that support sports moguls; the right of fans to see their interests represented before Congress; and the necessity of public disclosure of financial information by professional teams.[12] A similar organization, United Sports Fans of America, is a fan advocacy group. This group argues for a player code of conduct, a moratorium on franchise relocation, and modification of the NFL's home-market blackout rule so that the games will be televised locally if 90 percent of the tickets are sold instead of the current 100 percent.[13]

A third option is to financially support existing organizations that show promise in bringing about change. The Center for Study of Sport in Society at Northeastern University is an organization that works within the system to make sport more inclusive (race, class, and gender) and to make colleges and universities more responsive to the needs of student-athletes. It engages athletes in after-school tutoring programs for disadvantaged primary and secondary students in schools and community centers, and it promotes public awareness on such issues as men's violence against women and human rights.[14] Another important organization is the Women's Sports Foundation. This organization sponsors research, lobbies politicians, mobilizes pressure on decision makers, and provides information to the public—all with the goal of attaining gender equity in sports.[15]

Sport has an incredible grip on most people. It is compelling; it can be a magical, wonderful illusion. But even as sport excites and inspires, it has problems. Let's not get rid of sport. Let's make it better. For me, that means sport should be more fun, more inclusive, more humanized, and more ethical. My hope is that you will join me not only to understand these complex social arrangements called sport but also to work for their improvement.

Notes

1. Mike Lupica, *Mad as Hell: How Sports Got Away from the Fans and How We Get It Back* (New York: Putnam, 1996), p. 234.

2. Paraphrased from Claude S. Fischer et al., *Inequality by Design: Cracking the Bell Curve Myth* (Princeton, N.J.: Princeton University Press, 1996), p. 7.

3. For the history of the Branch Rickey/Jackie Robinson integration experiment, see Jules Tygiel, *Baseball's Great Experiment and His Legacy* (New York: Oxford University Press, 1983); Jackie Robinson, *I Never Had It Made* (New York: Putnam's, 1972).

4. Alex Ben Block, "So, You Want to Own a Ball Club," *Forbes,* April 1, 1977, p. 37.

5. This suggestion comes from Rick Telander, *The Hundred Yard Lie: The Corruption of College Football and What We Can Do to Stop It* (New York: Simon and Schuster, 1989), pp. 213–217.

6. Lupica, *Mad as Hell,* p. 236.

7. Ibid., pp. 186, 188.

8. Dean Bonham, "C'mon Fans—Put the Lid on Salaries," *Rocky Mountain News,* July 26, 1998, p. 13G.

9. Dan McGraw, "Big League Troubles," *U.S. News & World Report,* July 13, 1998, pp. 40–46.

10. Adapted from Jay J. Coakley, *Sport in Society: Issues and Controversies,* 6th ed. (New York: McGraw-Hill, 1998), pp. 520–522.

11. Thad Williamson, "Bad as They Wanna Be: Loving the Game Is Harder As Colleges Sell Out Themselves, the Fans, the Athletes," *The Nation,* August 10–17, 1998, pp. 40–41.

12. For a discussion of Nader's plan, see Lupica, *Mad as Hell,* pp. 214–219.

13. The USFA Internet address is www.usfans.com.

14. See, for example, the following publications by the Center for the Study of Sport in Society (Northeastern University, Boston, Mass. 02115): *Sport in Society Annual Report, National Consortium for Academics and Sports Quarterly Newsletter, Sport in Society News,* and the annual *Racial Report Card.*

15. Women's Sports Foundation, Eisenhower Park, East Meadow, N.Y. 11554.

Index

Adidas, 132
Adler, Patricia and Peter, 110
advertising, Super Bowl and, 2
affirmative action, for college sport, 108
African Americans, 18–23; in college sport, 19–20, 21, 108, 111; excluded from sports, 86; graduation of, 134; as leaders, 21–23, 137, 164–65; Olympics (1968) and, 26, 80; postathletic careers of, 135; in professional sports, 16, 136–39, 141; salaries of, 22, 132, 137; in school sport, 18–19; "unequal opportunity for equal ability" and, 22; University of Mississippi symbols and, 31–32, 38; women and, 21, 22–23, 137. *See also* race; *specific sport*
Agate High School, 42
alcohol abuse, 63, 88
Ali, Mohammed, 19
Allen, George, 11
Allen, Paul, 156
amateurism, 43, 86, 95–96, 120–21, 124, 126
amenorrhea, 62
American Basketball League, 139
American Express, 132
American Indian Movement (AIM), 33, 36
amphetamines, 63
anabolic steroids, 2, 46–47, 52, 63, 64–66

Anderson, Brady, 64
Angell, Roger, 21–22
announcers, gender divisions in sport and, 24–25
anorexia nervosa, 66
anticipatory socialization, 89
anti-inflammatories, 63
archery, 63
Arena League, 147
Arizona Diamondbacks, 146–47
Arizona State, 121
Arslanian, Sark, 87
Arvada West High School (Colorado), 64
Ashe, Arthur, 139
Asian Games, 65
Association for Women in Psychology Ad Hoc Committee on Sexist Language, 38
asthma, misuse of drugs for, 63
athletic directors, African Americans as, 21, 23, 164–65
athletic movement/revolution, 97–98, 162–63
Atlanta Braves, 29, 33, 152–53
Austin, Tracy, 70
Australia, 21
authoritarian, coaches as, 86–88, 97, 98–100. *See also* school sport, parallels between Soviet system and
automobile racing, 20, 83

About the Author

D. Stanley Eitzen (Ph.D., University of Kansas) is professor emeritus of sociology at Colorado State University, where he taught for twenty-one years, the last as John N. Stern Distinguished Professor. Prior to that he taught at the University of Kansas for seven years. He was editor of *The Social Science Journal* from 1978 to 1984. Although he is well-known for his scholarship in homelessness, social inequality, power, family, and criminology, he is best-known for his contributions to the sociology of sport. He has taught the course Sport and Society since 1972. He is the author or coauthor of seventeen books (including three on sport) as well as numerous scholarly articles and chapters in scholarly books. He is a former president of the North American Society for the Sociology of Sport. Among his many awards, he was selected to be a Sports Ethics Fellow by the Institute for International Sport in 1996.